D0065189

$ 7.93

FLASHPOINT TRIESTE

Flashpoint Trieste

The First Battle of the Cold War

Christian Jennings

This book is dedicated to the exceptional
and inspirational Kat Sacco and Giulia Mate.
The best of Italy.

Questo libro è dedicato a Kat Sacco e a Giulia Mate.
Un'ispirazione eccezionale, il meglio dell'Italia ...

First published in Great Britain in 2017 by Osprey Publishing,
PO Box 883, Oxford, OX1 9PL, UK
1385 Broadway, 5th Floor, New York, NY 10018, USA

E-mail: info@ospreypublishing.com

Osprey Publishing, part of Bloomsbury Publishing Plc

A CIP catalogue record for this book is available from the British Library.

ISBN: 978 1 4728 2170 6
PDF e-bookISBN: 978 1 4728 2172 0
ePub e-book ISBN: 978 1 4728 2171 3

Index by Zoe Ross
Cartography by Bounford.com
Typeset in Adobe Garamond Pro
Originated by PDQ Media, Bungay, UK
Printed in China through World Print Ltd.

17 18 19 20 21 10 9 8 7 6 5 4 3 2 1

Front cover images: Partisan, France, September 1944 (Photo by Mondadori Portfolio via Getty Images); Piazza dell'Unità d'Italia, Trieste (Tu xa Ha Noi).
Page 4: A policeman stands lookout outside Trieste, February 1952. (Photo by Walter Sanders/The LIFE Picture Collection/Getty Images)

Osprey Publishing supports the Woodland Trust, the UK's leading woodland conservation charity. Between 2014 and 2018 our donations will be spent on their Centenary Woods project in the UK.

Contents

Preface

This Land is My Land, June 2016

The view from the terrace of the villa, looking across the Gulf of Trieste towards Venice, is of the dark cobalt waters of the Adriatic. The sea shimmers and dances in the summer heat; hulking container ships from Odessa, Shanghai and Valencia wait out at anchor. Closer to land, yachts flit in graceful semi-circles, chasing the wind. The port and city of Trieste crouches with its face to the sea, its back to the mountains that rise behind it, sudden and steep. One of its main historical museums is housed behind the sea-front, in an old villa on a street that rises above the harbour. Lime trees crowd in on the museum's terrace. Seen from it, the city seems elegant, graceful, spires and twisting back streets. The architecture says confidently that Romans, Byzantines, Venetians and Austro-Hungarians have come and gone from here.

On a scorching June morning of blue sky, some pupils from the primary school that sits next door to the museum have gathered in a fast, giggling clump on the pavement. Spontaneously they start to sing. It's a pop song, one of the hits of the summer. Everybody across Italy has heard it a hundred times. In the bar, the supermarket, in the shops, clubs, in their apartments. In short, anywhere that people gather, where the radio is playing, where there's noise, movement and laughter. Which in Italy can be practically anywhere, except at the very dead of night. It's by the Roman singer Max Gazzè, a bouncy, satirical paean to girls and love and destiny and, yes, coffee. It's called '*La vita com'è*' – 'life as it is' – and everybody knows the words. The school-children sing beautifully in perfect time. Down in the port of Trieste, below the terrace, the cranes turn slowly in the heat. The leaves on the lime trees that stand round the villa are still bright green, not yet flattened by the heat of July and August. The wind is warm. It's lunchtime. Things look calm. One would never think, standing here, that this is a place over which World War III could have started.

The train to Trieste takes its time clicking along from Venice. The elegant, high-speed starlets of the Italian railway system are the Frecciabianca, Frecciarossa and Frecciargento – the White, Red and Silver Arrow, three types of high-speed train that dash at 180 miles per hour across the main points on the Italian compass: Rome, Milan, Turin, Genoa, Florence, Taranto. Onto the platforms of the station at Venezia Mestre, they disgorge thousands of German tourists, Swedish backpackers, the nervous parties of Japanese holidaymakers in their sunshade straw hats and surgical facemasks. But many of the tourists stop here. Those going further down the line cross to another platform and take the slower regional train, the Regionale Veloce that goes to Trieste.

At first, the journey plods, the train pulling through the flat swamp land that surrounds the lagoon of Venice. There are short, muddy canals, fishermen drinking beer from plastic bottles and trying to catch eels, trees and fields that even in midsummer somehow conspire to look sodden. The journey goes in a huge semi-circle, heading north-east around the top of the Adriatic. The sea is somehow lost to the right as the train clatters forward, the railway line suddenly running parallel to a motorway. Twenty-ton articulated Volvos and Scanias haul containers from Austria and Switzerland towards Slovenia, Trieste, Croatia and all points east. There are fewer people on this line, even in summer. But on listening to the conversations of the different travellers, it suddenly becomes apparent that at least a third of them aren't speaking Italian. And as the journey continues over the top of the Adriatic, the language mix shifts perceptibly at each station. The Trenitalia carriage, with its bright blue seats and crisp air-conditioning, fills with the vocabulary of Slovenia, Croatia and the Balkans.

The woman opposite is reading a copy of *Slobodna Dalmacija*, a daily newspaper from the Croatian Adriatic coast. She turns the pages, folding the paper each time she does so. Apart from the cookery pages and the promotions for holidays in Sharm el-Sheikh, it's evident from reading the domestic headlines displayed opposite that most of the articles consist of those four staples of Balkans journalism: the regional politics of ethnicity and nationalism, and the plans that NATO, the UN and the EU allegedly have for Balkans land. Next come articles about the legacy of the 1990s conflicts in Bosnia, Kosovo and Croatia. These focus on commemorations for the dead and anniversaries of key events in the war in question, as well as stories about people who are still missing, those thousands who disappeared during the different conflicts. Twenty years on from the civil wars of the 'nineties that tore apart the former Yugoslavia, you remember that memories in this part of the world are still fresh. But then you realise that these articles in the newspaper opposite are not all about what happened in 1992. Some concern the legacy of World War II. And the word 'Trieste' seems to appear in several headlines. What, one wonders, is this idiosyncratic, clearly still unsettled city towards which the train is travelling?

About thirty miles short of the Italian border with Slovenia, the landscape suddenly changes. One minute the train is pulling alongside a nondescript pine forest, the next the sea flashes up dark turquoise on the right, palm trees spin past the windows, and stark, white limestone hills rise above the Adriatic coast. It is like arriving in a different country. Past the shipbuilding town of Monfalcone, through a rushing alleyway of Wellingtonia trees and spiky palms, and suddenly on the right sits the Castello di Miramare, an Austro-Hungarian castle that looks like a wedding cake. Ten minutes later, the train hisses and clacks past silos and marshalling yards, and pulls into platform three at Trieste Centrale. The passengers alight, while the engine and carriages vent the brake system in explosive blasts of compressed air. The station clock says 12.32. It's ninety-three degrees.

Outside the station entrance is where Italy hits the Balkans face-on. One taxi driver is Italian, and says he is from a family that in the 1930s settled further south-east down the Adriatic coast in Yugoslavia. He calls his family's town of origin by the Italian name 'Fiume'. This means 'river'. In Croatian its name is Rijeka, which is what it is called today. It's more than seventy years since September 1943, when the Italian army surrendered and signed an armistice with the Allies. Italians then made up a large percentage of Trieste's population. But with the surrender of Mussolini's army, communist Yugoslav partisans took revenge on many Italians living in Yugoslavia in places like Rijeka. They were told to take what they could carry, and then hit the road west to Italy. Some were threatened with death. The taxi driver, like many other local Italians forced off property in Yugoslavia three generations ago, still considers their house and land his property, even though it's now firmly in Croatia. The problem is that the Croatian government doesn't. Despite the fact that they've agreed to pay Italy compensation concerning reparations from the World War Two period. The shaven-headed man with a broad smile, who's sitting at the wheel of the VW minibus near the station entrance, doesn't call the town Fiume. He calls it by its Croat name, Rijeka, because he's Croatian. He's waiting to pick up passengers who have come to take advantage of one of the very much lesser-known attractions of the Balkans: dental tourism. It's a region where the the political-economics can be successful but are fragile and idiosyncratic. At their worst they are beset with endemic corruption, nationalism and ethnic division, and regional development is hamstrung by recent history. So every conceivable source of revenue is to be explored. Cheap and good dentistry is one. The people of the former Yugoslavia are inventive and resourceful, as befits as region that is no stranger to conflict. When war hit Yugoslavia in 1991, and a million people fled as refugees, they ended up in unlikely places. Melbourne, Kuala Lumpur, Atlanta, San Francisco, Northampton. Among them were a fair number of teenagers, who were absorbed by the educational systems of their countries of refuge. And among these, some chose to study dentistry. When peace, of a sort, finally washed over ex-Yugoslavia in 1995, many of them came home and brought their qualifications with them. They had been trained excellently, and now found their home countries chock-a-block full of *stranci*: foreigners by the thousands, the soldiers, diplomats, aid workers and humanitarian staff from the North Atlantic Treaty Organization (NATO), the European Union (EU) and the United Nations (UN) who had arrived to rebuild the Balkans. These people enjoyed large, tax-free salaries, and needed good dentists. Thus a small homegrown industry was born. And the man at the wheel of the minibus outside Trieste station is waiting to ferry Italians off down the coast. They'll get a new set of dental implants or a child's prosthetic brace done at a third of the price, and the same quality, as it would cost them in Milan or Rome or Florence.

Rijeka is in Croatia. But many Italians still refer to it as Fiume, from the days when it had a sizeable Italian population. Both names in Italian and Bosnian-Croatian-Serbian, as the *lingua franca* of the Balkans is called these days, mean the same thing – 'river'. The city was part of the Austro-Hungarian Empire until 1919, and was annexed by Benito Mussolini in the early 1920s and occupied by the Germans in 1943. Taken back by communist Croatian and Slovenian partisans in 1945, it then became part of Yugoslavia, now resting in the modern state of Croatia. For fifty years its blood-mired story was one of the brutal politics of displacement and revenge. So Trieste, as the first-stop city next door, was a natural refuge for all three nationalities. And since 500 BC, it's also always been a big and important port.

So leaving the Italian taxi driver and the Croat dental ferryman sitting in their vehicles parked in the shade, a 300-yard walk from the station reveals different languages and different peoples. The Italian policewoman with her Ray-Bans and holstered Beretta 9mm, waving traffic across a zebra crossing, is obviously talking to a colleague in her native language. The three teenage girls, with their small backpacks with the names of their boyfriends and favourite bands inscribed on them in Tippex, are chattering in Slovenian. A man, woman and little child are speaking fast Mandarin. They're standing in front of a Chinese convenience store that sells everything from flippers and Batman beach towels to laser-dot pointers and plastic ashtrays sporting images of the Castello di Miramare. The men in tight T-shirts, heads shaved, counting handfuls of euro notes outside a betting shop, are muttering in Croatian.

The three men going back to their ship, whose T-shirts say that they work for a Rotterdam maritime salvage company, are laughing in Dutch. The Ukrainian merchant seaman on shore leave, sitting at the bus-stop, has made an early start on plastic bottles of Slovenian lager. He is staring at the Austrian couple next to him on the pavement who are trying to orientate themselves on their tourist map. The short and gaudily dressed prostitute is from Nigeria, almost certainly trafficked illegally into Italy.

Emerging from the small grid of streets around the station and the docks, the neo-classical and Austro-Hungarian architecture of the city's old centre bursts into view. Capturing it for posterity on their mobile phones are four American servicemen in civilian clothes. A waiter in a café speaks a local language, called Ladin, from up on the Austrian border. Here and there you can hear the occasional smatter of the Triestine dialect, a mixture of Dalmatian and Venetian. The city is nothing if not cosmopolitan.

The leaflets on the reception desk at the small two-star hotel inform the business traveller and tourist that there's no shortage of things to do, and see, in and around Trieste. Three miles out of town is the Castello di Miramare, the Austro-Hungarian castle you see coming in on the train. It was formerly the headquarters of some Allied units after the Second World War. Down on the coast there are some caves and grottoes with harsh orange stalactites, and a nearby beach with turquoise sea. A little hybrid tramway and funicular railway climbs a thousand feet from Piazza Oberdan, up to the town of Opicina on the mountain above the city. There's a guided tour to be had at the headquarters of the Illy coffee company down in the industrial area, what it calls the Università del Caffè. The manufacturer of Italy's most-favoured beverage claims that Trieste was where coffee beans first entered Europe. This is something the Venetians would dispute, but Illy employees and aficionados can even work at their headquarters for a Masters Degree in Coffee Economics and Science.

Then there's the ferry that travels down to the Istrian peninsula in neighbouring Slovenia, the castle of San Giusto, and no shortage of old Austro-Hungarian coffee bars. Not surprisingly, Trieste also has several fish restaurants. Its cuisine is like the city: an eclectic mix of Italian, Austrian and Slovenian, touched by the influence of the sea. In the suburb of Prosecco, sitting 800 feet above the sea, there's a lot of tasting to be done of the sparkling wine named after the village. Meanwhile there are churches and art and beautiful architecture. Plus four different museums dedicated to the history of the city. Like a slightly misunderstood and beautiful model, Trieste exudes a confident and individual air. The stones of the ancient port tell of cultural elegance and long-established history.

But of all the places to visit in the city and its surroundings, one stands out for its sheer historical singularity. Down in a southern suburb, near the motorway that leads to Slovenia, there's a reminder of the brutal German administration that ran the city from 1943 to 1945. An old concentration camp – 'the only camp in Italy with a working crematorium', states the promotional leaflet. The number ten bus, it says, will take you directly there.

The Piazza della Borsa is the second largest square in Trieste, only slightly smaller than the huge Piazza Unità d'Italia. On one side of it sits the seventeenth-century neoclassical palace housing the city's Chamber of Commerce. A multi-ethnic and multi-lingual city Trieste might be, but first and foremost it's always been a port, and a city of merchants. Shipping, insurance, banking, the coffee trade and wine are at its heart.

In the middle of the square, two men are standing with a banner. They look bored. A child is taking a photo of them on a mobile phone. One of them holds a blue clipboard, on which is attached a list of seven signatures. 'The Free Territory of Trieste' says his banner. On it is the coat-of-arms of the city, the red shield with the silver halberd in the middle, pointing upwards. It commemorates the silver lance of St Sergius, a Roman soldier martyred in Syria in the third century AD for being a Christian. When he was put to death, says tradition, his halberd fell out of the sky and landed in the main square in Trieste. Kept in the cathedral of San Giusto, the weapon has reputedly never rusted, its metal refusing to accept gilding.

What do the two men want? A Free Territory of Trieste, is the answer. One of them passes over a leaflet. Italy, it says in brash, loud type, has occupied the city and surrounding land illegally. A law passed in 1945 by the Allied Commission in Rome declared the city a free territory. Italy has no rights over it. Trieste must have its own seat at the United Nations, a tax-free economic status within the European Union, and be a free port and independent trading zone. The city is hugely multi-ethnic, says one of the two men, thumb stabbing his list of seven signatures. It's 'a cold-weather Jerusalem'. But doesn't it formally belong to Italy, after the 1954 London Treaty returned it to Italy? And didn't the 1945 law divide the city into two zones of military occupation, one American and British, one Yugoslav? And the 1947 United Nations Security Council Resolution that he is quoting merely recognised this? He shrugs. Things are more straightforward than that, he says. Italy invaded in 1947, and it's time for her to go. He has written several times to the UN in New York about this, and sent petitions to the European Union in Brussels.

Have they replied? He shrugs. No. But you know, he says, they're busy these days. Syria. North Korea. He gestures over at a building on the other side of the square, tall and glass-fronted. The ground floor is occupied by a shop, the smart, slick window displays of the Tezenis underwear chain. Even at midday in summer, the lighting captures the mannequins in the window just so, the pink bras, the men's boxer shorts, the teenagers' pyjamas with rabbits on them. The eye is drawn automatically to the shop windows. What it isn't drawn to is the office on the floor above, where the windows hold huge lettered banners. 'Free Territory of Trieste: Trieste Libera,' they shout. Is anybody listening?

No, says the grinning barman two doors down. Not any more, not these days. He is balancing a tray on his right palm, bearing two very popular Venetian cocktails. They are Spritzes, large balloon glasses filled with nearly a pint of deep orange Campari and sparkling Prosecco wine. The ice clinks and reflects in the sun. A small bowl of crisps, and four purple olives the size of damsons accompany the drinks. What does he think of his neighbours and their petition? He laughs, twisting his index finger clockwise and anti-clockwise on his right temple in a classic Italian gesture.

'*Pazzo*,' he says. Mad. Then pauses and starts laughing. '*Sono squilibrate!*' They're unbalanced.

St Sergius' silver halberd on its red shield is much in evidence on the walk through the city. Mugs, mouse-mats, postcards, tea-towels, beach towels, baseball caps, lighters. It's also emblazoned on the little flag that waves from the top of the cab of the number ten bus. The vehicle's route goes up and around the front of the castle of San Giusto, built originally by the Romans, and then changed and adapted and added to by the Byzantines and Venetians and Austro-Hungarians. The bus clicks and hums as it rides the slope upwards, picking up the electrical current from the lines of wires overhead. Then there's a sharp plunge downwards; the Adriatic explodes in a turquoise spark when glimpsed between two walls, before the bus turns left into a longer, greyer boulevard. It gets more industrial with each hundred yards. A cemetery on the left, supermarkets and garages on the right. Pensioners on the bus reading the morning copy of Trieste's most popular paper, *Il Piccolo*, 'The Small One', so-called for its original tabloid format. The teenagers on the bus in their shorts and Converse All Stars are heading for the beach down in Slovenia. But before that there's a stop on Via di Valmaura, a wide boulevard that leads to an industrial estate. A supermarket on the corner, an empty street, and then on the right high walls, and a six-storey red brick building.

La Risiera di San Sabba. The San Sabba Rice-Processing Plant. Italy's only wartime concentration camp with a fully functioning crematorium. Through the big steel doors, and on the left-hand wall are a series of huge marble and metal plaques. From the World Holocaust Remembrance Centre at Yad Vashem in Jerusalem, the Italian Holocaust Survivors' Association, Trieste's Lesbian and Gay Community, the National Association of Partisans, they march along the wall. There's a dark tunnel of an entrance, and two doors on the left to the toilets and the bookshop. The architecture of the bathrooms seems very non-Italian, something horribly institutional and penal in the layout and structure of the Ladies' and the Gents'. The Germans re-designed them in 1943, says the helpful curator a few minutes later. To their own specifications, and kept prisoners' stolen possessions in there. Of course, he says, when the camp was liberated in 1945 by the partisans, it had dead bodies all over the place. He takes you through to the bookshop. In the camp courtyard, overlooked by six storeys of the old factory, it is boiling hot. This is where the building housing the crematorium stood. The actual incinerator was underground, reached by a set of steps. And on the left is a huge chamber with wooden beams, where rows of small, cramped stone cells stand in a row. Inmates have scratched and written messages on the plaster, in Italian and Slovenian.

'This really is the end ... I only hope the SS keep me alive.'

'Celestin Rodela, from Istria, born on 2nd October 1914, brought here on 26th April 1945.'

A scratched portrait of a female cellmate, drawn in red crayon before she was killed.

'*Pomozi Bog!!*' (God help us!)

The bus ride back to the city centre thirty minutes later suddenly seems full of crackling life, smiles and abundant happiness.. The curators at the camp have a certain number of documents and records, they say, but have suggested a visit to one of Trieste's more erudite and least-visited museums. The Istituto Regionale per la Storia del Movimento di Liberazione nel Friuli Venezia Giulia. IRSML, thankfully, for short. The Regional Institute for the History of the Resistance in Friuli Venezia Giulia. And so two hours later I'm on the terrace of the villa under the lime trees, listening to the school-children sing. When it comes to archives, the IRSML is the real thing. A large detached house set in a beautiful garden; the entire first floor and basement are all one archive and library. Focused very firmly on a single topic: Trieste from 1939 to 1947. The helpful, softly spoken co-curator explains carefully what is in the archives.

Well, she says, everything to do with World War II in Trieste of course. Slovenian, Croatian and Italian partisans, missing persons, SS atrocities, Yugoslav atrocities, Italian fascist atrocities. Mussolini, the Allied occupation of Trieste, the post-war Allied Military Government, all the international fears about another war starting here. She counts off on her fingers. Oh, and deportations, refugees, Italian Holocaust deportees, and what happened after the war. We've got material from MI6, the CIA, OSS, SOE, Yugoslavia's OZNA, stuff from the Germans.* There's the entire documentation of the Allied Military Government, and 3,000 books on Trieste alone. Oh, she adds, and a basement full of files from the American National Archives that almost nobody ever goes to look at. ('It's cold down there,' she says by way of warning, 'even in summer.')

Sitting at her desk, she appears mildly distracted. It must be the busy publishing work she is doing, I suggest, looking at the book manuscript she is copy-editing. The museum has its own small and erudite publishing imprint. The pages she is working on detail a very thorough, day-by-day account of the operational activities of some

* MI6: Military Intelligence Section 6, the British foreign intelligence service .
CIA: Central Intelligence Agency, the US foreign intelligence service since World War II.
OSS: a US foreign intelligence service during World War II, superseded by the CIA.
SOE: Special Operations Executive, the secret British organisation created during World War II to carry out sabotage and encourage resistance in enemy territories overseas.
OZNA: Department of National Security, Yugoslavia's security service from 1944 to 1946.
Gestapo: Geheime Staatspolizei (Secret State Police), the secret police force in Nazi Germany.
Abwehr: the German military intelligence service from 1921 to 1944.

German units in Slovenia and north-eastern Italy, from September 1943 to April 1945. Most visitors to the museum and archives come in spring and autumn, she says. Of course, in summer everybody's on the beach, and in winter it's too cold.

And she is right: all the material is there. The diplomatic cables, the Yugoslav intelligence reports, the Allied Military Government's notes, MI6's operational priorities, war crimes investigators' progress and interviews written down. Original German documents from and about the Gestapo and Abwehr. The details of how Marshal Tito's partisans shot down American Dakota transport aircraft. Churchill's and Harold Alexander's and Harry S. Truman's memos back and forwards. Cable after cable from British ambassadors in Rome, Cairo, Belgrade, Vienna, American agent assessments by the OSS and CIA, and endless analyses on Stalin's and Tito's intentions. All often in original form, sitting in cardboard containers and old box files. The sheer volume of material, and its organisation, is impressive. The woman's colleagues are walking encyclopedias of information. The archive on the thousands of Italians, Slovenians, Croats and Germans who went missing and were reportedly murdered or deported between 1943 and 1945 is around 15,000 pages alone.

Six weeks after the end of the war, in July 1945, the second Allied military governor of Trieste arrived in the city to take up his posting. An American lawyer working for the US military, he wrote the following in his diary of the moment when he rounded the headland leading along the Adriatic, and saw the city for the first time:

> Trieste is fairyland. The stuff dreams are made of. It is possible at that moment (of seeing it) to imagine that everyone living in such a place would be so happy to be there, that he would be filled with love for his neighbour, and all about him.

When the time came to write his autobiography about his time in Trieste, drawing on diary entries, he was to write the following:

> If this, the Cold War, was a war, then where was its opening, partially decisive engagement? I assert without equivocation that this engagement occurred in Italy in the Po valley and the north Adriatic littoral of Trieste. I further contest that its focal point as an element of the Cold War was the political and doctrinal confrontation at Trieste.[1]

And after months of reading the lost, hidden, deserted documents in the IRSML archive, one understands that the calm view from the villa's terrace is very deceptive. I realise that Trieste is a place over which World War III could have started. And the archives in the villa explain exactly how, and why.

Author's Note

This book was written on the Adriatic coast in Trieste, at Bardonecchia in the Italian Alps, at Finale Ligure on the Mediterranean, and at the Circolo dei Lettori at Palazzo Graneri della Roccia in Turin. Thanks and acknowledgements go to many people, but particularly to the following: my brothers Anthony, James and Martin, my sister Flora, and my niece Valeria. Also to my journalist friends Carlotta Rocci and Giulia Avataneo in Turin, the literary translator Serena D'Auria in Caltanissetta, and Dr Fulvia Benolich at the Istituto Regionale per la Storia del Movimento di Liberazione nel Friuli Venezia Giulia in Trieste. I would particularly like to thank Sara Skondras for her help in Turin. Fiammetta Rocco was extremely encouraging from the beginning, while Andrew Lownie's agenting skills were exceptional. Many thanks as well to Kate Moore at Osprey Publishing, who from the start saw the secret of this book.

Maps

Northern Italy and the Adriatic, April 1945, showing the Allied advance before the race for Trieste

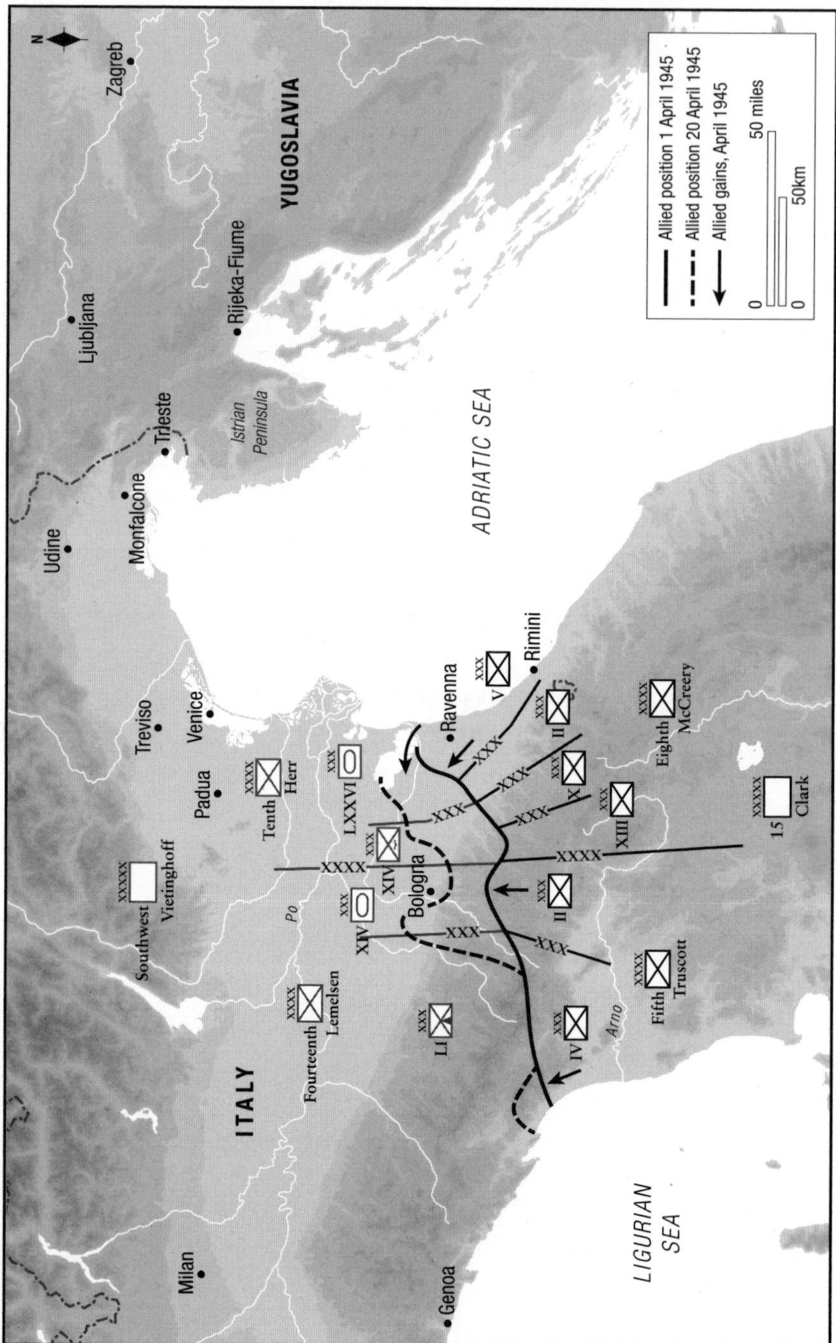

Trieste and surrounding territory

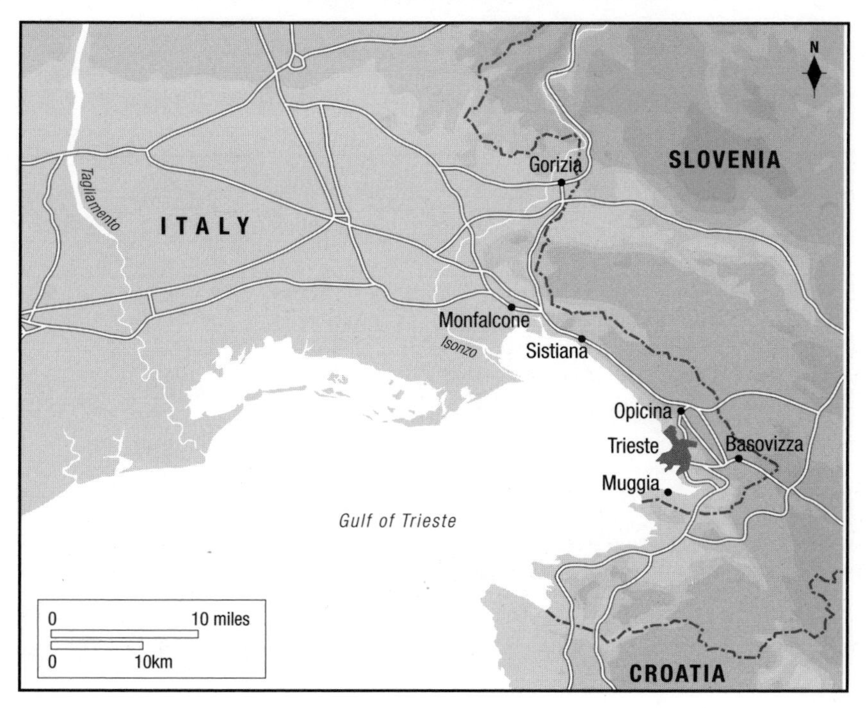

TRIESTE, THE MORGAN LINE AND INTERNATIONAL BOUNDARIES FROM 1937 TO 1954

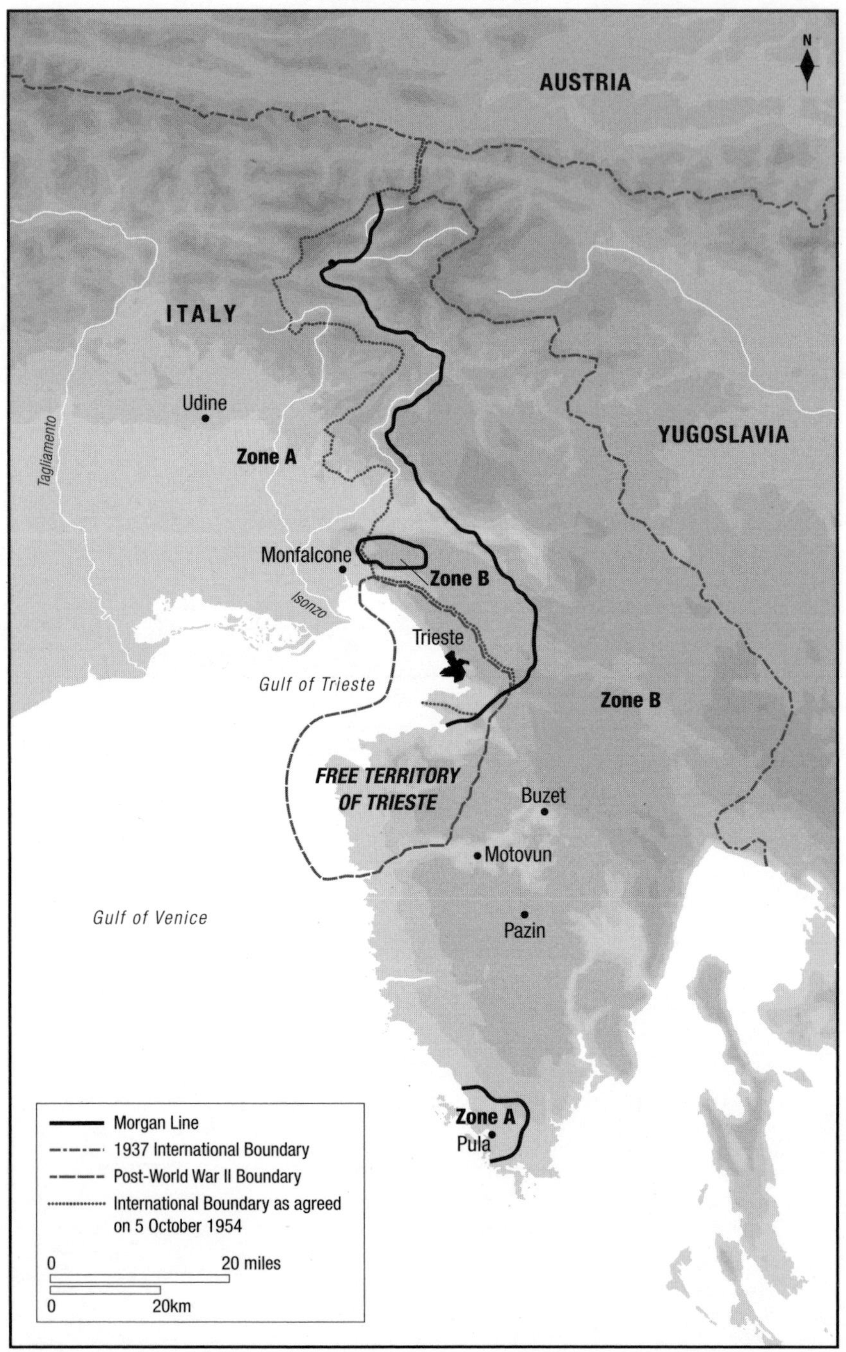

Trieste and the region of Friuli Venezia Giulia

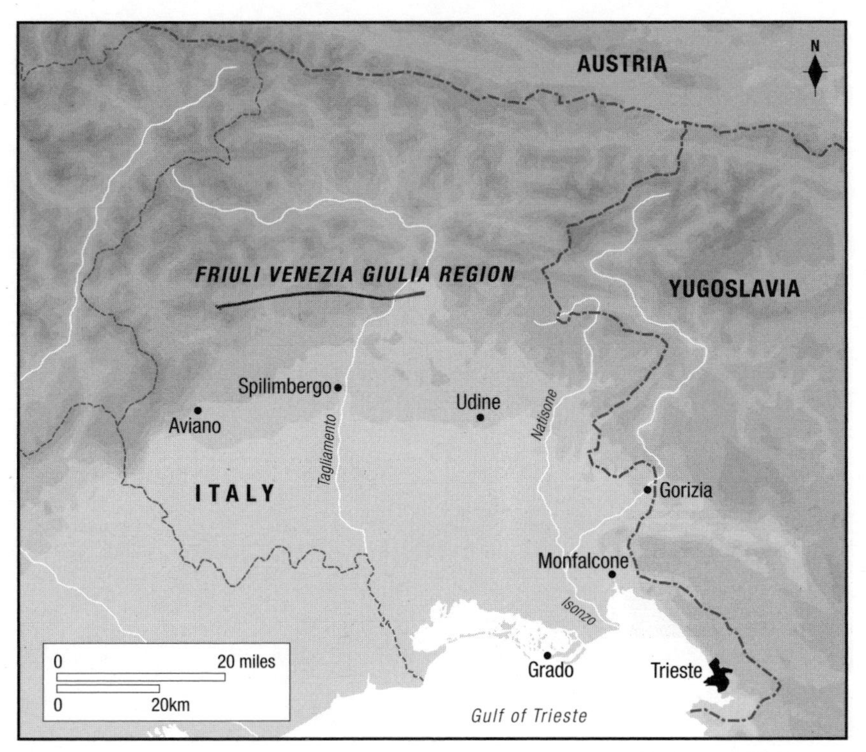

THE BORDER AREA BETWEEN ITALY, AUSTRIA AND YUGOSLAVIA, 1945

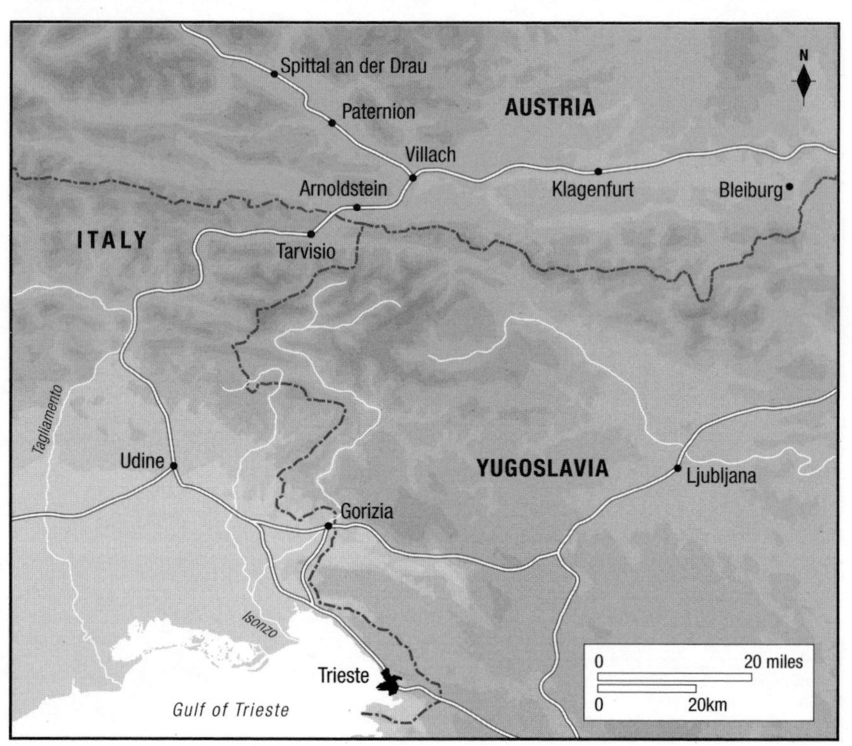

Trieste and the Istrian peninsula

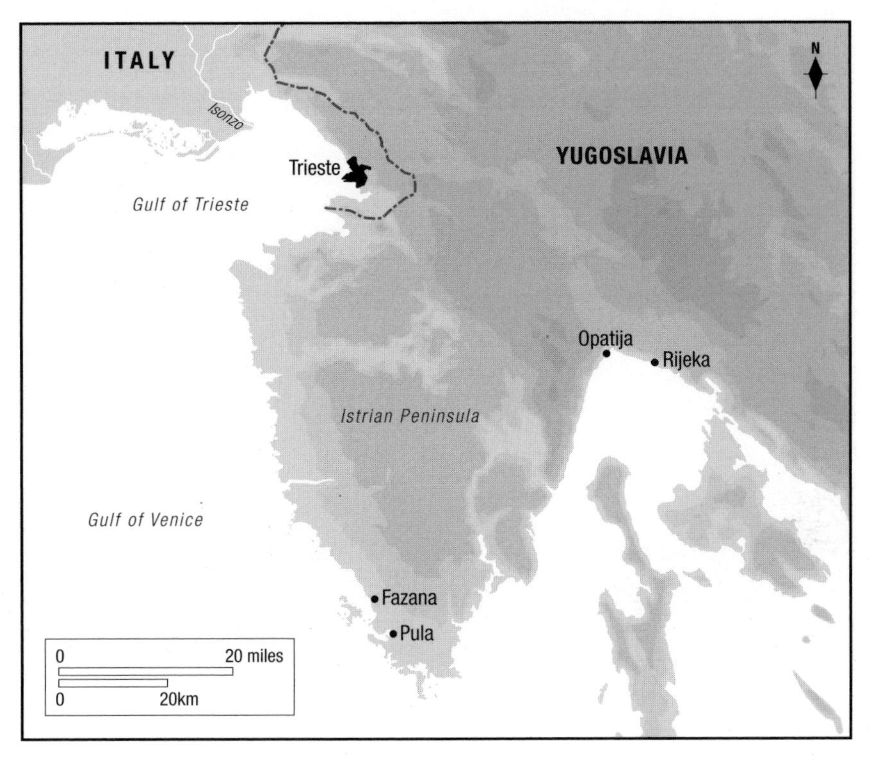

Trieste, the Adriatic and Yugoslavia

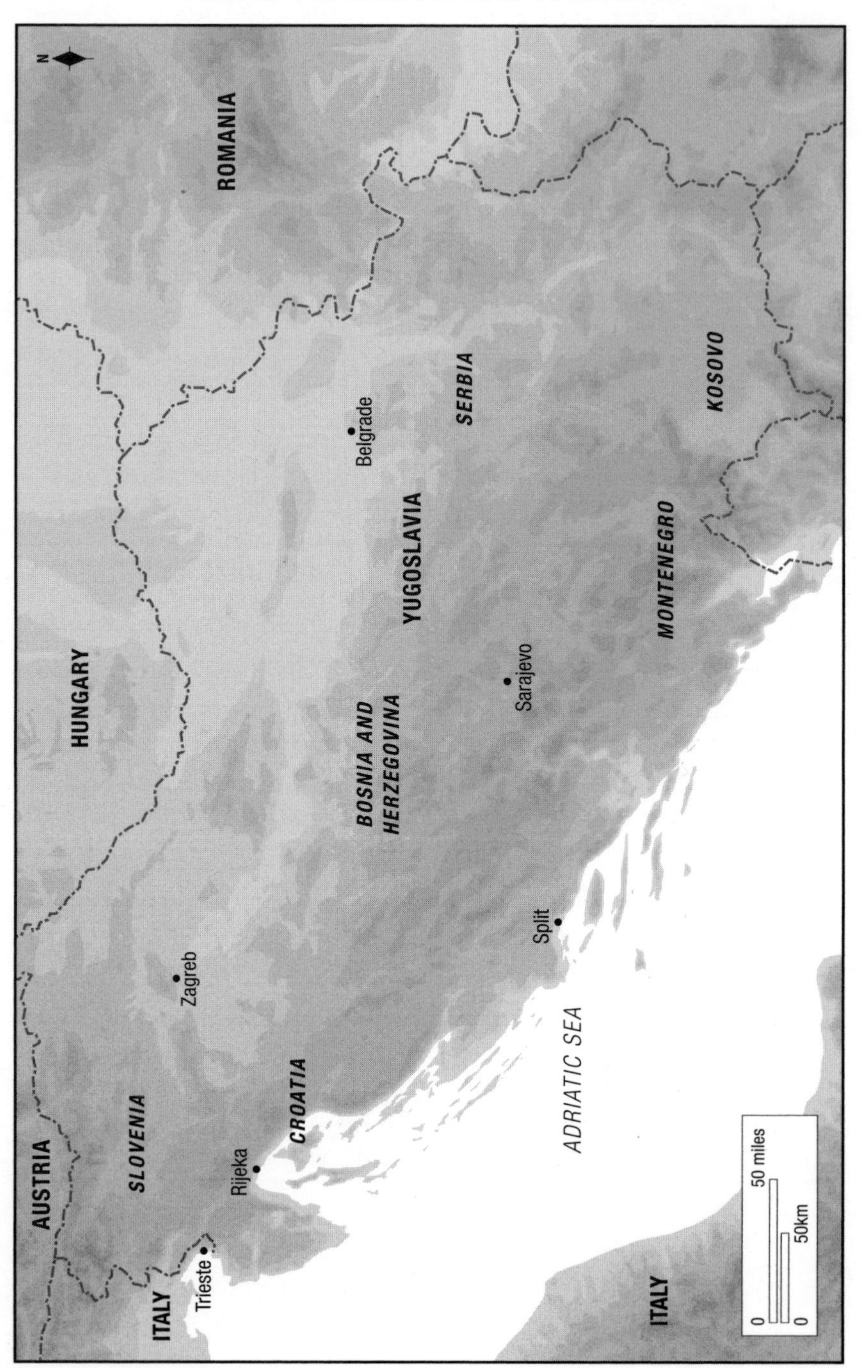

Part One

THE FALL OF TRIESTE

1

The Race for Trieste, April 1945

On his first day in office, President Harry S. Truman summoned his new Secretary of State and instructed him to provide a summary of every problem that the United States faced in their dealings with the rest of the world. It was 13 April 1945, and Hitler still had two and a half weeks to live. The Russian troops of General Georgi Zhukov were shelling Berlin. One month earlier, Operation *Meetinghouse*, a night raid on Tokyo by US B-29 bombers, had killed around 100,000 civilians in a single night: as many as would later die in Hiroshima. Edward Stettinius Jnr had taken over as Secretary of State in December 1944, and he had seen American foreign policy evolve during four years of war. His boss, President Franklin Delano Roosevelt, had died of a cerebral haemorrhage the previous day in Georgia, *en route* to the founding conference of the United Nations in San Francisco. Stettinius was astute and always saw the wider political-economic picture. He came from mixed English and German ancestry, and had married into a wealthy southern family in Virginia. He had been Under-Secretary of State in the previous administration under Cordell Hull, was experienced, and possessed an obsessive love of detail and responsibility inherited from his German ancestors.

So the summary he wrote for the new President was long and thorough.[1] He concentrated on five countries: Imperial Japan, Nazi Germany and Fascist Italy, with whom the United States had been at war since December 1941. Italy was now out of the war; Germany would inevitably capitulate in a matter of days. But the situation in the Pacific was less clear, for the Japanese military appeared determined to resist to the last man and woman. It seemed that a full-scale invasion would be required, with anticipated American casualty figures as high as a million.

Then Stettinius turned to the United States' allies: the Soviet Union and Great Britain. Roosevelt had met British Prime Minister Winston Churchill and Soviet Marshal Joseph Stalin at Teheran in November 1943, and again at Yalta, just a few weeks before his death. After the first meeting, he stated that Stalin would work with the United States for a post-war world of justice and democracy. When he attended the Yalta Summit in February of 1945, he was dying, and his position had changed dramatically.

Roosevelt now agreed with Averell Harriman, his ambassador to Moscow, who believed that Stalin's regime represented totalitarianism, and the end of democracy and personal liberty. Events quickly gave weight to these suspicions. It took only a month for Stalin to renege on promises made at Yalta to grant Poland a democratically elected government. By March he was openly accusing his American and British allies of brokering a separate peace deal with the Germans, side-lining the Soviet Union.

By mid-April 1945, the Red Army had taken Vienna and Budapest, and was fighting on the Seelow Heights outside Berlin. Yugoslavia was under the control of Marshal Josip Broz Tito and his communist partisans. If these proxy allies could annex parts of Austria and north-eastern Italy, including the key port of Trieste, Stalin could command the Adriatic. He would establish a stranglehold on access from central Europe to vital Mediterranean shipping lanes leading to Egypt, Greece, the Suez Canal and India. The Allies were determined to prevent this, and desperate to help Poland maintain some kind of independence. But they could not afford to antagonise Stalin, whose assistance was still considered vital in concluding the war against Japan.

So when he came to summarising the threat posed to the United States by Italy, Edward Stettinius was blunt. Firstly, there was the catastrophic economic distress that saw parts of its population almost starving. As important was to prevent the forcible Yugoslav occupation of parts of the north-east of the country. Trieste, lying at the top of the Adriatic Sea, had suddenly assumed enormous strategic importance. A Yugoslav occupation of the city, and of the border provinces of Austria and Italy, could only lead to what the no-nonsense new Secretary of State from Virginia called 'serious trouble'.

Harry S. Truman had been Roosevelt's last running mate, and had watched his wartime foreign policy at one remove, but he grasped the important problems quickly. He had served in France in World War I on the Western Front, as an artillery officer with the Missouri National Guard, and had seen war. On reading the exhaustive memo, the new President wrote that 'we had another explosive situation on our hands that could become serious, and that was in the Trieste area'.[2]

The basic problem, he recorded, lay in the nationalistic ambitions of the Yugoslav partisan leader, Marshal Josip Broz, whom everybody called 'Tito'.* After the Germans invaded Yugoslavia in 1941, the British Special Operations Executive (SOE) and the American Office of Strategic Services (OSS) had first provided weapons and advisors to Serb nationalists allied with the Yugoslav monarchy. The head of this dynasty, King Peter II, had been in exile in London since 1941. The Allies had at first supported these Serbs. But then they decided Tito and his men represented a more effective opposition to the Germans. So the SOE and OSS then switched support to Tito and his partisans to help them in their fight against their common enemy. By late 1944, 90 per cent of arms and supplies being air-dropped to Tito's National People's Army came from the SOE and OSS. The latter was headed by General 'Wild' Bill Donovan. Marshal Tito had established himself as the head of the Yugoslav National Provisional Government. According

* The latter was a false name he gave himself – his name and surname were simply Josip Broz.

to intelligence reports provided by the OSS and SOE liaison officers working with the Yugoslav partisans, Tito was a highly capable resistance leader who ran a liberation movement and socialist dictatorship.

Tito was a communist and a liberator, and a very effective military commander-in-chief of the National People's Army. This comprised nearly 750,000 Yugoslav soldiers and partisans, and was by far the largest group of men and women in Yugoslavia then under arms against the Germans. Tito combined these qualities with an appeal not just to the undistilled patriotism and nationalism of everybody from his country, their *nacionalizam*, but to a strong regional characteristic they called *inat*. This was a complex brand of pride that said that nobody, however strong, would take away from a Yugoslav person or peoples anything that was rightfully theirs. Over 500 years, the previous Ottoman rulers of parts of Yugoslavia had learned from bitter experience what *inat* could do. And Tito and his partisan commanders were firmly convinced that the Slovene and Croat-speaking areas in and around Trieste, as well as in parts of Austria, could lawfully be said to belong to Yugoslavia. As they had done until the end of the First World War, under the Austro-Hungarian Empire. So he decided to make a pre-emptive land-grab for the harbour city and the surrounding area of Venezia Giulia.

Trieste was one of the oldest and most strategically vital ports in the Mediterranean. It was particularly important because it had a major deep-water port forming an outlet into the Adriatic from landlocked Austria, Hungary and southern Germany. Tito was also intent on claiming the Austrian border provinces of Styria and Carinthia, and was moving his troops towards them. This flew straight in the face of American and British plans for the future of post-war Europe.

Edward Stettinius and Winston Churchill knew that the Soviet Union also supported and influenced Marshal Tito. It hadn't been that way for the entire war. The British and Americans had cemented strong links with Tito since 1941. They had dispatched liaison officers from the OSS and SOE, but most importantly they had parachuted or flown in nearly 90,000 tons of arms, food, medicines and logistical equipment. But the Allies' failure to break through the German defensive positions in northern Italy, called the Gothic Line, had disappointed Tito. He had thought that once the British 8th and American 5th Armies had liberated Rome in June 1944 it would be a matter of weeks before they arrived in northern Italy – and then hooked right into Yugoslavia. Indeed, then-General Harold Alexander had written to Churchill in June saying that he estimated the Allies would be the other side of the River Po in northern Italy within twelve weeks. It was to take nearly a year. Marshal Tito was expecting the Allies to be across the Po, and into Yugoslavia, by Christmas 1944. Their failure to be so was one reason he was increasingly allying himself with the Russians.

Yugoslav partisans and the Bulgarian Army, with assistance from the Red Army, had liberated Belgrade from the Germans on 20 October 1944. Watching Yugoslav partisans celebrate by firing enormous amounts of ammunition into the air, a watching OSS officer asked a Yugoslav colleague if he didn't think this was a waste of precious ammunition. Oh no, came the reply, now the Russians are behind us they'll give us all we want. And we won't have to rely on you Americans and British. So although a firm nationalist, and nominally autonomous, Tito was influenced by Moscow. Both sides wanted, and needed, productive and mutually friendly relationships.[3] Tito liaised closely in Belgrade with officers from Russian military intelligence (the Main Intelligence Directorate of the General Staff, Glavnoe Razvedyvatel'noe Upravlenie, or GRU), and from the People's Commissariat for Internal Affairs (Narodnyi Komissariat Vnutrennikh Del, or NKVD), the Russian Communist Party's law enforcement arm.[4] Moscow wanted Tito to take his partisan advance as far west as possible before the war in Europe ended. Stalin, as a Georgian, understood the burning absolutes of Slavic nationalism and ethnic rivalry. He understood the geo-political benefits for his regime of fomenting division among the different ethnic and political groups in countries he was trying to control. He had done this to effect in the Ukraine. And had no qualms about doing it in

Yugoslavia. But Tito was a member of the Comintern, and a de facto ally of Moscow. Stalin thought he was on his side, ideologically, militarily and politically, and could be controlled. Who knew – the Italian Communist Party, under the leadership of the pro-Moscow Palmiro Togliatti, had fifteen brigades of partisans operational in the field in northern Italy, and stood ready to link up with Tito's men once they had crossed into Italian territory. Maybe, thought Moscow, the territory they controlled through Tito could now extend into north-eastern Italy and southern Austria?

In the way of this plan stood the 300,000 men of the enormous 15th Allied Army Group, commanded by the American General Mark Clark. By mid-April 1945, the American 5th Army and the British 8th Army, including Canadian, Polish and Indian divisions, had reached the industrial heartland of northern Italy around Milan, Bologna and Turin. On the right flank in the north-east of Italy, heading for Padua, Venice and Trieste, was the 8th Army, led by British Lieutenant-General Richard McCreery. In the forefront were the 'Kiwis' of the 2nd New Zealand Division, commanded by Lieutenant-General Bernard Freyberg, who had won the Victoria Cross on the Western Front in France in 1918. The Allies' immediate post-war plan was simple. Once the Germans had surrendered, the British and Americans would run the whole of Italy through a central Allied Commission devolved into regional Allied Military Governments (AMGs) until such time as the country could hold proper elections.

So on 27 April Churchill sent Truman one of his regular cables.[5] Churchill used to do much of his correspondence with the Americans late at night from London. He would often sit up in bed drinking brandy, smoking a cigar and wearing his red and black silk Chinese dressing-gown, his favoured 'dragon kimono'. That evening he wrote to Truman that he was still waiting to hear from Washington about the proposed plans for the occupation of Trieste, and the Venezia Giulia region around it. Could Truman make a decision as soon as possible? 'It seems to me,' wrote Churchill:

> vital to get to Trieste if we can do so in the easy manner proposed, and to run the risks inherent in these kinds of political-military operations. The great thing is to be there before Tito's guerrillas are in occupation, and therefore it does not seem to me there is a minute to lose. The actual status of Trieste can be determined at leisure. Possession is nine points of the law. I beg you for an early decision. [6]

That day, Truman and Stettinius consulted the American Joint Chiefs of Staff; the machiavellian Secretary of State had already obtained a consensus of opinion from them before meeting the President. So they were in full agreement, and authorised the Allied Supreme Commander in the Mediterranean, Field Marshal Harold Alexander, to carry out Churchill's plan for the occupation of Trieste and Venezia Giulia. Alexander received his cabled instructions while sitting in a commandeered seventeenth-century villa in Siena, *en route* from Rome to the Allied front line just outside Milan. The plan was simple: Alexander was to establish a formal Allied Military Government in the region of Venezia Giulia, and to occupy Trieste. Neither Tito nor the Russians – ostensibly their allies – had been told by Truman or Churchill that the British Field Marshal, along with 125,000 soldiers, was heading for territory that they intended to occupy as well. Truman and the Americans had decided they would only inform Stalin once the 8th Army had actually taken possession of it. Churchill had last minute concerns about this, and said so to Truman:

> The military part seems to me very good; but it is surely a delusion to suppose the Yugoslav government, with the Soviet government behind them, should agree to our entering or taking control of Venezia Giulia? They will undoubtedly try to overrun all this territory and will claim and occupy the ports of Trieste, Pola and Fiume, and once they get there I do not think they will go.

Churchill added:

> Therefore, I hope that Alexander will be left to carry out the plan, which the Chiefs of the Combined Staffs have approved, as quickly and secretly

> as possible and that above all we shall try to take possession of Trieste before informing the Russians or Yugoslavs. [7]

Truman, Stettinius and the American Joint Chiefs of Staff stressed that there was no need to obtain prior Russian consent. They conceded that the wisest thing to do would be to inform Marshal Tito that the Allies were arriving in Trieste as they were actually doing so. And to explain to him that if any of his forces remained in that area they must necessarily come under Alexander's command. Truman then added one final last caveat to this highly confrontational plan:

> Alexander is directed to communicate with the American Combined Chiefs of Staff before taking further action in the area in question, if the Yugoslav forces there fail to cooperate. I think this is important, for I wish to avoid having American forces used to fight Yugoslavs or being used in combat in the Balkan political arena.[8]

The stage was thus set for the first confrontation between the Western Allies, the Russians and the Yugoslavs. It was 3pm on 30 April 1945. Hitler would commit suicide that afternoon. Two days before, Italian dictator Benito Mussolini had been shot by Italian partisans. Field Marshal Harold Alexander radioed the 8th Army Headquarters of Lieutenant-General Richard McCreery, outside Verona, and told him to 'race for Trieste with all speed and men'.

The radio message was passed straight through to the 8th Army's spearhead, the 2nd New Zealand Division. This formation was divided into three brigades, of about 2,500 men each, with accompanying medical, engineering, signals and artillery units. A brigade was then sub-divided into three infantry battalions. One of 2nd Division's hardest-fighting and most individual units was the 28th Battalion. Most of its soldiers and officers were Maoris from across the north and south islands of New Zealand. Raised in 1939 as part of the New Zealand Expeditionary Force, the battalion had fought with distinction in Crete and North Africa. General Montgomery was full of praise for their combat record. After the Afrika Korps faced the Maoris in North Africa, Field Marshal Erwin Rommel's chief of staff, General Siegfried Westphal, is reported to have said, 'Give me a Maori battalion, and I will conquer the world.'[9]

They were tough people – farmers, stockmen, cowboys and factory workers – from a very tough country. They lived and fought according to Maori tradition, and they believed deeply in their ancestors, in their spirits, and in an afterlife. As one of their chaplains in Italy, Padre Wi Huata, wrote:

> In battle they won respect for their fiery courage, and their most light-hearted contempt of danger. I believe that the 28th Maori Battalion was so good at fighting because they had a strong spiritual side to their lives – a simple belief in their ability to fight and a real belief in the Hereafter.[10]

Across the deserts of North Africa, and all the way up Italy from Taranto in the south to the River Po in the north, a unit church service was held whenever possible. The battalion padre would parade the men, often before dawn, particularly before going into combat. When out of the line, the Maoris loved singing, playing sports, swimming and drinking. They swapped their rations with Italian civilians for large amounts of red and white wine, which they transported in their lorries in five-gallon petrol jerrycans. This was in the faint hope that their officers – also mostly Maori – would think it was fuel. 8th Army regulations banned the eating of any Italian civilian food or consumption of any Italian alcohol, for fear of poisoning. The Maoris broke both rules, particularly the second, with spectacular regularity.*

* The extremely detailed daily entries from 1942 onwards in the 28th Battalion's War Diary are a colourful litany of daily wartime operations, gallantry and extra-curricular activity involving Maori soldiers on and off the battlefield in North Africa and Italy. The diary can be found at www.28maoribattalion.org.nz; see also J. F. Cody's *28th Maori Battalion* (Wellington, New Zealand: Historical Publications Department, 1956).

Collecting German and Italian pistols and machine guns from captured enemy soldiers was seen as obligatory; hard to discipline but extremely obedient, they got on very well with other Allied soldiers like themselves: the Gurkhas from Nepal, the Indians, the Canadians, the African Americans. The Germans were simply the enemy – the Hun, Jerry, or Teds (short for the Italian *tedeschi,* meaning 'Germans'). They were there to be fought, attacked, killed, captured and over-run. From the time of their arrival in Italy in November 1943, the Maoris of the 28th Battalion had tried to do this at every given opportunity. They were frequently decorated for gallantry. They were predominantly kind and considerate to the Italian civilian population, particularly in the countryside. Both sides recognised each other as farmers and stockholders, so bartering was common. Cigarettes and rations went one way, wine, fruit and occasional livestock the other. An officer remembers a ten-man section of Maoris marching along a dusty road, a dead chicken swinging from each man's web equipment. One Maori emerged after a German artillery bombardment had destroyed a village. He was wearing items he had looted – a fur-collared overcoat and polished riding boots – and was carrying an umbrella and a mandolin.

The enemy's watches, weapons, lighters, belts, insignia, equipment, vehicles and horses were there to be taken as loot. When the Maoris had crossed one river in north-eastern Italy, they had even formed an *ad hoc* cavalry platoon from captured horses. The tough New Zealanders liked the hardy, no-nonsense Italian partisans as well, particularly the thousands of women who fought with them. As they liberated a town in northern Italy in April 1945, a female partisan caught the eye of one non-commissioned officer (NCO):

> One, in particular, stood out from among the others by her bearing and her beauty. This be-pistolled (she carried two, one a Beretta and the other a Luger) trousered daughter of Italy bore a bandolier, well filled with ammunition, cowboy-like, encircling her waist, with another, equally cumbersome, wound around her deep bosom, from shoulder to waist, almost completely hiding the heaving chest behind it.[11]

When the order arrived over the radio to head for Trieste as fast as possible, the 28th Battalion had advanced as far as the outskirts of Padua, near Venice, in the extreme north-west of Italy. The unit's commanding officer, Lieutenant-Colonel Arapeta Awatere, was sitting in his Willis jeep. He had a .45-calibre Webley revolver in a canvas holster at his waist, the ribbons of the Distinguished Service Order and the Military Cross on the left-hand breast of his faded khaki shirt, and a large garland of flowers around his neck. They were a gift from a grateful Italian woman. She had planted them around the neck of the stocky Maori officer as he and his men were driving through a small town two hours earlier. The German defences across northern Italy were collapsing, but resistance was stiff. Everybody knew the war was very nearly over. But despite the German retreat, they were still fighting at every opportunity, and the Maoris had been in continuous action for three weeks. Awatere had been wounded in North Africa, had survived, and had commanded first a company, and then his battalion, as it fought all the way up Italy. He was determined that neither he nor any of his men were going to become casualties in the last forty-eight hours of the war. And absolutely determined that they were not going to take a bullet in the chaotic period of post-war liberation. So he told his officers and men to be on their guard over the next three days as they drove for Trieste. And that everybody – Germans, Italian fascists, Yugoslav partisans, Serb Chetnik irregulars, Italian communists – should be treated as the enemy. The battalion's intelligence officer summed up the operating environment in a dispatch:

> Only a pen wielded by the Prince of Darkness could do justice to a situation where, besides the US Fifth and British Eighth Armies moving forward like juggernauts, two bitterly hostile forces from Yugoslavia – communists under Tito and Serb monarchists under Mihailović – slaughtered one another when they were not shooting Germans. Italian partisans murdered upholders of the Mussolini regime and burned their own cities to smoke out the German garrisons. Mussolini, the author of it

> all, was by now hanging by the feet in front of a wayside petrol station in Milan, like a pig waiting to be dismembered. But now the 2nd New Zealand Division had a pursuit role – strike hard and fast for Trieste.[12]

The 30th April, the day of the advance, was a Monday. The Maori soldiers had had a Sunday church service the day before where nearly 600 men turned out. But the following day, Padre Wi Huata brought the men together again in the shade of some plane trees in a small town south-west of Padua. Both officers and men had been issued rations and equipment the previous night: 120 cigarettes per person, one bottle of gin between two officers, tots of warm rum for the men, chocolate, biscuits, and one bar of soap between four. Four hand-grenades each, .45 cartridges for the Thompson sub-machine gunners and those carrying pistols, and .303 rounds for the Bren light machine guns and the Lee Enfield rifles. It was late spring, and the ubiquitous Italian insects were already at work. The men took Atabrine tablets against malaria and used repellant creams to ward off the bites of malarial mosquitoes. In Sicily in summer 1943, the number of American combat casualties had been exceeded only by the number of men who caught malaria, and 8th Army regulations made it a disciplinary offence not to take anti-malarial tablets, even though they made men feel sick and nauseous.

The Italians waved as the New Zealanders drove off. Some just stood and stared. Through villages on crossroads, past country mansions hidden in trees, the convoy of soldiers rumbled forward as fast as they could. They passed through Padua at dusk. The city was burning in a dozen places, most of the German garrison had been killed by the partisans, and as the Maoris drove past, they saw collaborators being dragged towards firing-squads. By the time the moon came out, they were driving through Mestre, where the road forked right for Venice, and led straight on to Trieste.

Lieutenant-Colonel Awatere gave orders to his officers and senior NCOs by the side of the road. The men could smell the sea air. Rifle and machine-gun fire cracked and buzzed on the road ahead, and artillery rounds whooshed overhead like breathless trains, on the way to hit German positions in front of them. Yugoslav partisans were reported to be heading down into Trieste from the mountains above it, said the colonel. It was imperative the Allies got there first, he'd been told. Confused and conflicting reports were coming in over the radio from British and American SOE and OSS agents operating with partisan groups on the road ahead of them. The Yugoslavs, and Russian advisers, had reached Trieste. No they hadn't, said another contradictory report. There was fighting in the seaport between Germans and partisans. The New Zealanders would make a full-frontal attack with tanks, accompanied by an amphibious landing onto the docks of Trieste. The situation changed by the hour.

The convoy drove on past Venice, turning right and heading east as they curved around the top of the Adriatic coast. It was now 11pm on 30 April. Suddenly a group of German artillery guns, pulled by hot and panicking horses, trundled towards the Maoris. Some of the anti-tank guns were drawn by cream-coloured oxen with huge horns, panting in the warm night. A long line of German infantry followed them, their boots crunching along the road as they marched under the moonlight. The Maoris jumped down from their trucks, cocking their weapons. A Bren gunner took cover behind the trunk of a plane tree. Then a lone New Zealand soldier materialised out of the darkness, and walked up to one of the officers from the 28th Battalion. This entire column of men were all his prisoners, he said, smiling. He'd captured them by himself up the road. The Maoris let him take his huge personal column of prisoners, and loot, back towards Venice, and then drove on. Trieste was still sixty-five miles away. Sometime after midnight the column halted by the River Piave, which ran into the Adriatic, at a right-angle across the battalion's line of advance. The men posted guards and fell asleep in the ditches by the side of the road. It was the early hours of 1 May.

One person in the Allied armies who could have predicted what might happen in Trieste, and in the Venezia Giulia, was a British lieutenant-colonel called Peter Wilkinson. A child of the British Empire, he was born in India where his father was serving in the army. After studying at Cambridge University in the 1930s, he had been one of the earliest recruits to the Special Operations Executive in 1940. He had served in Poland just before the Germans invaded. When they did, he made a report to the British War Office detailing how effective were their Blitzkrieg techniques. London rejected the assessment, telling him bluntly that such warfare would never work in western Europe. When the Germans reached Paris in 1940, the War Office rescinded this criticism, and decorated Wilkinson. He then served in France, from where he rescued the Polish General Sikorski, and was posted to Crete in 1941 just as German paratroopers started dropping. Evacuated by the Royal Navy under repeated German bombing runs, he served in Egypt before being posted to Yugoslavia. He trekked across the country with the partisans, met Marshal Tito, and took a party of Slovene partisans into Austria to try to create a resistance network against the Germans. On the Allied side, Wilkinson knew more than almost anybody else about Yugoslavia. When the Germans managed to crack the SOE mission's cipher codes, he was pulled out by RAF aircraft and returned to Italy. He then created and led SOE's Number 6 Special Force in north-eastern Italy. This was a group of officers and men, experienced in guerrilla warfare, whose task was to coordinate resistance against the Germans across the border in Yugoslavia. They also had to try and find effective methods of dealing with the immediate post-war period in the country.*

On the morning of 1 May 1945, Wilkinson was waiting outside Venice for a fellow officer to return from a reconnaissance mission into the city. He had gone to find out if various SOE agents had

* Wilkinson wrote an autobiography after the war, entitled *Foreign Fields: the Story of an SOE Operative* (London: I.B. Tauris, 2002). He also wrote a history of the SOE and General Gubbins, who commanded it. Documents detailing Wilkinson's operations and career as a soldier and as a post-war diplomat are also in The National Archives, the Imperial War Museum in London, and the IRSML in Trieste, the Istituto Regionale per la Storia del Movimento di Liberazione nel Friuli Venezia Giulia.

survived the liberation. This brother officer from SOE had taken not only Wilkinson's staff car, but also his sleeping kit and haversack. So he was biding his time in a small town, carrying nothing but his webbing equipment and a Colt Compact, a shortened model of the popular 1911 Colt .45 automatic pistol.

Out of nowhere, a Willis jeep suddenly pulled up in front of the headquarters where he was standing, and a British general told him to get in. The young lieutenant-colonel from SOE could not refuse. The general's chest was emblazoned with combat decorations, including three Distinguished Service Orders and a Military Cross. It was Lieutenant-General Sir John Harding, who commanded the British XIII Army Corps, the parent unit of the 2nd New Zealand Division. With Harding at the wheel, the jeep accelerated off at high speed down the road towards Trieste. The ebullient general was an erratic driver, and the roads were full of British and New Zealand troops heading as fast as they could for the Adriatic seaport. In quick succession, Wilkinson and his high-ranking driver had two collisions with other vehicles. They were unscathed. As they drove, General Harding swerved as he overtook trucks, tanks and armoured cars, while keeping up a steady stream of questions to the SOE officer about what he thought would happen in Trieste. Over the noise of the engine, of accelerating tanks, and the wind, Wilkinson tried to explain. He thought that the Allies' failure to break through the German defences on the Gothic Line in northern Italy in winter 1944, and thus push on to liberate Yugoslavia, had severely disappointed Tito and his partisans; and that it had pushed them decisively into the arms of the oncoming Red Army. The partisans saw the Soviets as allies. Wilkinson said he thought that if the Allies did not want to relinquish Trieste and the Venezia Giulia region to the Yugoslavs – and by extension the Russians – they would have to fight for it.

Regardless, said Harding, returning the salutes of passing officers as he steered the jeep one-handed, his orders were to take Trieste as quickly as possible. So he was accompanying Wilkinson further up the road to introduce him to the commanding officer of the New Zealand Division, Lieutenant-General Bernard Freyberg, who was leading the race for the crucial seaport. Church bells were ringing as they drove, and Italian civilians lined the road, cheering and offering the passing soldiers bottles of wine, baskets of tomatoes and melons. But the conversation did not only focus on Trieste. Harding knew Theresa, Wilkinson's new wife, who was in the Women's Royal Naval Service, or Wrens, based at Allied Headquarters outside Naples. Although she was a naval NCO, and not an officer, class made them close adherents. Harding and Theresa would often go riding together, and on hearing of her forthcoming wedding, the general had lent her his staff car so she could drive into Naples and buy a hat.

Shortly, the two officers rumbled over the River Tagliamento, and arrived at Freyberg's temporary headquarters at the side of the road. The two generals conferred, while Wilkinson chatted with Major Geoffrey Cox, a New Zealander he had last seen on Crete in 1941. Cox was Freyberg's chief intelligence officer. As a journalist he had covered the Spanish Civil War in Madrid, the Winter War in Finland, and then the so-called 'Phoney War' in France in 1939. He had subsequently joined the army, served in Greece, Crete and North Africa as an intelligence officer on Freyberg's staff, and then worked as a diplomat in Washington. 1944 saw him back in uniform at Monte Cassino, from where he fought the war up Italy with the New Zealand 2nd Division. By the time he stood at the side of the road at the beginning of May, he had been twice Mentioned in Dispatches, and been made a Member of the military division of the Order of the British Empire.

Having ordered Freyberg to get to Trieste and seize the city and its port facilities as quickly as possible, Harding drove back towards Venice, accelerating away erratically in a cloud of dust.

Freyberg, Wilkinson and Cox then climbed into a jeep and pushed on towards Trieste. As they drove, they passed truck after truck laden with New Zealand soldiers, who waved and shouted ecstatically when they saw that the driver of the jeep was none other than one of their national military heroes. If Harding, with his long war experience and list of decorations, was popular with the soldiers, Freyberg was an icon.

Freyberg had been born in Britain, but the family moved to New Zealand when he was two years old. A keen competitive swimmer, who had initially trained as a dentist, Freyberg had reportedly fought in the Mexican revolution in 1913 before joining the British Army at the outbreak of World War I. By its end, he had fought at Gallipoli and on the Western Front, won the Victoria Cross and three Distinguished Service Orders, been wounded in action six times and Mentioned in Dispatches five, and was the youngest general in the British Army. He had rejoined the army in 1940, and led the New Zealanders in Crete and North Africa. Churchill called him 'my Salamander', from his ability to pass through fire almost unscathed. Freyberg would have been the first to admit he was not a political man – he saw military action as the easiest solution towards problems in wartime. Harding and Alexander had chosen him to lead the advance on Trieste specifically because he and his men would address the problem like a bull at a gate.

At that point, however, Wilkinson knew three things very clearly. Firstly, that the combination of hundreds of thousands of Allied, Italian, German, Russian and Yugoslav forces converging in and around Trieste made the strategic and tactical situation one of the most militarily and politically complex of the war. Secondly, he had firmly promised his new wife serving in Naples that after five years of fighting this would be the last combat operation of his war. Lastly, he had limited trust for the Yugoslavs he knew waited in front of him. His best friend from his parent regiment in the British Army, the Royal Fusiliers, was an aristocratic major who had also joined the SOE. He had disappeared in highly suspicious circumstances the previous winter while serving alongside Slovenian partisans in Austria. Wilkinson thought it quite possible that Yugoslav partisan commissars, or intelligence agents, had murdered him.

As he and the two British officers drove towards Trieste, they began to pass groups of Italian partisans, some of them waving the green flags of the Catholic Osoppo group that operated north-east of Venice. Then the flags started changing to the red flags of the communist Garibaldi partisan brigade. The two sides were sworn enemies: in the village of Porzûs in February that year, a group of Catholic Italian partisans from the Osoppo group had been murdered by Slovenian rivals from the Garibaldi group. As the British officers and the New Zealand war hero accelerated on, bumping over the cobbles of small town squares, raising dust as they cornered heavily on the avenues lined with plane trees, the local reception changed. The civilians were suddenly silent at the sides of the road, the partisans now giving the communist clenched fist salute. Signs on houses and streets started appearing in Slovenian. The jeep, driving faster than the New Zealanders' trucks, reached the head of the Allied column, alongside the advance armoured car squadron of the British 12th Royal Lancers. The three officers crossed the River Isonzo, which up until the end of World War I had marked the frontier between Italy and the Austro-Hungarian Empire. Which had included what was now Yugoslavia.

They rounded a long corner by a pine forest just before the shipbuilding town of Monfalcone. And then General Freyberg and his two passengers suddenly saw the dark cobalt of the Adriatic Sea, and, some twenty miles in the distance, the towers and spires of Trieste. But they also saw something else. A hundred yards in front of them, blocking the road, were two motorcycle dispatch riders and a group of army officers in drab serge uniforms, red stars set in the centre of their forage caps. These were not Italian partisans, noted Wilkinson immediately. This was the Yugoslav National Liberation Army.

General Freyberg dismounted from his jeep, and the Yugoslavs approached. One of the officers recognised Wilkinson from his time with the partisans, and shook his hand. The situation was gently tense. The New Zealand general explained, with the two Allied officers translating into German and halting Serbo-Croat, that he was advancing on Trieste and expected no opposition.

That, said one of the officers, was just not going to be possible. The Yugoslav National Liberation Army, with around 100,000 troops, had already occupied the city and its surroundings. The Allies could proceed no further.

2

Holding Trieste, 29 April–1 May

Friedrich Rainer and Odilo Globocnik left Trieste in a hurry. The two SS generals were the most senior Nazi party officials in the city, and were desperate to escape before the Allies or the Yugoslav partisans arrived. They knew they faced a war crimes trial from the former, with the death sentence almost a certainty. A firing squad was just as likely from the latter. The atrocities carried out during their regime in Trieste had seen to that. If there were two German men the Slovenian partisans would most dearly like to catch, they were SS-Obergruppenführer Rainer and SS-Brigadeführer Globocnik.*

When Italy had signed an armistice with the Allies in 1943, and the Germans occupied the country, Hitler had appointed Rainer as the *Gauleiter,* or administrator, of Trieste and the coastal areas of Istria and Venezia Giulia that surrounded it. Globocnik had been the head of the SS and police.

* When the Germans fled Trieste, they left behind vast amounts of paperwork and documentation from their time in Trieste and Venezia Giulia, some of which is now in the IRSML in Trieste and National Archives in Ljubljana. Information also comes from accounts from Italian Fascist officials, German Wehrmacht and SS men who, under questioning, provided information on Rainer to American and British investigators. They form part of the Nuremberg trial archives. Rainer also wrote an autobiography about his time as a witness, *My Internment and Testimony at the Nuremberg War Crimes Trial,* published by Edwin Mellen Press in 2006. Documents from his trial in the former Yugoslavia are held in Ljubljana.

Together Globocnik and Rainer had carried out the Final Solution in Trieste, killing or deporting most of the city's Jews to concentration camps. The SS men had also overseen a two-year campaign of atrocity and reprisals in the region against Slovenian and Italian partisans and communists, as well as anti-Fascists. The Germans had constructed a concentration camp in Trieste too, at an old rice-processing plant in the suburb of San Sabba.[1]

So, as he prepared to flee, Rainer knew two things. The Allies would certainly want to detain him as he had direct command-and-control responsibility for what had happened in Trieste. He was also absolutely sure the Americans, British and Yugoslavs would want to apprehend Odilo Globocnik. Prior to arriving in Trieste in 1943, the latter's senior role in Operation *Reinhard* had led to the killing of hundreds of thousands of Jews in Poland, mainly in the camps of Bełżec, Majdanek, Sobibór and Treblinka.

So on the night of 29 April, the Nazi *Gauleiter* and the SS general decided to flee the city under cover of darkness. They planned to drive northwards back to Rainer's native Austria. There they would hide out for the summer in high Alpine villages, surrounded by sympathetic supporters who could offer them sanctuary. There was only one escape route they could take. It would be madness to drive directly north-east from Trieste into Slovenia, cut past the capital, Ljubljana, and then head towards Klagenfurt in Austria. The country was enemy territory, half-occupied by Yugoslav partisans and soldiers, and inhabited by Slovenians. So that route was out of the question. An escape by sea was also impossible. Where would they go? They could only sail in two directions. South-east along the coastline of Istria would lead them further into Yugoslav, and south-west across the Gulf of Trieste towards Venice would take them straight into Allied-controlled territory. So the only option was to keep just inside the Italian border, and take the road that ran north-westwards from Trieste to the small city of Udine. Then they would head to the Austrian frontier and the town of Villach. It was a journey of 120 miles, and the British and Americans were closing in fast. Italian partisans were also operating all over the area through which they would drive. There was one ray of hope – in this complicated territory of competing factions and allegiances, there were also pro-German militias made up of Serbs and Cossacks. The two officers estimated that the trip could be done in four hours, and if they didn't run into trouble they could be in Villach before daybreak.

The two had commandeered five Italian and German lorries, and a staff car. SS-Sturmbannführer Ernst Lerch, a native of Klagenfurt, travelled with them. He had worked with Globocnik in Poland, and been his chief of staff in Trieste. His boss had been his best man at his wedding to a female Gestapo agent. With him was SS-Sturmbannführer Hermann Höfle, second-in-command to Globocnik on Operation *Reinhard*, and Austrian as well. The third high-ranking SS man with them was Georg Michaelsen, a *Sturmbannführer* who had served in Poland and Trieste too. They would travel in civilian clothes, armed. Globocnik formed a personal escort of sixteen loyal men and women from the Ukrainian SS, who had operated with him in Poland. He had originally brought ninety-four of them to Trieste and along with Italian Fascists, some of them had worked as guards at the San Sabba concentration camp.[2] Now this small squad would guard him and Rainer as they broke north.

They would also guard another cargo that Globocnik ordered them to load into the backs of the trucks. From the ghettos and camps in Poland, Globocnik had reportedly taken an unauthorised personal cut of the jewellery, gold sovereigns, currency and personal valuables taken from hundreds of thousands of Jews. He had brought this personal hoard back with him to Trieste.* He had also worked closely with the German *Kunstschutz*, the cultural 'conservation' programme. From autumn 1943 to spring 1945, they had transported some stolen works of art from the city's two main museums, and its

* As head of Operation *Reinhard*, Globocnik wrote detailed reports to Himmler about the value and quantity of goods taken from Jewish and other prisoners that were transported back to Germany from Poland. The gold bullion and gold coins alone weighed 4,700 kilos, or 4.7 tons. (Nuremberg Trial Document NO-059/60, reports from Globocnik to Himmler on 'Valuables turned in from Operation Reinhardt'.)

largely Jewish art dealers, to caches in nearby Austria guarded by the SS.[3] The lorries and staff car pulled out of the cobbled streets of the ancient seaport, and headed for the main railway station. Then they joined the highway that curved around the docks before turning north for Udine. Ahead of them the night sky was cut with artillery explosions, the undersides of the clouds blossoming yellow and orange with the reflected detonations of air raids. The two SS generals knew the Third Reich was in tatters, and the war over. Like many of their colleagues, they'd considered plans to head for Spain or Argentina. But for now, the immediate imperative was to get to Austria alive.

They left their former fiefdom at the mercy of the advancing Yugoslavs and Allies. It was woefully under-defended. Most of the SS troops in Trieste disappeared north or westwards the moment their two senior officers bolted. Two German generals and one colonel from the Heer,* the regular army, stayed behind to defend the seaport and its surroundings. Between them, Major-General Hermann Linkenbach, General Kübler of the Adriatic Coastal Command, and a composite infantry battle-group, Kampfgruppe Berger, mustered five German regiments. These were equivalent in size to large Allied infantry battalions. They included the 901st and 902nd Infantry Regiments, the 1088th Artillery Battalion, and the 30th and 313th Engineer Battalions. The 10th SS Police Battalion was stationed at Gorizia, thirty miles north-west of Trieste, but on hearing that their commanders were fleeing towards Austria, they joined them.[4]

The German defence of Trieste and its coastal surroundings thus consisted of a maximum of 5,500 men, many of them naval ratings, cooks, anti-aircraft gunners, engineers and inexperienced soldiers. The positions they were holding stretched along twenty miles of coastline from Monfalcone in the west, where General Freyberg and Lieutenant-Colonel Wilkinson had been halted, to the furthest eastern suburb of the city of Trieste. Some 20,000 soldiers and

* The Wehrmacht, or German armed forces, comprised the Heer (regular Army), Kriegsmarine (Navy), and Luftwaffe (Air Force).

partisans from the 9th Slovenian Partisan Corps, and the 20th Division of the Yugoslav People's 4th Army, were advancing towards them from the north and east. From the west, the 2nd New Zealand Division spearheaded the entire British 8th Army. The Royal Navy had complete control of the seas, and the British and American air forces owned the skies. The Germans were completely trapped.

One moment the SS troops and their leaders were there, noticed Linkenbach, and the next they were gone. So on 30 April he and the two other senior Wehrmacht officers split their troops up as best as they could, hoping to delay by at least a few hours the two simultaneous advances from east and west. Linkenbach, at fifty-six a veteran of the First World War, thought that with two regiments of 1,500 men he could defend Trieste against an amphibious landing for up to a fortnight. But he knew he was powerless against a vast, triangulated land assault by tanks, artillery and 30,000 experienced infantrymen coming at him from three different directions. His dire defensive situation then got worse.

Following the departure of the SS administration of Trieste, the German XXXIV Army Corps in the Slovenian capital, Ljubljana, took overall command.[5] It was vital, they told Linkenbach, that the infantry men of Kampfgruppe Berger held the line south-east of Trieste to stop the Yugoslavs advancing up the Adriatic coast. But Colonel Berger, a veteran of the Russian front, knew all too well what could happen if he and his men were taken prisoner by Tito's troops. So the battle-group left their positions, and drove as fast as they could towards Trieste itself, aiming to surrender to the advancing Allies. They left behind a skeleton force of some 600 men to defend thirty miles of the mountainous, craggy Dalmatian coastline. Berger's troops headed for one of the oldest and most easily defendable buildings in Trieste, the Castello di San Giusto. The city is built in the shadow and on the slopes of a mountain, which climbs a thousand feet above it to a rocky plateau. The castle, built by the Romans and enlarged by the Venetians in the 1300s, commands a dominating view of the port and its surroundings. For hundreds of years it had seen attackers and defenders from the Roman, Phoenician, Venetian, Ottoman and Austro-Hungarian empires fight in and over Trieste. On 30 April 1945, it was where many of the Wehrmacht troops inside the city decided to make a stand.

Major-General Linkenbach's few remaining troops included some sailors from the German Kriegsmarine, so he posted them at defensive positions on the harbour of Trieste, which is built around a man-made lagoon. Two long moles, enlarged jetties, curve around it like crabs' pincers. A group of five German E-boats, armed with 20mm canon and a few torpedoes, were docked here. The exit from the port was half-blocked by three Italian merchant ships, bombed by the Royal Air Force, which had semi-capsized and now lay on their sides in the Adriatic waters. There were also many other submerged and semi-sunk vessels in the much wider area of the harbour and lagoon stretching around Trieste.

Three miles further west, on a limestone spur pointing out into the sea, stood the Miramare castle. The elegant, baroque palace and its forty-acre garden had been built in the mid-1800s by Ferdinand Maximilian of the House of Hapsburg, the younger brother of the Emperor of Austria. It had been a present for his wife. The trees and shrubs that filled the botanical garden came from the Middle East and Central America. Friedrich Rainer had used it as a training school for army officers, but had never turned it into a defensive position for fear the Allies would bomb it. An atrocity-prone National Socialist though Rainer was, he was also an art-lover and aesthete. Linkenbach had no such luxury of choice: the castle provided the perfect observation position from which to spot Allied troops approaching by land or sea, so he sent an understrength company of his men to occupy it. Within an hour, they were digging their MG-42 machine guns into the sandy earth beneath the enormous cedar trees, that a hundred years before had been transported from Lebanon.

On the night of 29 April the San Sabba crematorium, and the building housing it, were dynamited by the Germans. They were hoping to dispose of some of the evidence. Three to five thousand-odd Italian Jews, captured Italian, Slovenian and Croatian partisans and civilians, suspected communists, Italian soldiers with anti-Fascist sympathies, Roma and homosexuals had been killed in the camp. Others had been imprisoned there before being transported to other camps elsewhere. Before leaving, the Germans mixed some of the human ashes that remained in the crematorium with the rubble. Parts of these remains were left in three large paper sacks in the ruins of the crematorium building. The guards and officers then jumped into trucks outside. Those victims inside the camp who were still alive were left locked in cramped, lice-ridden cells and on the upper floors of the building, which had been used as barracks for the guards.[6] A combination of German, Ukrainian, Italian and Austrian troops had worked at the camp. Those who remained in the city on the night of the 29th then either fled, or drove as quickly as they could towards another of the city's strongpoints.

Trieste's law courts, the city's Tribunale, were built in the nineteenth century in an enormous five-storey building in the centre of the city, near the sea. The walls of the building were three feet thick, and on four sides it faced access roads leading into the centre of the town. It was a perfect defensive position. The camp guards, the Italians and two mixed companies of SS men barricaded themselves inside. There were around 800 of them. They had a lot of ammunition, food, red wine, and plentiful supplies of looted cognac and *grappa,* Italian brandy. But the Italian communist partisan groups, waiting in the city for the arrival of Tito's men, quickly did something decisive. They cut off the water supply to the huge building. The beginning of May on the Adriatic is hot, and no weather to fight defensive urban warfare, without water, inside a very large municipal building with the windows closed. The SS men suddenly began to question their choice of defensive location, but it was too late. Two opposing groups of Italian partisans, communists who supported the Yugoslavs, and Catholics who supported the Allies, were fighting each other in the streets outside. The Germans had no escape.

The small town of Opicina sits half-way up a mountain a thousand feet above Trieste. It lies on the slopes of the Karst plateau which runs above the city, and south-east along the Adriatic coast of Yugoslavia. The fierce north-east wind that gusts down into Trieste at all times of year barges its way through the town's elegant piazzas, and the narrow back streets that climb in serpentine curves up through the city. The wind starts up on the mountain above Opicina. Called the *Bora,* it frequently gusts at speeds exceeding 100 miles per hour and causes the temperature to plummet; legend says it drives foreigners and strangers mad. This vicious wind has had a profound influence on the architecture and layout of Trieste. In Roman times, when the city was part of their empire, many of Trieste's cobbled streets were built narrow and winding as a barrier against the *Bora*. They climb in charming curves that rise up through the city. It makes the city easier to defend, as well. And much harder for those trying to attack it, however superior their numerical strength.

So on the morning of 30 April, men and women from the Yugoslav National Liberation Army stood on the mountain slopes above Trieste, around the town of Opicina, and tried to work out the best way to attack the city below. Many of them had been fighting the Germans for three years. Like everybody in the partisans and the Narodno-oslobodilačka Vojska, the Yugoslav National Liberation Army, they thought of themselves as Yugoslav.*

Wasn't that what Marshal Josip Broz said? The partisans and soldiers all knew that 'Tito' was simply his nickname, or an assumed name, that had somehow stuck with the Allies and everybody else. As for Tito and his men and women? When the political commissars

* Extensive documentation on the 9th Partisan Corps and the 4th Yugoslav Army is in the IRSML in Trieste, and in the Arhiv Republike Slovenije, the Slovenian government archives in Ljubljana, as well as in the National History Museum in Belgrade. A lengthy and thorough account of the operational activities of the Slovenian partisans is in Maks Zadnik's *Istrski Odred,* published in 1975 by Nova Gorica Slovenia. The title translates as 'Istrian Detachment', and it is cited in this book as *Istrian Detachment.*

weren't around, they respectfully and ironically called him *Deda,* or 'grandpa'. Everybody from Yugoslavia was included in his army and partisans, from all ethnicities. The 1st Tank Brigade in the 4th Army was typical. Montenegrins, Serbs, Italians, Jews, with Croats and Slovenians in the majority. They had all been taught in training that their army and resistance was a socially egalitarian operation, representative of true people's communism. Class-wise, they knew, it was the same: 65 per cent of the officers were industrial workers or peasants, and 27 per cent came from a grouping called intellectuals, merchants and clerks. Only 10 per cent of the officers were actually former soldiers. The rank-and-file were over 80 per cent workers and peasants, but a good 20 per cent were intellectuals and merchants. The partisan officers knew their figures and their training. They had to. It kept OZNA, the secret police, off their back.* And everybody knew the old, dark, saying. *OZNA sve dozna.* OZNA can find out anything.

The Yugoslav soldiers looked down from Opicina into the heart of Trieste. It was a city they considered theirs. Hadn't Slovenes, Croats and Austrians made up the majority of the population in the port, and the surrounding region, for several hundred years under the Hapsburgs and the Austro-Hungarian Empire? And wasn't it only because the British and the French had backed the Italians in the First World War, and then allowed them to annex Trieste, that the city was now part of Italy at all? That, said the Yugoslav divisional commanders, was about to change. The British and New Zealand soldiers, with their huge numbers of tanks and artillery pieces, were blocked fifteen miles west of the port, on the old Austro-Italian border at the River Isonzo. The partisans and the Yugoslav soldiers were a day ahead of them. Opicina was the last barrier before they could storm down the winding streets all the way into Trieste.

The Yugoslavs saw no reason they would want to shoot at the British and Americans, particularly at this late stage in the war. Unlike

* Odjeljenje za Zaštitu Naroda, or Department for National Security, was the wartime Yugoslav security service that existed between 1944 and 1946.

the Germans, the Italian Fascists and non-communist Italian partisans who the National Liberation Army regarded as their enemy. For every Yugoslav partisan and soldier whose friends, colleagues and relatives had either disappeared, been killed or captured since the Germans arrived in 1943, this was pay-back time. They knew that truth of what had happened under the Germans would be plain for the world to see, once they arrived in Trieste and opened the gates of the Risiera di San Sabba.

Nobody in the partisans knew exactly what had been happening inside the old factory for two years, but nobody who had gone into it seemed to come out alive. The first commander of the camp in late 1943 had been a brutal German *SS-Sturmbannführer* called Christian Wirth. The communist Garibaldi Brigade partisans had tracked his movements as the German major was driven around Trieste in a staff car. One day in May 1944, he drove across the line into neighbouring Slovenia, the car pulling hard as it climbed up the winding roads through the suburbs of Trieste. Just outside the village of Hrpelje, his driver slowed to take a bend. The car was hit out of nowhere with several ripping bursts of partisan machine-gun fire. The car crashed into a large olive tree at the side of the road. Wirth was killed.

The mountain town of Opicina, and Trieste, were going to prove a hard target. The Germans in Opicina had prepared a network of defensive bunkers that held 88mm anti-aircraft guns and 75mm Pak anti-tank guns. The Yugoslavs had no idea how many Germans were defending the town. But they remembered what their Red Army and partisan instructors had told them at the training camps outside Ljubljana and elsewhere. Three to one superiority in numbers for the attacker. Five to one if you can possibly manage it, especially when street-fighting. So the commanders of the 4th Army and the 9th Corps from the National Liberation Army waited until just after midnight on 30 April, and then went for broke. They threw three whole brigades into Opicina, nearly 9,000 men.

The Germans defending the small town knew that they had almost nothing to lose. The war was as good as over. Even if they escaped from the Slovenian attack, they still had to get down to their colleagues barricaded into the city below them, and try to surrender to the Allies. Against the German bunkers, the partisans and Yugoslav soldiers had M3 Stuart tanks, supplied by the Allies, as well as some T-32s and self-propelled guns from the Russians.

So when they attacked that morning, they stalked the German bunkers in pairs. Then the men attacked in small groups, throwing hand-grenades, then charging positions firing their huge mixture of weapons – Russian, Italian and German bolt-action rifles, Russian PPSh and German Schmeisser sub-machine guns, as well as British Sten and Bren guns air-dropped behind the lines. It was fighting at close quarters. Up narrow, steep streets, across rocky limestone slopes that led up the mountain, through back gardens draped with tanglesome vines, over walls on which climbed roses and thorny bougainvillea. It was impossible to simply by-pass the German bunkers, as they would only be able to open fire afterwards on other units, or on any vehicles reinforcing the partisans from the Slovenian border above Opicina.

By the time the sun was up over the Adriatic Sea, the partisans and Yugoslav soldiers had counted thirty-six German bunkers, of which they had knocked out perhaps twenty. Twice they reached the railway station, the school and the church. Twice they had to retreat under extremely accurate German machine-gun and anti-tank fire. By mid-morning their commanders had sent another brigade to join the attack, and by midday it had pushed the Germans out of the old white stone porticoes of the railway station. Half the town was still in German hands. Then, out of the blue, there came a moment of relief and respite for some units. Their battalion and brigade commanders ordered them to withdraw away from the German positions. The rest of the brigade would take care of Opicina. They told them to join up with another brigade group, which had gathered in a small piazza and along a road leading down the steep hill to the city itself.

They left the Germans in Opicina with their backs against the wall fighting the numerically superior partisans. This second brigade was to advance down the slope as quickly as they possibly could. And head straight for the centre of Trieste. They were told to capture it as soon as possible, regardless of casualties. Allied tanks and infantry had been spotted fifteen miles away, approaching fast. There was no time to lose. The sun was overhead, and the early summer bounced off the Adriatic Sea in the harbour below. It was just after midday on 1 May, 1945.

3

The Capture of Trieste, 1–2 May

A day before Hitler committed suicide on 30 April, the Germans signed a document agreeing to a ceasefire and surrender of all their forces in Italy and Austria. This would come into effect at 2pm on 2 May, and the number of troops covered by it came to nearly a million. The agreement was signed at the headquarters of the Supreme Allied Commander of Mediterranean Forces, British Field Marshal Harold Alexander. SS-Obergruppenführer Karl Wolff represented the Germans at the ceremony. It took place at the Allied Headquarters in the Palazzo Reale in Caserta, originally built for the Bourbon Kings of Naples. Wolff was signatory on behalf of Generaloberst Heinrich von Vietinghoff, commanding German forces in Italy.

Under the codename of Operation *Sunrise*, the canny SS general had also been negotiating a secret peace deal with the Allies in Switzerland since late February that year. The British and Americans had informed the Russians of the early peace overtures made by the Germans; but Stalin and his foreign minister, Vyacheslav Molotov, had strongly suspected they were being excluded from the talks by the Western Allies. Taking monumental offence at this perceived diplomatic slight, the Russians had then accused both the British and

Americans of trying to arrange a peace deal with the Germans behind their backs. It had caused a major division between Stalin, Roosevelt and Churchill, and had seen the collapse of any real remaining trust between the West and Moscow.

Into the bargain, the Russians were not aware of the surrender arrangements agreed at Caserta. Field Marshal Alexander hoped to take them and Marshal Tito by surprise. If the latter thought his men and women were still in active combat against German units in Yugoslavia and Italy, they would have considerably less incentive to open fire on Allied units as they arrived to take over Trieste. So shortly after midday on 1 May, Alexander sent a radio telegraph to Marshal Tito in Belgrade. He was diplomatic. He said simply that, should the Allies encounter any of Tito's partisans or soldiers during their ongoing operations in the Venezia Giulia and Trieste, Alexander presumed that Tito would have no objection to these men falling under Allied command. Alexander was an excellent officer – the American general Omar Bradley was quoted as saying that he was 'the outstanding general's general of the European war'.[1] But Alexander was also cautious, and was keen to avoid confrontation with Tito at the precise moment when the latter had just occupied territory the Allies saw as rightfully theirs. Sending a telegraph to Churchill shortly after his message to Tito, Alexander then eschewed tact and diplomacy. Tito's forces were fighting inside Trieste as he wrote, and he thought it impossible that the Yugoslavs would withdraw their forces from the city unless the Russians told them to. If he (Alexander) was told by the Allied Combined Chiefs of Staff to occupy the whole of Venezia Giulia by force, he could do so; but, he said:

> ... we shall certainly be committed to a fight with the Yugoslav Army, who will have at least the moral backing of the Russians. Before we are committed I think it as well to consider the feeling of our own troops in this matter. They have a profound admiration for Tito's Partisan Army, and a great sympathy for them in their struggle for freedom. We must be very careful therefore before we ask them to turn away from the common enemy to fight an ally.[2]

As Alexander dictated this dispatch, the Allied troops advancing on Trieste were trying to find what cover they could from the sun. Under the cypress and plane trees that lined the road eastwards from Monfalcone, a huge, sprawling, dusty python of armoured cars, trucks, jeeps, personnel carriers and towed artillery guns lay motionless in the midday Adriatic heat. Sudden summer rain squalls came and went. They were waiting for orders to move forward. The Maoris of the 28th New Zealand Battalion had just been diverted northwards to help take the town of Udine. The vanguard of the Allied advance was now made up of other battalions from the 2nd New Zealand Division, and the British armoured cars of the 12th Royal Lancers.

Lieutenant-Colonel Peter Wilkinson, accompanying General Freyberg, was near the head of the column. They were talking to Yugoslav officers. Also with them was Geoffrey Cox. It was now around 3pm on 1 May, Wilkinson noted in his diary.[3] The SOE officer was worried that the New Zealand commander might decide to stage a full-frontal attack on Trieste, thus bringing the Allies into direct combat with Tito's men.

So when the Yugoslav officers suggested a meeting at 7.30pm that evening with the Allies and their own commanders, Wilkinson was relieved. The first imperative now was to brief Freyberg before they met the commander of the Yugoslav 9th Corps. Wilkinson and Cox found some shade, and tried to explain the strategic, tactical and political lie of the land to the ebullient and aggressive Freyberg. It took twenty minutes. The Slovenians who made up a percentage of the Yugoslav 9th Corps regarded swathes of territory east of the River Isonzo as theirs. This river now lay just behind the Allied spearhead. This land had originally been part of the old Austro-Hungarian Empire, and had only been ceded to Italy at the end of the First World War. The focal point of this land, and the Yugoslav claim to it, was Trieste. Wilkinson now thought it likely that Tito's men would fight for the port. Freyberg wanted the forthcoming meeting that evening to focus on military matters, and to avoid the political. Wilkinson and Cox both thought this unlikely, if not impossible.

Privately, the former also thought that it was improbable that the 9th Corps commander would show up that evening. Decisions of this strategic magnitude would have to be decided by Tito himself. The meeting at 7.30pm proved him right. The Yugoslav commander didn't appear. The Allied column stayed put. As the hot, sweating, dusty, exhausted soldiers stopped for the night, they brewed tea. Squalls of summer rain came in. They ate an idiosyncratic supper of army ration bully beef and dried biscuits, supplemented by tomatoes and melons given to them by the grateful Italian civilians they had passed on the road further west. General Freyberg arranged for Wilkinson to be given a tent and some blankets: his SOE colleague who had been dispatched to Venice had still not reappeared with his staff car and bedding roll. Wilkinson had only the dusty battledress he was wearing, a water-bottle, his 1911 .45-calibre Colt automatic pistol, four magazines of ammunition, a compass, notebook, pencil and his identity card. The thoughtful Freyberg augmented these. He sent an orderly over to the SOE officer's tent, bearing one of his own personal handkerchiefs. The sun slipped below the horizon. The smashing thumps and blurting bursts of artillery, small-arms and mortar fire coming from north, east and west punctuated the warm velvet cloak of the Adriatic night. The 1st of May 1945 became the 2nd.

But the pensive and well-informed British lieutenant-colonel couldn't sleep. His thoughts kept turning to his SOE counterpart who had vanished the previous year at the hands of Slovenian partisans. And his loyalties were also torn: he had operated with other groups of Slovenians, and he completely understood how their territorial claim to Trieste made sense to them. Wasn't it, he remembered them saying constantly, land that belonged to them under the Austro-Hungarian Empire, that Italy had since stolen? Hadn't Mussolini banned any Slovenes living on Italian territory from speaking their own language? Wasn't it obviously time to reclaim this city, and the land around it? Wilkinson could identify strongly with the Slovenian cause, far more so than any other British officer he could think of. So as the night progressed, he started writing a heartfelt letter to General Harding arguing that the Allies should make a more balanced consideration of Yugoslav territorial claims. He slept for less than two hours.

By the morning of the following day, the advance units of British and New Zealand troops called Wilkinson repeatedly to their *ad hoc* headquarters. Nearby Allied units, including the British Lancers, were taking the surrender of increasing numbers of Serb nationalist fighters. The Chetniks* were a loosely grouped formation of Serbian fighters loyal to their leader, Colonel Draža Mihailović. Their very broad and opportunistic aim was a Greater Serbia achieved through whichever means presented itself, be it collaboration or resistance.

When the Germans had invaded the Kingdom of Yugoslavia in 1941, the country had done what the Balkans characteristically do when a rigid, unifying central power is removed. It had started fighting against the invader, and also within itself. The Serb Chetniks who were loyal to the King at first resisted the Germans, and cooperated with the Allies. But Churchill found them too prone to inaction and collaboration, so switched his allegiance to the much larger and better organised Yugoslav National People's Army. This was led by Tito and had multiple partisan adherents. Tito and Mihailović then split, disagreed, opposed each other, and then fought. Some Chetniks remained independent, some allied themselves off-and-on with the Germans and Italians, while some fought them. It was a mess. They also fought Tito's men, and the Croats who made up the nationalist Ustashe.† This was the Balkans: the endless permutations for agreement and violent disagreement in the ethnic *bouillabaisse* were limitless.

What was certain, however, was that the Chetniks were desperate not to be taken prisoner by Tito's Yugoslav partisans or soldiers. The past operational behaviour of all sides, in tit-for-tat killings and revenge atrocities, meant that a firing-squad could be the answer for the Serbs if

* The word derives from the Serbo-Croat *ceta,* meaning a band, or group of guerrillas.

† The Ustashe were a fascist, ultra-nationalist Croat political group with armed units, which existed from 1929 to 1945. Their aim was the establishment of a Greater Croatia, and they allied themselves with the Germans to achieve this aim. Among other numerous excesses, they established and ran the concentration camp at Jasenovac, south of Zagreb, in which an estimated 80–100,000 Serbs, Bosnians, gypsies, non-fascist Croats and others died. The word derives from the Croatian verb *ustati* meaning to rise up, or rebel.

captured by Tito's men. But other partisans captured from opposing units in the war had often just been co-opted in joining the National Liberation Army. So that day outside Trieste the Serbs were not taking any chances, and were turning themselves in to the British as fast as they could. And as one of the few Allied officers who could speak their language, the SOE colonel kept being called upon to interpret.

Meanwhile Cox, the soldier and diplomat, was busy drafting an operational battle plan that would enable Freyberg to take Trieste and the surrounding land. The intelligence officer could see clearly what was happening. 'Trieste was the first major confrontation of the Cold War,' he was to write later.[4]

In Wilkinson and Cox, Freyberg could not have hoped for a better intelligence adviser or special forces officer who could liaise with the partisans. Between the two of them, they had lived and served in Spain, Finland, France, Greece, Crete, North Africa, Poland, the United States and now Italy. They could field French, Spanish, a smattering of Finnish and Polish, Italian, Serbo-Croat, German and two distinct brands of English. What was crucial – and differentiated them from almost every other officer serving in the Allied forces – was that they knew the difference between the various brands of communism across Europe. They knew what each regional, national and ethnic variation of it meant, from Madrid to Moscow, and Rome to Belgrade. Whether it meant land, money, access to power, idealism, workable socialism, a faux-paradise for the workers, outright autocratic totalitarianism, or simply all of these. They knew that the difference between extreme left and fascist right blended into this totalitarianism almost instinctively when under attack from outside. The ideologies of left and right pulled in a circle where both extremes actually met each other face-on.

Things then sped up. As Wilkinson and Cox had breakfast on 2 May, the Yugoslavs sent a messenger. He announced that the commander of the Yugoslav Army's 9th Corps wanted to meet with Freyberg at 11.30am. The appointment was at the same nearby farmhouse where they had convened, fruitlessly, the previous evening. Half-past eleven arrived and the meeting began. Freyberg explained to the Yugoslav general that Field Marshal Alexander had ordered him to take Trieste and its port facilities, and that he intended to do just that. Tito's officer explained, nervously, that his men already held the port area. If Freyberg was insisting on taking and holding something that was *already* taken and held, well then, he'd have to consult with his superior, the commander of the 4th Army of the National Liberation Army. This, he said, was General Petar Drapšin. A name Peter Wilkinson knew all too well from his days operating with Tito's men.

The thirty-one-year-old partisan general was the son of peasant farmers from Srbobran in northern Serbia, close to the Danube. He had fought in the Spanish Civil War, and been interned in France. In 1939, he escaped to Zagreb in Croatia, and when the Germans invaded Yugoslavia in 1941, he was given his own command in the newly formed National Liberation Army. A hardline member of the Yugoslav Communist Party, he exceeded his operational remit in 1941 and 1942 in the region of Herzegovina in southern Bosnia. Entrusted with leading communist rebellion in the area, he reportedly reacted ruthlessly against local civilians who refused to embrace his own brand of hardcore revolutionary communism. The stories about him and his men were legendary among the partisans and Yugoslav soldiers. About how in spring 1942 his men had executed sixty villagers, and then danced around their murdered corpses, in front of their relatives. The brutal aim was to remind the local Bosnian population of the absolute power held by the communist Yugoslav National Liberation Army. The incident earned Drapšin official sanctions from party headquarters, but his ruthless combat ability against the Germans saw him promoted again and again, being given a battalion, then a division, then a corps, and now the 4th Army. One writer and historian who served with the partisans was to describe Drapšin as 'a psychologically unstable person whose condition bordered on complete insanity'.* It was he, Wilkinson

* Sava Skoko was a Bosnian Croat from Gacko in Herzegovina, a region of southern Bosnia. He was a partisan in his twenties, and after the war he documented abuses carried out by the Yugoslav National People's Army, and partisans, against the civilian population of Yugoslavia. His account of the killings carried out by Drapšin's men is included in his book *Krvavo Kolo Hercegovacko,* published in Podgorica, Montenegro in 1995. The title translates as 'Bloody Dance of Herzegovina'.

knew, who had just taken control of the Dalmatian coast, the Slovenian region of Istria, and Trieste itself. His record of treatment of non-communist opponents, fascist or otherwise, did not bode at all well for many of the population of Trieste who now found themselves under his control.

Before the meeting broke up, General Freyberg told Drapšin's deputy that he would be perfectly happy to 'clean up' any pockets of German resistance that lay between his current position, outside Monfalcone, and the centre of Trieste. Wilkinson and Cox were interpreting between them in a mix of English, German and Serbo-Croat. Wilkinson used the German verb *reinigen*, literally meaning to cleanse, or purify. Confused, the Yugoslav general replied that the question was tactically academic, as there were no German forces between Monfalcone and Trieste, clean or dirty. Freyberg gave orders to resume the advance. But then another messenger arrived, and a meeting was offered with Drapšin himself at 2.30pm that afternoon. Freyberg agreed. He waited with his staff for twenty minutes, but then the Yugoslav leader did not arrive. So, determinedly, the New Zealand veteran gave clear orders to head straight for the centre of Trieste.

The campaign in Italy had ended officially at 2pm on 2 May, as agreed in Caserta. But this did not apply to German forces east of the River Isonzo, which included those defending Trieste. The New Zealanders of the 9th Brigade of the 2nd Division, accompanied by British tanks and armoured cars, continued along the coast road towards the port. The 22nd New Zealand Battalion was in front. Shortly after 2.30pm they came level with the grandiose display of Austro-Hungarian architecture that was the Castello di Miramare, three and a half miles from the centre of Trieste. 'A' Company of the 22nd New Zealand Battalion liberated it. Before they did, low-level airstrikes by Spitfires attacked anti-aircraft positions in the area north of the castle and the coast road beside it.

The German commander in the *castello* was a naval officer of coastal artillery. He said that his men had just intercepted a radio transmission issued by Admiral Doenitz in Berlin. Hitler had appointed him to command the Third Reich in the aftermath of his death. The German commander at Miramare said that his senior officer further east down the coast, at Fiume, had ordered him to fight on. But he refused, and so fifteen German officers and 600 men gave themselves up. The Kiwis of the advance guard removed the large German flag that flew on top of the castle, and signed it. The New Zealand troopers who had survived the war put their names on captured flags every time they liberated a position *en route* to Trieste. Just behind them in the advance, Freyberg announced that he would make his headquarters at the castle. At this point, Geoffrey Cox felt the urgent call of nature. He ducked behind a nearby bush. Suddenly there was the sound of a dusty, confused scuffle behind the leaves, before the intelligence officer emerged with his Webley .38 revolver pushed into the back of a German prisoner – who said, rather forlornly, that he was the last German between Miramare and Trieste. This was almost true. A few minutes later a roadblock a mile beyond the castle was demolished by Allied Sherman tanks of the 20th Royal Tank Regiment. 'The drivers then accelerated, the last few miles were covered at a grand pace, and at three o'clock on that sunny and momentous afternoon the regiment's first tanks, the spearhead of the Division, entered Trieste.'[5]

The Italians provided an ebullient and joyful welcome. Columns of Yugoslav troops and partisans, some in Stuart tanks, watched more silently. Snipers were at work. Wilkinson accompanied Freyberg a short way towards the city, before the general returned to the Miramare castle. The SOE colonel then pushed forward himself in a jeep with a New Zealand brigadier. The streets were crowded, and the enormous Piazza dell'Unità d'Italia, bordering the Adriatic, was packed both with Italian partisans and civilians, and Yugoslav partisans and soldiers. Enormous red, white and blue Yugoslav flags, with the red communist star in the centre, were everywhere. Wilkinson could hear shooting, single shots, pistols, sub-machine guns. It came from every side street, every curving alley that snaked up the mountain on which the city sat, every glossy quay by the sea, every backstreet cobbled piazza. But he couldn't see anything specific, such as who was shooting whom, or how or where. Then a radio message suddenly arrived, and the SOE officer ordered his driver to head up the hill for the northern part of the city. A German unit was trying its best to surrender to a company from the 22nd Battalion, who were convinced they still had fight left in them. 'Surrender to a New Zealander, and you lose your watch,' went a saying popular with the Germans that day. 'Surrender to a Yugoslav, and you lose your life.' Wilkinson arrived at the side of the road, and made a simple suggestion to the major commanding the Allied company. Let the Germans surrender, and you can have their watches. What on earth do we want with a bunch of 'fucking Teds'? was the answer. The New Zealanders only wanted their watches, and didn't want to be burdened with more prisoners, just as their advance was taking them right onto their objective.

Part of the mixed German force of Kampfgruppe Berger, meanwhile, was holed up in the Castello di San Giusto, in the centre of the city. The castle was surrounded by partisans, Yugoslav soldiers, and Italian civilians. They were all desperate to capture it and take the Germans prisoner, to be dealt with as General Drapšin and his headquarters saw fit. The Germans were under no illusions what might happen if they gave themselves up. So when a company of the New Zealand 22nd Battalion, accompanied by tanks, arrived to take their surrender at around 5.30pm, the Germans can only have felt they had at least an even chance of seeing another sunrise. Nevertheless, a German bazooka fired at, and missed, one of the Allied Shermans. The partisans and Yugoslav soldiers were firing at the castle, and threatened to open fire on the Allied troops if they tried to enter the gates. But the New Zealanders drove in, and found to their surprise only 170 German men and twelve officers, who immediately surrendered. Then almost as quickly offered to join forces with the Allied troops to fight the Yugoslavs outside. In one of the curious twists of irony that war produces in a lightning sleight-of-hand, both New Zealanders and Germans posted joint guards that night on the walls of the castle. The Allied company commander told the German admiral commanding the castle that his New Zealanders had not eaten since that morning. So the German officer asked the exhausted Kiwis to eat with his men. Supper was horsemeat stew. The New Zealand company commander dined with the German officers, also on horsemeat casserole, but washed down with bottles of Scotch whisky. The Kriegsmarine officers had taken them from the Allies in 1942, when they re-captured Tobruk. The Scotch had lasted them through all the intervening war, and they had brought the last bottles with them to Trieste.

The German defenders of the Tribunale building in the centre of Trieste were in no mood to give up, however. The commanding officer of the 22nd New Zealand Battalion described their commander as an SS officer who was 'humbugging undecidedly and was apparently under the influence of alcohol.'[6] So the New Zealanders and the Yugoslav troops and partisans outside took matters into their own hands. They cleared the area around four sides of the building, and surrounded it with eighteen Sherman tanks. At ranges from twenty to fifty yards, the armoured vehicles then simply blew holes in the building with their 75mm main armaments and Browning .50-calibre machine guns. The Germans took cover in the cellars, but 'humbugging' ceased within thirty minutes. General Drapšin's men took over the building, spent the night clearing it, and at dawn were seen emerging with 200 prisoners. Along with the other occupants of the building – German and Ukrainian guards from the nearby concentration camp, two companies of SS men, and 400 Italian Fascist policemen – these men were reportedly never to be seen again.

The welcome given to the liberators in Gorizia said everything about the chaotic fighting and confused loyalties that day. The town was about twenty miles north-west of Trieste, right on the Yugoslav border. The New Zealanders arrived on the afternoon of 2 May, to find that Tito's men had got there before them. The Yugoslav Marshal had ordered his men to occupy Venezia Giulia as far west as the River Isonzo. This flowed into the Gulf of Trieste about ten miles diagonally opposite the port itself. It had huge symbolic value too: in the First

World War, the Italians and Austro-Hungarians had fought a dozen very bloody battles along this river between 1915 and 1917. Half of all the casualties suffered by Italy in the war – 300,000 out of 600,000 – were taken on the Isonzo. So in May 1945, the streets of Gorizia were full of parading demonstrators:

> Yugoslav Communist bands carrying red, blue, and white flags with the red star prominent in the centre were shouting 'Death to the Fascists. Death to the Italians. Long live Tito. Viva Stalin. Viva the Allies.' Parties of Italians answered them with 'Gorizia for the Italians, Viva America, Viva England' and carried the red, white and green flag of Italy. Both factions carried the Union Jack and the Stars and Stripes.'[7]

The official surrender of the Germans to the Allies happened that evening, around 10pm on 2 May. An Austrian civilian arrived at the headquarters of the commanding officer of the New Zealand 22nd Battalion. He delivered a message. The German commander of Trieste, General Linkenbach, wanted to surrender his troops to the Allies, with a guarantee they would not be handed over to Tito's men. The lieutenant-colonel devolved responsibility downwards, and sent his intelligence officer, a second lieutenant, to meet Linkenbach. The German had his headquarters in a villa in the northern part of Trieste, overlooking both the Adriatic and the port. His terms were simple: let us surrender to the Allies, and we'll do whatever you want. The New Zealanders immediately saw the strategic ramifications of a complete German capitulation, on their terms. Linkenbach's surrender would mean the Allies could retain some degree of control over a tactical situation in Trieste where the upper hand was rapidly devolving to the Yugoslavs. Once questioned and debriefed, the German general would also be a vital source of intelligence. He would almost certainly be able to provide testimony at forthcoming war crimes trials. So Linkenbach and the New Zealand subaltern returned to the Allied headquarters.

At 4am the following morning, 3 May, 120 New Zealanders arrived and formed the prisoners into a column. This consisted of eight staff cars full of German officers, eight lorries of prisoners, 300 men on foot, and three sitting on and in a motorbike and sidecar combination. The New Zealanders had built an impromptu prisoner-of-war (POW) 'cage' in Monfalcone, and the Germans were put into it. Their first rations as POWs were just some of the huge amounts of melons and tomatoes given to the advancing Allies by the Italian population along the road of advance.

By late that evening, Lieutenant-Colonel Wilkinson had seen for himself that both Allies and Yugoslavs had firmly occupied Trieste, and World War III had not yet started. He could relax a little. The transfer of some German prisoners to Monfalcone was a relief: Wilkinson had spent enough time operating with the partisans in the two preceding years to know what was going to happen to their German prisoners. A firing squad was a possible answer. Another was a long, slow confinement in one of the Yugoslav detention camps on the Danube. Or they would be worked almost to death in the lead mines of the Trepça complex at Kosovska Mitrovica, in southern Serbia. So he had returned to the Castello di Miramare in high spirits. Where he learned three things. Firstly, that the SOE liaison officer who operated with General Drapšin had arrived in Trieste, and was now liaising with General Freyberg. Which meant that Wilkinson's presence was no longer needed. So he could now hold firm to his promise to his wife, Theresa, that Trieste would be his last operational mission. A young subaltern was standing in the ankle-deep, cream-coloured crunch that was the gravel in front of the Castello di Miramare. He told Wilkinson the war in Italy was over. The signature on the Caserta agreement had come into effect at 2pm that day. The third piece of news was that his SOE colleague had finally arrived from Venice with his staff car, and his sleeping kit. That night his batman, Corporal Jewels, made up a bed for him in one of the state rooms in the Castello. As Peter Wilkinson fell asleep beneath two portraits of the Austro-Hungarian Emperor and his wife, the scarlet walls of the room all around him, he had one last thought. Who on earth had been shooting whom that afternoon with such ferocious determination in the centre of Trieste?

But the following morning, any hopeful thoughts that he and other Allied officers might have had that the story of Trieste would end peacefully were smashed. The Allies' worst fears were realised. Something happened that everybody had feared would occur. From Edward Stettinius, to Churchill and Harold Alexander, right down to infantry platoon commanders on the dusty roads outside Trieste. Allied soldiers came into an armed firefight with the Yugoslavs and Germans at the same time, and a New Zealander was killed. In minutes, the whole strategic and operational dynamic changed. And it shifted in favour of the Yugoslavs, and not in the direction of the Allies or the thousands of captured Italian and German prisoners.

At around 8.30 on the morning of 3 May, the commander of the German garrison in the town of Opicina sent a message to the Allies. Some of the Yugoslav soldiers and partisans who had attacked the town had by-passed the remaining German bunkers in their rush to occupy the city of Trieste. The Germans who were still in Opicina, some 1,200 of them, wanted to surrender. And they only wanted to surrender to the Allies. So a company of New Zealanders, around 120 men, drove up the hill in lorries, accompanied by three Sherman tanks. The road up to Opicina is long, winding and steep, and climbs more than a thousand feet to the top of the mountain overlooking Trieste and the Adriatic. Only two tanks could make it up the slope, as one broke down. The infantry's three-ton lorries then couldn't get past a blown-up road-block. So thirty of the soldiers dismounted, and in two groups of fifteen, climbed onto the two remaining Sherman tanks. These clattered off up the hill.

Foot-slogging infantry, with sore, tired feet, hefting heavy personal equipment, were always relieved to climb on the back of a tank. It gave them respite from arduous physical exertion, even if the ride was no more than a few hundred yards. It meant that for a moment, however brief, they weren't marching, but sitting. So for men who might have been awake for two days, enduring combat, high temperatures, thirst, and the endless tramp-tramp-tramp of marching, a lift on a tank was a relief. There were hidden dangers, though. The driver of the tank couldn't see the men sitting on the back of the engine housing. So it took clear radio communication to make sure that any infantrymen climbing onto, or dismounting from, the tank didn't get feet caught and torn off in spinning tank tracks, fall, get left behind, or touch or sit on or near very hot pieces of metal.*

Thus, on the road up to Opicina, the two tanks set off again with the infantry sitting on the back. Their tracks slammered and scrunched across the detritus on the road's surface: branches of olive trees ripped off by shell-fire, cartridge-cases, ammunition boxes, bricks, pieces of wire fence and shreds of vines. There were German, Yugoslav and civilian corpses lying twisted and butchered as well, their limbs splayed hither and thither in the way dead bodies have, their clothing ripped.

As the Germans were willing to surrender to the New Zealanders, but not to the Yugoslavs, the company commander started negotiations. As he did so, a Yugoslav mortar position opened fire on the German positions. Rifles and machine guns joined in. The Germans and New Zealanders were sitting ducks, and one Kiwi lance-corporal was killed. The New Zealand company wanted to attack the Yugoslavs instantly and destroy their positions. The company commander, and the German officers, saw instantly what could happen as a result: a sudden, full-blown firefight with Tito's men, which would envelop all of Trieste, escalating into artillery barrages between both sides. The New Zealand company commander yelled at his men to hold their fire, they and the Germans took cover instantly, while out in the open by the edge of a road the dead lance-corporal sprawled twisted and bleeding. His body represented a stark and dramatic turn of events. It demonstrated what would happen over the next decade in the city that lay a thousand feet below where his corpse now lay.

As mortar fire continued, the New Zealand captain struggled up to the Yugoslav brigade and divisional headquarters on the edge of Opicina – it was from here that the attack on the town had been coordinated. The commander of the Yugoslav division, a British SOE

* The author's father commanded a troop of four Cromwell tanks in France, Belgium and Holland in 1944, and often mentioned this pitfall.

liaison officer stationed with him, and the captain drove off to hammer out a deal with Freyberg's chief of staff, Brigadier William Gentry. This courageous and highly organised staff officer had been awarded the Distinguished Service Order twice, in North Africa and then Italy, and was the perfect foil to Freyberg's strategic and tactical aggression. He decided that, rather than risk more lives, the New Zealand company should withdraw to their positions. The Yugoslavs should then take the Germans prisoner. This pull-back to positions west of Trieste was then extended to the rest of the New Zealand 2nd Division and the British armoured and artillery units supporting them. Meanwhile thousands of Germans continued to try to surrender. General Drapšin and his troops were given operational free rein to take these prisoners, and oversee what happened in Trieste. Their fate, and that of the idiosyncratic Adriatic port, were sealed. The 'Forty Days of Trieste' had begun.

Part Two

REVENGE IN TRIESTE

4

Kidnapped by the Partisans

From the Austro-Hungarian Empire to Yugoslavia

The area around Trieste, the Venezia Giulia, Istria and the north-western coast of Dalmatia had always had a chequered history. Especially since the nineteenth century. By 1871, all of Italy had been united into a single country. The political and social process called the *Risorgimento* had brought all the different states into one. Rome became the capital. Only a few contested parts remained, in the north-eastern regions of the south Tirol and the Friuli Venezia Giulia. The new, united Kingdom of Italy wanted to incorporate Trieste, the Istrian peninsula and the Adriatic port of Rijeka into its territory. But they were part of the Austro-Hungarian Empire. In 1915, Italy allied itself with the British, French and Russians in World War I. The Treaty of London, signed in April that year, promised the majority of these Adriatic territories to Italy on condition of a victory by the Entente Allies against Germany and the Austro-Hungarian Empire. Italy fought against the Austro-Hungarians in the war, and suffered 600,000 casualties in the subsequent fighting. Half of these were in a string of bloody battles in the far north-east of the country, along the River Isonzo and in the mountains of the Dolomites. 100,000 alone were at the battle of Caporetto in October 1917. The Italians felt that they had paid for the north-eastern parts of the Venezia Giulia in blood.

When World War I ended, the Allies honoured the Treaty of London and ceded to Italy the promised territories around Trieste and on the Dalmatian coast. Meanwhile the Austro-Hungarian Empire ceased to exist. A new country came into being: Yugoslavia, the Kingdom of the Serbs, Croats and Slovenes. It immediately began to lay covetous eyes on territory that Italy saw as its own. The Austro-Hungarians had encouraged Slovenes and Croats to settle in and around Trieste, knowing that the influx of non-Italian populations would help insulate against border claims by Italy. The port's population had risen from 80,000 in 1846 to 229,000 in 1910. A census in that year numbered the city's population as an ethnic mix of 148,000 Italians and 56,000 Slovenians. Each national grouping naturally felt strong economic, social, cultural and geographical ties to, and claims on, the city.

In 1919 the Treaty of Saint-Germain-en-Laye gave the region of Venezia Giulia, the city of Trieste and the town of Zara to Italy. The port of Rijeka remained in Yugoslavia. Italians were hugely upset that the Paris Peace Conference handed over this city, which they called Fiume. So in September 1919, a flamboyant fifty-six-year-old poet, pilot, soldier and Italian nationalist called Gabriele D'Annunzio took action. He got into his red Fiat sports car, and, followed by several lorries carrying 200 supporters, drove to and seized the city. Two thousand supporters joined him. D'Annunzio declared Fiume as an independent entity, the Italian Regency of Carnaro. But then he went one step too far. He declared war on Italy itself. This led to his surrender in 1920 after the Italian Navy bombarded the port. The Treaty of Rapallo then created the independent Free State of Fiume. This was then changed in 1924 when the Treaty of Rome was signed by both Italy and Yugoslavia. Fiume was given to Italy. The Adriatic region was like a chessboard where the white and black pieces were being constantly upended and replaced at different ends of the board.

In Trieste, discrimination by parts of the Italian population against Slovenes was rampant. In 1924, the wife of a Slovenian clerk gave birth to a son. What happened was typical. The father applied for a birth

In this World War I-era propaganda poster celebrating the return of the city to Italy, Trieste, in a red gown, kneels before a white-gowned Italy. 'Finally', says the caption. (Photo by Galerie Bilderwelt/Getty Images)

Marshal Josip Broz Tito talking from his mountain headquarters in Bosnia, circa 1943. At his feet is his pet Alsatian 'Tiger', killed during a German air strike which also wounded Tito. (Bettmann/Getty Images)

Marshal Tito meets Winston Churchill, Naples, 1944. In the back row, second from left in a kilt, is Fitzroy Maclean. (Photo by Hulton Archive/Getty Images)

Advance to Trieste: New Zealand machine-gunners in action on the Silaro River, April 1945. (Photo by Mondadori Portfolio via Getty Images)

Italian Fascist propaganda poster depicting Allied and Russian soldiers as rapists and looters: the caption translates as 'How long will you let this continue?' (Photo by: Photo12/UIG via Getty Images)

The Red Army arrives in Belgrade, 20 October 1944. (Photo by Voller Ernst/ullstein bild via Getty Images)

Tito signs the Russia–Yugoslav Friendship Treaty in April 1945; Stalin is behind him, and Russian Foreign Minister Molotov on the far right. (Photo by: Sovfoto/UIG via Getty Images)

US Secretary of State Edward Stettinius (centre), British Foreign Secretary Anthony Eden (right) and Russian Foreign Minister Vyacheslav Molotov (left), San Francisco, 1 May 1945. (Photo by PhotoQuest/Getty Images)

An Allied jeep races towards Trieste on 1 May 1945, cheered on by Italian and Yugoslav partisans and civilians. (Photo by Mondadori Portfolio via Getty Images)

Above: A boy drinks from a fountain in Trieste, May 1946. (Photo by Nat Farbman/The LIFE Picture Collection/Getty Images)

Opposite top left: Friedrich Rainer, the German Gauleiter of Trieste, with a duelling scar on his left cheek. (Photo by Heinrich Hoffmann/ullstein bild via Getty Images)

Opposite top right: Odilo Globocnik, taken when he was Gauleiter of Vienna in 1938. (Photo by ullstein bild/ullstein bild via Getty Images)

Opposite: Italian refugees flee their village to escape fighting. (Photo by © Hulton-Deutsch Collection/CORBIS/Corbis via Getty Images)

A young female Italian collaborator is led away by partisans, Lombardy, April 1945. (Photo by Keystone/Getty Images)

Yugoslav partisans, 1945. (Photo by Roger Viollet/Getty Images)

certificate, intending to name his son 'Gorazd'. The Italian municipal clerk refused to enter this Slovenian name, instead writing the Italian version, 'Gerardo'. The father protested in court. His case was dismissed. He took it to a higher court of appeal. This court rejected it, saying:

> The fact is that the obstinacy with which G.M. (the clerk) insisted in bestowing a Slavic name upon his son in this historic moment when everybody ought to take pride in Italianicizing everything ... arouses justifiable suspicion that a more or less concealed purpose lurks behind it ... the right of paternity may not reach so far as to constitute an abuse to disturb the public order, or to offend the national consciousness. Case dismissed.[1]

Benito Mussolini, the leader of the Italian Fascist Party, became Prime Minister of Italy in 1922. He instituted a policy of 'Italianisation' of the land around Trieste and in the Venezia Giulia. This extended as far as the western boundaries of the Istrian peninsula, which lay just south of Trieste. The Paris Treaty had given this peninsula to the new Kingdom of Yugoslavia. Mussolini wanted to extend this swathe of 'Italianicised' land further eastwards down the Dalmatian coast, to link up with the port of Fiume, which sat by itself, separated from Italy by the Istrian peninsula, now part of Yugoslavia. So he re-settled thousands of Italian families across the Venezia Giulia, and banned the use of the Slovene language, which an estimated 60 per cent of the population there used. Industrial contracts and political placement went to his Fascist supporters. Communists and Slovenes found themselves increasingly marginalised. And the industrial town of Monfalcone, fourteen miles west of Trieste, was a political microcosm of Mussolini's policies towards this north-eastern Adriatic region.

YUGOSLAVIA BREAKS UP

On 6 April 1941, Mussolini's chance to realise his territorial ambitions arrived. As part of their Balkans campaign, the Germans and Italians invaded the Kingdom of Yugoslavia. The campaign was swift and decisive. Yugoslavia surrendered on 17 April. It was militarily overwhelmed, and had made the strategically disastrous decision to try to defend all of its borders simultaneously. The country was then divided up amongst Germany, Hungary, Italy and Bulgaria, the latter all allies of the Third Reich under the Tripartite Pact. The Croatian fascist leader Ante Pavelić, backed by the Italians and supported by his extreme nationalist militia, the Ustashe, declared the Independent State of Croatia (the Nezavisna Država Hrvatska or NDH). The German troops in Yugoslavia, who had allied with these violently nationalist Croats, installed their new allies in the Independent State of Croatia. Together they stepped up aggressive anti-partisan operations. The rest of the country split into two predominant factions: the Serb nationalist Chetniks, who resisted and then sometimes collaborated with the Axis; and the majority of the Croat, Bosnian, Serb, Montenegrin and Slovene remainder, whose loyalty lay with the Yugoslav National Liberation Army, in which they served. This was commanded by Josip Broz Tito, and was comprised of regular soldiers and partisan units.

The westernmost province of Yugoslavia was Slovenia, whose borders ran into the Adriatic just a few miles south-east of Trieste. The communist Slovene partisans, loyal to Tito, allied themselves with one of the Italian communist rebel groups who were operating in the mountains on the Italian side of the frontier. This group called itself the Garibaldi Brigade, after the leader who had unified Italy in the 1860s. They were fighting the Germans and their Italian Fascist allies, loyal to dictator Benito Mussolini. Feeling it marginally safer to operate from inside the Italian border, many of Marshal Tito's partisans from the province of Slovenia decamped across the frontier line. They hid out in the mountains above Trieste and in the suburbs and villages around Monfalcone.

By late 1941 Mussolini's fortunes were turning: the British 8th Army were defeating him roundly across the sands of Egypt and Libya. Il Duce's much-vaunted 'African Empire' had come down to beleaguered parts of Abyssinia and Ethiopia. The supposedly invincible battleships and cruisers built in Monfalcone and Livorno in the 1930s – like the *Zara*, *Fiume* and *Pola* – had proved frighteningly vulnerable to torpedoes launched from British aircraft, to the guns of the Royal Navy and to the Malta-based submarines of the Royal Navy's 10th Flotilla. There was also one crucial thing that the Italians didn't fit to their warships, that Britain did. Radar. During the battle of Cape Matapan, fought off the Peloponnese islands on the night of 28 March 1941, battleships of British Admiral Sir Andrew Cunningham's fleet managed to close to within 3,500 yards of three Italian heavy cruisers. This was point-blank range for battleship guns. The Italians never saw them coming. It was pitch dark without a moon. The first the Italians knew was when the piercing beam of the huge searchlight on the battleship HMS *Valiant* was illuminated. A young Greek midshipman had given the order to switch it on.* With the Italian cruisers lit up like Christmas trees, the British opened fire. *Fiume*'s gun turrets, weighing nearly 200 tons each, took direct hits and were blown fifty feet into the air. The sleek, modern heavy cruiser went to the bottom of the Mediterranean in three minutes. It was the final reversal of Mussolini's naval hopes.

THE ITALIAN ARMISTICE AND THE GERMAN OCCUPATION

In August 1943, the Italian government did exactly what Hitler had feared it would: it secretly negotiated an armistice with the British and Americans. By the autumn of that year the Allies had already invaded Sicily and were about to land on the Italian mainland at Salerno. The Fascist regime of Benito Mussolini had lasted for twenty years, but by 1943 it was falling apart. The British, their Commonwealth allies and the Americans had defeated Italy militarily in North Africa, Ethiopia and Eritrea. Britain's Royal Navy had either crippled, or sent to the bottom of the Mediterranean, several of their finest capital ships. The remainder of the Italian fleet was effectively confined to port. The Germans were deserting their allies as well. When the Third

* He would go on to marry the future Queen Elizabeth II, and become Prince Philip.

Reich's military commander in southern Italy, Field Marshal Albert Kesselring, successfully withdrew 60,000 Germans troops back from Sicily to the Italian mainland in August 1943, they left behind 230,000 Italians to surrender to the Allies. And the collapse of Italy was about money too – Il Duce's grandiose military, cultural and territorial designs for Italy were based on economic sand. The country was bankrupt. He had sent 235,000 soldiers to fight alongside the Germans in Russia: 80,000 of them had not returned from Stalingrad. The Italian Army and the Italian nation took this very badly indeed.

They were frightened of the Germans. They had seen from the early 1930s what Hitler wanted to do, and it scared them. But Mussolini, the snake-charmer of nationalism, had also encouraged Italy to dream dreams of unattainable glory, so the Italians understood Hitler's appeal, even if they didn't like it. But Russia? It was Africa with worse weather. Why help Hitler invade it? OK, said the elegant middle-class industrialists and artisans in Milan and Florence and Turin, the supporters of Fascism. Communism is like smallpox – everybody knows it's got to be stamped out. But sending our boys to Russia to do it? Everybody could see that was a mistake, from the noblest Roman intellectual to the humblest Sicilian *contadine,* the peasant smallholders who made up much of the country's agricultural backbone.

Nevertheless, Mussolini did send some twelve divisions, around 235,000 soldiers, to Russia. They came from the finest divisions in the army. These included the *Alpini,* the elite mountain units from Piemonte who'd learned their winter warfare in the wind and blizzards at 10,000 feet in the Italian Alps. The Tridentina, Julia, Cuneense and five other divisions. But mountain warfare training had not prepared them for fighting against Red Army tank divisions. Their Italian Carcano rifles malfunctioned in the freezing snows on the River Don. The bolts froze shut. The soldiers had thin greatcoats, poor food, and inadequate supplies. By the time they broke out of Stalingrad in January 1943, only 4,000 men out of a column of 40,000 Italian, German and Hungarian stragglers and wounded could raise a weapon. Struggling through snow drifts to reach German lines, on 26 January

1943 they found their route blocked by an entire Red Army division in the frozen hamlet of Nikolayevka. Undeterred, the Tridentina Division led a human wave assault, and forced the Soviets out of their path. But by the time the pride of the Italian Army sludged its freezing, frostbitten and starving way back into German trenches, there were only 5,650 soldiers left from three divisions of 45,000 men.

And by July 1943 the Italian mainland was already being bombed by the Allies. The country's Catholics risked vicious reprisals if the Pope protested too loudly about what was happening to Europe's Jews. The Allies spent time hatching their plot: secret talks with Italian politicians, members of the royal family, the army and the navy took place in Lisbon, Algiers and Sicily. The British wanted an unconditional surrender: the Italians wanted to meet in the middle. The Americans didn't care so long as Mussolini went. Which, on 25 July 1943, he did. The Grand Council of Fascism told him in short order that it was transferring control of the armed forces to the ineffectual King Victor Emanuel and the despised Prime Minister Pietro Badoglio. Mussolini was then deposed, and led into exile guarded by 200 Italian policemen still loyal to the King. While the Allies hesitated for several crucial days in August, Hitler and the Oberkommando der Wehrmacht (Armed Forces High Command, or OKW), transferred 100,000 experienced troops from Austria, France and Yugoslavia into Italy. After a short-lived fight by Italians loyal to the King, Rome was occupied by the Germans on 9 September 1943. Field Marshal Kesselring declared open season on partisans and their sympathisers.

The Italian Army collapsed into three pieces. They dumped their weapons, took off their uniforms, and walked home; joined the anti-Fascist partisans; or swore allegiance to Mussolini. 'Il Duce' was taken by a group of Italian policemen to a deserted hotel in the Italian Apennines, on the vast, windswept plateau of the Gran Sasso. His stay was short: Himmler dispatched a team of SS commandos and paratroopers who rescued him in a dramatic and successful operation. Mussolini and the commander of Operation *Eiche,* or Oak, flew to

Berlin to meet Hitler. SS-Brigadeführer Otto Skorzeny received the Knight's Cross of the Iron Cross. Hitler allowed Mussolini to set up his own puppet state in territory in Italy controlled by the Germans. He called this the Italian Socialist Republic, more commonly known as the 'Salo Republic' after the northern town where it had its headquarters.

Across the whole of Italy, the number of partisans exploded. In Monfalcone, the shipyard town west of Trieste, fifteen hundred men walked out of the yard in their blue work dungarees. They announced the formation of their own partisan group. Being the territory geographically closest to Yugoslavia and Austria, the land around Trieste was the first to be taken over by German troops when they occupied Italy. *SS-Panzergrenadiers* were on the streets of Rome in September 1943, while *Fallschirmjäger*, or parachute troops, dug trenches overlooking the Allies' landing beaches at Salerno. The Third Reich had already decided that the land around Trieste and the Adriatic was not going to be part of Italy anymore. So Hitler decided to form an operational area called the 'Adriatisches Küstenland'. This was the 'Adriatic Coastal Area' or 'Litorale Adriatico'. It was made up of Trieste, Italian territory around it, and parts of western Yugoslavia. So a big chunk of north-eastern Italy and western Yugoslavia, linked to Austria and with three main deep-water ports, was now a single German-controlled administrative area. It provided a political, economic and strategic buffer zone between the southern Reich, Italy and the Balkans. It was strategically vital land. German troops in southern Italy, Greece and the Aegean Islands could be supplied by sea from Trieste, after reinforcements were moved by rail from Austria and Bavaria to the Adriatic port. The area was economically powerful too, and provided a perfect place to re-settle Germans.

YUGOSLAVIA AFTER THE ITALIAN ARMISTICE

Hitler knew that in Yugoslavia the communist partisans of Marshal Josip Broz Tito, although nominally independent of external influence, sided with both the Russians and the Allies. By late 1943, the Yugoslavs were fighting the Germans and their hated, atrocity-prone Croatian Catholic Allies, the Ustashe, across much of the country. The latter had set up a network of concentration camps on some eighty square miles of territory they controlled around the town of Jasenovac, sixty miles south-east of Zagreb. Tens of thousands of Serbs, Jews, communists, Roma and Slovenes were imprisoned and then murdered. Conservative estimates of the number of victims range from 77,000 to around 100,000. Among all of the German SS's willing national accomplices, from Latvia via the Ukraine to the Balkans, none exceeded the levels of cruelty of the Ustashe. Hitler's plenipotentiary in Croatia, General Edmund Glaise von Horstenau, was to say in his memoirs that: 'These camps have reached the height of hideousness here in Croatia, under the Ustasha leader installed by us. The greatest of all evils must be Jasenovac, which no ordinary mortal can glimpse.'[2]

Tellingly, a Gestapo report in 1942 had expressed substantial concern that the violence perpetrated by the Croats against ethnic Serbs at Jasenovac was pushing large numbers of Serbs into joining the partisans. The report cited such Ustashe practices as the cutting off of Serb womens' breasts with kitchen knives.

THE SS ARRIVE IN TRIESTE

On 1 October 1943, Hitler gave control of the new Adriatisches Kustenland, the Adriatic Coastal Area, to two senior Nazis with proven track records in implementing the Final Solution, both mentioned earlier in this book. He gave governing powers to an Austrian Nazi who was already the *Gauleiter,* or administrator, of the Austrian province of Carinthia. SS-Obergruppenführer Friedrich Rainer was forty when he arrived in Italy, and virulently hated Italians. He quickly decided that the region of Friuli Venezia Giulia was basically not Italian, but Austrian, and that he should separate it from Italy immediately. Any parts of the population who didn't conform to his regional social and eugenic planning – Jews, communists, Slovenes, Yugoslavs, anti-Fascist Italians – should be displaced, killed or imprisoned. The anti-Fascist and Slovenian partisan colleagues were firmly in his sights.

To help him in this task Rainer had a willing deputy. SS-Brigadeführer Odilo 'Globus' Globocnik was originally from Trieste, and was born in 1904. He moved from Trieste to Austria, joined the SS in the 1930s and became administrator of Vienna. He was a fanatical SS officer and National Socialist, who hated Jews, communists and particularly Catholics. He was also extremely corrupt. In 1938, SS-Reichsführer Heinrich Himmler had stripped him of his position in Vienna after he was caught making illegal foreign currency deals. He was made a lowly corporal in the Waffen-SS, and fought in the invasion of Poland. But in a swift *volte face,* Himmler had pardoned him later in 1939, recognising that this ruthless Austrian was extremely useful. So he had made him a general.

Before arriving in Italy, Globocnik had been involved in organising *Aktion Reinhard*, the operations that had already killed over a million Polish Jews in a variety of ghettos, and in the German-run camps at Bełżec, Sobibór, Majdanek and Treblinka. He brought with him to Trieste some of the men who had helped him do this. They included ninety-four personnel from Einsatzkommando Reinhard, many of whom were Ukrainian SS troops, male and female. *Einsatzkommandos* were sub-units of *Einsatzgruppen,* or 'action groups,' responsible for dealing with those described as 'elements hostile to the Reich behind front-line troops'. This included Jews, Polish gentiles, anybody suspected of being a communist, Roma and partisans. The *Einsatzgruppen* were run by the Central State Security Office, the Reichs-sicherheitshauptamt, or RSHA. This was controlled by the Ministry of the Interior, headed by SS-Reichsführer Heinrich Himmler.

After Poland, Himmler sent Globocnik to Trieste. He became Rainer's appointee in charge of the SS and policing. He also had under his command a complicated grouping of local police and militias made up of Fascist Italians, still loyal to Mussolini and his Salo Republic, and anti-communist Slovenes. They were called the Territorial Defence Militia, and included the Special Inspectorate of the Venezia Giulia State Police. This was founded in April 1942 with the specific task of repressing partisan operations and controlling workers in large factories. Globocnik and his subordinates were also in charge of dealing with the Jews who still remained in and around Trieste.

Just after the Italian Armistice a third high-ranking SS man arrived in Trieste. SS-Obersturmbannführer Christian Wirth was fifty-eight in 1943, and was one of the earliest members of the Nazi Party. He brought with him some of the men who had taken part in *Aktion Tiergarten 4* – the liquidation, started in 1939, of Germans, Jews and communists suffering from incurable physical and mental diseases. Rainer and Globocnik knew that they were going to need a large detention, transit and interrogation centre for their security operations in the Adriatic Coastal Area. So they took over the rice-drying factory in San Sabba. The Germans brought back in the engineers who had installed the factory's drying and heating installations, and gave them new instructions: put in a working crematorium.

ONDINA PETEANI AND THE TOWN OF MONFALCONE

The Italian industrial seaside town was dominated by its communist trade unions. The shipyards, whose dry-docks jutted out into the Adriatic, had always built warships for Italy and the Austro-Hungarian Empire. Mussolini's rise to power and the preparations for war in the 1930s saw the area around Monfalcone and Trieste industrialised on an enormous scale. The former grew from a village to a town, with a population of a few hundred in the late 1920s that increased to 19,000 by 1942. One of the people who worked in the dockyards that produced battleships was a seventeen-year-old girl called Ondina Peteani.[3] She was born on 26 April 1925 in the city hospital in Trieste. Her story was to be the story of that city, what had happened in and around it before World War II, and what would happen during it.

Shortly after Ondina was born, her mother, Valentina, returned to the family house in Vermegliano, a village outside Monfalcone. She rejoined her husband Antonio and the seven other children in the family. Antonio Peteani was a farmer who had fought in the First World War on the side of the Austro-Hungarian Empire against the Italians, and made it clear to all those who would listen that his nationalist sympathies still lay with the former. He had five children by a first marriage. His second wife, Valentina, born in 1888 near Udine, north-west of Trieste, was an energetic and open-minded woman.

After the First World War finished, those who had survived drifted home to re-build their lives. Valentina Peteani got a job cooking for a rich Austrian family miles away from home in Marienbad, a fashionable spa town in the modern-day Czech Republic. While she was there, she had an affair with a wealthy local government official in 1924, and got pregnant. She decided to keep the baby. She wrote a letter to her husband Antonio, back in Italy, explaining the situation, and apologising profusely. He displayed a flexibility and altruism of spirit that was impressive, particularly by the standards of the hierarchical, conservative Catholicism of 1920s Italy. He wrote back to her saying that he was happy with this unorthodox situation, that he didn't care if anybody disapproved, and that he would help raise the new child as his own, giving her the family name. This was Ondina, a dark-haired little girl.

From a non-conformist, independent-minded mother and a big-hearted father came a single-minded and rebellious daughter. She grew up in what she would later describe as a 'politically stimulating environment, surrounded by women who had worked in factories and fought for their rights'. She read fairy tales and romantic novels, but graduated quickly onto Jack London and Victor Hugo in her early teens, drawn in by their descriptions of social problems. She got her first part-time job when she was twelve, working in a printing press next to a local bookshop. When she turned fifteen in 1940, it was time to drop out of school and help provide income that would feed the ten mouths in her family. Fiercely loyal to her father and mother, she understood why she had to go to work in the noisy, crowded, dirty and rough shipyard, even though she hated it. The blue-collar industrial working environment sparked an interest in her fellow working man and communism. This was also 1940, and if you were from a poor working-class background in one of Trieste's suburbs, there was only one place you went, boy or girl, to find a job. The Monfalcone shipyards.

Like every teenager she had daydreams of a different, more glamorous life. But hers went beyond the average sixteen-year-old's. She dreamed of being kidnapped by communist partisans. It was now 1941 in the Italy of Benito Mussolini, and she was growing up fast, beautiful and idealistic. The Italians were fighting the British Army in North Africa, and their navy in the Mediterranean. Ondina, her fellow workers and her supervisors employed in the vast Monfalcone yard were always whispering that anybody suspected of harbouring communist sympathies faced one of two terrible fates. The first was that Il Duce's paramilitary supporters, the *Camicie Nere*, or 'Black Shirts', would come to the factory and take you away to be fined heavily, and then beaten for being a troublesome subversive. The second fate was reputed to be even worse. The Slovenian and Italian communist partisan bands that hid out in the limestone caves in the mountains above Trieste would hear about the communist sympathisers themselves, or through their vast network of informers. Then, at night, they would descend from their hideouts on the plateau above the coast and kidnap the person in question. They would take them away and force them to become a partisan, living a life of quasi-penal socialist slavery, never to be seen again. Such were the rumours buzzing around the dry-dock and shipyard where Ondina worked ten-hour days, and where thousands of men and women worked on the huge battleships and cruisers of the Italian Navy. These ships went off to face Britain's Royal Navy in the Mediterranean, off Crete, Malta and Sardinia.

But as the independent and rebellious Ondina would say to those close to her, she dreamed of being kidnapped by the partisans. Anything had to be better than spending endless days in a ship-manufacturing plant working on a lathe that, her bullying supervisors kept telling her, made parts of Italy's finest battleships. She wanted to be at school with her girlfriends. She wanted to be at home. She even wanted to be working with her poor father on his small farm, much diminished in size since the Fascist authorities had confiscated half of the land because he was suspected of being 'anti-Italian'. But what she really wanted to be was Monfalcone's first female partisan. It fitted in with every image she had in her adolescent mind. Bicycling furiously from one secret band to another, in her knapsack copies of *Unita,* or 'Unity' and *La Prossima*, 'Next', the partisans' forbidden, underground newspapers. There would be messages too, arranging meetings where socialist trade union leaders met covertly with communist partisans. In Ondina's mind they'd get together in huts high in the mountains, and they would come up with madly brave plans to overcome the hated, arrogant, land- and business-owning middle-class *Fascisti.* Many of this social class swore allegiance to Mussolini's party in return for employment, for big business contracts and social advancement, while families like Ondina's struggled to support their children. It was the *Fascisti* who were behind the brutally repressive policies against the Slovene-speaking minority around Trieste. But what the Black Shirts hated more than anything were communists and the trade unions. And even as a sixteen- year-old Ondina stood for both.

But as 1941 turned into 1942 she knew she just had to wait, and that her time would come. She was convinced of it. Sooner or later, promised the forbidden communist newspapers, the working population of the region of Friuli Venezia Giulia, around Venice, Trieste and the northern Adriatic, would rise up against Mussolini's Fascists. It would be the moment that she and her family had waited for.

COMMUNISM AND INDUSTRIALISATION IN TRIESTE

Many of the population of Monfalcone were low-paid and badly treated industrial workers whose opposition to Fascism, and embracing of communism, was instinctive. Socialists and communists launched leaflets against Mussolini's war in Ethiopia in 1935. In 1937 they released a hot-air balloon whose sides were emblazoned with the words 'Long live the USSR. Death to the Fascist criminals.' A social collective called 'Red Aid' sprang up in 1936. It collected money from workers in Monfalcone, which was then distributed to the families of political activists in the shipyards who had been arrested by the police. The shipyard also had a secret printing press. Copies of *La Prossima* were smuggled in from Padua, 200 miles west of Trieste. Meetings of communist cells took place in people's homes, with a lookout posted on the roof or in the garden to warn of approaching police or *Camicie Nere*.

By 1942, aged seventeen, Ondina was already loyal to the partisan cause. She was accustomed to taking the train from the halt at Monfalcone, with its staggering view from the platforms of the whole Gulf of Trieste and the northern Adriatic. She'd sit in a third-class carriage, cotton scarf knotted on her head, a picnic of fresh bread and bacon fat to accompany her. Very occasionally there'd be a small rind of Parmesan too, to keep her company on the three-hour rail journey west to Padua, or an hour north to Udine. She would return with copies of *La Prossima* and *Unita* in her basket, which would be distributed around the shipyard. This mixture of 'bread and communism', as Ondina described it, was not for the faint-hearted. The seventeen-year-old girl faced imprisonment if she was caught, with her family constantly harassed by the police for bribes to keep her fed in jail. Families whose children had been 'kidnapped' by the partisans were subjected to endless reprisals. Ondina's adolescent enthusiasm was such, though, that she even told people she'd offer the partisans her address so they could come and get her at night.

The Italian communist partisans decided that they needed a liaison officer to coordinate operations with their Slovenian counterparts. To her delight and amazement, they chose Ondina Peteani. They gave her the *nom-de-guerre* of 'Natalia'. And so began her life as a real partisan. Her job was to be a runner. Her partisan commanders assumed, correctly, that Italian Fascist patrols would be less likely to stop an innocent-looking teenage girl. Into the bargain, as good

Catholics and family men, they would certainly never submit her to a body search. Her bicycle became her new best friend, and every day before and after work she would pedal between different groups of Italian partisans in Monfalcone, and the Slovenian group camped out in a forest above Trieste. For six months her life seemed to be as romantic as she had imagined it would be. There was a tough, good-looking partisan leader to whom she looked up; the groups carried out guerrilla operations by the textbook, and the frequent firefights against the fascists saw both sides evenly matched. Ondina saw her first fighting at a roadblock where two of her colleagues were killed, while she escaped on foot, half-terrified, half-thrilled by the incredible experience. But the endless summer of her partisan idyll, like all summers, had to come to an end. And in September 1943 it did, in the most brutal possible way. Italy fell apart and the Germans invaded. The gloves came off.

5

Revenge and Reprisals on the Dalmatian Coast

By 1943, the daily menu of violence in Trieste, the Venezia Giulia and along the Dalmatian coast was one of reprisal, revenge, further reprisal and more revenge by all parties. On one side, there were Italian Fascists, Germans and their hated Croat Ustashe proxies. On the other side were the Croat, Slovenian and other partisans and soldiers from the Yugoslav National Liberation Army, and Italian communist partisan gangs, like the Garibaldi Brigade, to which Ondina Peteani belonged.

In the middle, by accident of birth and allegiance, were trapped such people as Norma Cossetto. She was Italian, from the same generation as Ondina Peteani; they were born only fifty miles apart, and both were clever, ambitious women. But they were separated by a brutal front line of wartime politics. What happened to each of them served to spur on their colleagues, and their enemies, into an increasingly extreme and vicious circle of revenge and counter-reprisal. Each side could use the others' behaviour as a hideous example. They could say, in many ways legitimately: this is what will happen to you and your families and friends if the Slovenian communists, Italian Fascists, Italian communists, Croat militiamen, Yugoslav soldiers or German SS arrive and stay in power. So from 1943 onwards, the story of what happened to Norma Cossetto was used by the Italian Fascists, and the Germans, to fire up signal flares of warning about the appalling fate that waited in store for anybody who fell into the hands of communist partisans.

THE *FOIBE*

Born in 1920, Norma was an Italian. She lived in the hamlet of Santa Domenica, near the town of Visinada on the Istrian peninsula, which sat some twenty miles due south of Trieste. Istria was then in Yugoslavia. By the time Mussolini's Italians occupied the peninsula in 1941, Norma's father Giuseppe was the head of the local Italian Fascist National Party and the mayor of Visinada. He was thus a man of political and social consequence. He also joined one of the various armed Fascist militias, and after the armistice between Italy and the Allies in 1943, he was posted to Trieste. Norma, her sister and her mother stayed behind in Istria.

By this time Norma was twenty-three. She had a degree in Italian Literature from the University of Padova, where she had also enrolled in the students' Fascist union.

Following completion of her degree course, she had moved back to Istria, and started working as a teacher in the seaside resort of Parenzo. During the summer of 1943, she was working on her university thesis about her home region, which she had entitled *Istria Rossa,* or Red Istria. It was a reference to the local dark orange-brown rocky soil that held a high content of bauxite. She was used to touring round local towns and villages on her bicycle to carry out interviews and gather information from people.

The signing of the armistice between the Italians and the Allies in July 1943 immediately made the partisans in Italy and Yugoslavia feel empowered. Norma's sister, Licia Cossetto, said that straightaway the family began to receive threats from Yugoslav and Italian communist partisans. On 25 September 1943 their house was robbed and vandalised. The following day the partisans called her to an interview in their new headquarters in the former *carabinieri* (police) barracks in

Visignano. Their terms were blunt: join the partisans. Her answer was straight. No. Nor, she said, would she deny her allegiance to Fascism. But she was released. Two days later, however, she was arrested again. She was taken to a former Italian barracks in Parenzo, from where her sister Licia tried to get her released, unsuccessfully. A few days later, this being the immediate aftermath of the armistice, the Germans marched into Istria, and so the partisans moved her and other captives to a nearby school. Norma was separated from the other prisoners in a room by herself, tied to a table, tortured, and repeatedly raped. On the night of 4/5 October, she and the other prisoners had their hands tied with wire, and were walked to a nearby village.

There, in the darkness of a field, the female prisoners were raped again. Their partisan captors walked them over to a dark, looming opening in the ground. The rocks seemed to split open and a large black entrance, like a ravine, became apparent. It was a *foiba*, or sinkhole, a cross between a mineshaft, a cave and a ravine, hundreds of feet deep. The limestone Karst plateau above Trieste and the rugged Dalmatian littoral were littered with them. Their hands still tied, the prisoners were shot in the back of the head, and pushed into the gaping crevasses. In a close-knit community where the Italian victims were almost all Catholic, news of the shameful and brutal death of Norma Cossetto spread instantly, and to exactly where the partisans most wanted it. To Cossetto's father, the Fascist official in Trieste. The message was simple: Italians, get out and get off land that is Yugoslav, or this is what will happen to you, your friends, and particularly your female children. It was an early, and brutally effective, example of ethnic cleansing. Just under a month later, the message was reiterated. Three Italian sisters, Albina, Fosca and Caterina Radecci, were killed and thrown into a nearby *foiba.*

The brutal behaviour towards Italians like Cossetto also owed much to the behaviour of the Italian Army in western Slovenia. They had occupied it after 1941. General Mario Roatta commanded the Italian 2nd Army in Slovene and Croat-occupied areas of Yugoslavia in the Second World War. He was notorious for his violent repression of the civilian population. He issued an operational memo on

1 March 1942, called Circular 3C. It outlined a policy of reprisals for partisan actions in areas under his command: the results of it were hostage-taking, executions, destruction of villages, confiscation of civilian property, and wholesale deportations. A total of 25,000 civilians from western Slovenia were taken to *ad hoc* detention centres that the Italians built on the Dalmatian island of Rab, and around such towns in the Venezia Giulia as Monigo and Gonars. Roatta's directives saw the deportation of an estimated 7.5 per cent of the population of the Slovenian province of Ljubljana. Thousands of them died.*

ONDINA PETEANI GOES ON THE RUN

The German occupation of Italy had begun in the early autumn of 1943, and along with the vicious treatment meted out as high-profile warnings to people like Cossetto, partisan life for Ondina Peteani around Trieste began to change. German soldiers were now everywhere. Returning on the train one day from Udine to Monfalcone with a consignment of paper for the partisans' printing presses, she and two girl friends were stopped by German soldiers. Luckily, they were more easygoing troopers from the Wehrmacht, and not from the Waffen-SS. The three teenage girls pushed their luck, and gave the Germans their heavy packages of paper to carry off the train for them. But by October, Ondina's luck had started to change. She was stopped and arrested by the Fascist militia twice, bluffing her way out the first time, and running away the second. The third time her good fortune ran out. A paramilitary policeman from the *carabinieri* came to her parents' house to arrest her. She kept her nerve, and explained to him that before she could accompany him to the police station, she needed to change her clothes. She went into her bedroom, climbed out of the window, and for a brief moment considered stealing the policeman's bike. But it had a flat tyre. So she ran.

* Neither Italians nor ex-Yugoslavs can agree on an objective or balanced judgement about Roatta, his policies and crimes. The documentation of his *in absentia* trial for war crimes in Italy in 1945 provides some, however; as does Davide Rodogno's *Fascism's European Empire: Italian Occupation during the Second World War* (Cambridge: Cambridge University Press, 2006).

As she did, she knew she was condemning her parents and brothers and sisters to the possibility of reprisals, deportation or possibly death at the hands of Globocnik's SS men and allied Italian militiamen. But she had no choice. She knew she had been betrayed. And that first and most importantly she needed to escape into the forest above Monfalcone, to contact her partisan colleagues and warn them to move location instantly. The next most important thing was to track down the informer and deal with him – or her. When she reached them, her commanders insisted that they had to have sufficient proof before they killed one of their erstwhile colleagues, and so they laid a series of traps in which the informer repeatedly incriminated himself. In January 1944, the commander of Ondina's unit decided they had enough proof. Five partisan fighters, including Ondina, followed the traitor, who was nicknamed 'Blecchi'. But Italian Fascist militiamen had tipped him off, and Ondina's group was ambushed. In the firefight one of her close colleagues was shot. Ondina escaped. She made her way back to the little village of Vermegliano where she had grown up, still following the informer. By now it was 29 January 1944. On a sloping track in the village two of her partisan colleagues arrived on push-bikes as 'Blecchi' crossed the road in front of them. They moved forward, shooting him from a mounted position at point-blank range as they wheeled past. The traitor collapsed to the muddy ground. Ondina and the two men fled on two bicycles, Peteani sitting on the saddle of the second machine as her colleague stood up and pedalled. But 'Blecchi' survived, as underneath his shirt he was wearing a primitive form of bullet-proof vest made of iron plates. He managed to make his way, with help, to the hospital in Monfalcone, where a German military doctor operated on him.

A few hours after the operation, the doctor told him he was out of mortal danger, but would have to stay in bed at the hospital for at least three further nights. A nurse tipped off the partisans immediately, and for a second time her commanders sent Ondina to do the killing. She went into the hospital with one other partisan on the night of 2 February. The nurse who had provided the inside tip about 'Blecchi' led the two up the hospital stairs, and along a corridor to the ward where the informer was lying in bed. To the partisans' and nurse's surprise, his mother was with him at his bedside. As Ondina and her colleague pushed their way into the room, raising their guns, 'Blecchi's' mother first tried to raise the alarm, and then tried to take the handgun off Ondina by force. But the girl from the shipyard, who had grown up reading Victor Hugo and then cherishing a vision of becoming a partisan, was no longer a day-dreaming teenager. She shot the mother, and then her traitorous son, in the head and chest with heavy, soft-nosed pistol bullets. Both were dead before the partisans had left the building. As they ran down the front steps to their waiting bicycles, they saw a huge, spreading orange glow stretching into the sky from the direction of Merne aerodrome two miles to the north-east.

While the two had been inside the hospital in Monfalcone, reinforcements from the Trieste Battalion had been in action. Fifty-four experienced Sardinian soldiers, who had deserted the preceding month from the Fascist Army of the Republic of Salo, had attacked the aerodrome. One of their former officers, codenamed 'The Raven', was leading them. Using incendiary bombs they managed to destroy eight German fighters and bombers. As a result of this, and the audacious killing of 'Blecchi' the informer, Odilo Globocnik's SS soldiers and police officers stepped up the tempo of their operations against the Italian partisans.. These fighters had, by now, taken to hiding out in underground tunnels that Austrian soldiers dug during World War I into the sides of the limestone slopes above Monfalcone. Ondina would take groups of female partisans down the slopes of the mountains on logistical missions. They went to collect clothing, food, medicines, weapons and ammunition. They gathered it from all of their different contacts, couriers and allies down in the city of Trieste, in Monfalcone and in some of the smaller villages. By early 1944, the weapons at their disposal were no longer limited to the Beretta machine guns and Carcano rifles of the Italian Army. They also included captured German Schmeisser MP-40 machine pistols and K-98 rifles, British Bren and Sten guns, American Garand rifles and

Browning .30-calibre belt-fed machine guns. The British SOE and the American OSS were also parachuting and delivering weapons to partisans in neighbouring Yugoslavia by the plane-load.

On the night of 11 February 1944, Ondina was returning up the mountain to her unit when she ran straight into a German patrol. She was immediately taken to the SS headquarters on Piazza Oberdan in Trieste. She was captured alone, and so at first tried to persuade her captors that she was on her way to visit her boyfriend. Refusing to say any more, and with the SS men in no hurry to find out anything, she was simply simply left in their cells for three weeks – then moved to the central Coroneo prison in Trieste. SS-Brigadeführer Globocnik found that the easiest and quickest way to carry out effective reprisals was to have a pool of hostages on hand in the cells for when retribution needed to be taken. Ondina was now among this random group of prisoners. While she was in her cell, resistance operations, and subsequent German reprisals, continued across the whole region of Trieste and the Adriatic coast. On 27 March the Germans hanged four partisans in public; the resistance followed this up with an attack on a German position in the town of Opicina, in Trieste's northern suburbs. Odilo Globocnik's SS men strung up seventy-two hostages in retaliation a week later. Then at the end of April, five German soldiers were strolling along Via Ghega, which leads off the ornate gardens of the Piazza della Libertà in front of Trieste's central station. A car drew up alongside them. Two hand-grenades saw the Germans dead and dying on the pavement in under twenty seconds.

As a reprisal, the SS took fifty prisoners from their pool of hostages at Coroneo prison. They included Italian partisans and civilians, Slovenians, and ethnic Croats from the port of Fiume–Rijeka, further down the Adriatic coast. (As this city had now become part of Yugoslavia, due to the Italian surrender, its name had reverted to the Yugoslav version.) Their captors took them to the indoor courtyard of a municipal building where the stairwell stretched up and around the cobbles below. The Germans then attached ropes to the various stone pillars that supported the stairwell, which climbed up and round the courtyard for four storeys. They knotted nooses into the ends of the ropes, and put them around the prisoners' heads. Then they pushed the prisoners off the banisters.

Ondina escaped this round of executions, and another on 11 May, when the Germans killed another eleven of her friends and colleagues. An interpreter who worked for the Germans told her that it was probably preferable for her to be deported away from Trieste. Even to a work camp somewhere far away, as it would be much, much better for her than to end up in the rice factory, the Risiera, over in San Sabba. He had heard that truly appalling things were taking place there. On 31 May 1944, she and 239 other prisoners from Coroneo prison climbed into trucks outside on the street and were driven to Trieste's central station. There was a bit of a walk past the normal passenger platforms, which confused most of the prisoners. Where were the normal trains? But their guards led them round to the side of the goods' marshalling yard, past the industrial silos, away from the sight of other people on the main platforms. Their transport was waiting for them there. A long row of dark brown cattle trucks.

THE RICE PLANT

San Sabba is a southern suburb of the city of Trieste, and its name translates literally as 'Holy Sabbath', or 'Holy Sunday'. It sits close to the Adriatic Sea. It is very near to the boundary and frontier that the city shared first with the Kingdom, and then, after 1941, with the People's Republic of Yugoslavia. In 1913 a rice-processing plant was built there, a six-storey red brick building with a courtyard, high walls and a large entrance gate that made it almost impossible to see inside. When the Germans arrived in 1943, they immediately saw its potential as a prison camp. At first they called it Stalag 339.* They initially used it to house Italian soldiers who, after the armistice in September 1943, refused to fight for Mussolini's Facists, or alongside the Germans.

* Stalag was a word used by the Germans to refer to POW camps: it is a shortened version of the word Stammlager.

Apart from holding, and killing, its inmates the camp also served as a transit centre. Some of those Italian Jews being transported to the Mauthausen–Gusen camp complex outside Linz, in Austria, and to Auschwitz, passed through it. As the war against the Italian and Slovenian partisans became more intense, and reprisals carried out by both sides more numerous and extreme, so the number of inmates at San Sabba increased. They represented a cross-section of those people in the region the Third Reich considered their enemies.

Guiseppe Karis was a partisan from the Garibaldi Brigade arrested towards the end of 1944 by the *Camicie Nere.* Taken to cell number six at the Risiera di San Sabba, he was interrogated and tortured by both Italian Fascists and the SS. There were Jews like David Fischbein, Levi Grunwald, and the seventeen-year-old Herty Wessel. Their eventual destinations were Auschwitz, Mauthausen and the women's concentration camp at Ravensbrück. In cell number ten, a woman called Olga Fabjan left her signature scratched into the cream-coloured plaster. She was accused of being a partisan. The SS and Gestapo tortured her, shut her up in a cell for seventeen days, and then moved her to one of the upper floors of the building. One of the women arrested with her was a Slovenian called Albina Skabar, who was twenty when the SS arrested her and her father in March 1945. Again, she was taken to the Risiera di San Sabba:

> They began to interrogate and beat me. They undressed me and hit me some more, and hit me hard enough so that three teeth were knocked out. I was bleeding a lot, and they finished the interrogation by kicking me out of the door brutally. I felt terrible, I leaned on my father and fainted. I don't know when I came round. I was seated on two wooden boards in a small cell, alone in the dark. There was no light and no window, and I didn't know whether it was day or night. The screams were terrible, particularly from the first cell, and from in front of the cells.*

* All three survived the war. Their names survive on the walls of the cells at the former camp,and their testimonies are recorded in the book *Scritte, Lettere e Voci* (Writing, Letters and Voices) from the Civil Museum of the Risiera di San Sabba; published in conjunction with IRSML in 2014.

Eventually the building proved too small to house all of the inmates, so from the end of 1944 onwards the cells and dormitories in which they lived became desperately overcrowded. The guards at the camp were predominantly Ukrainian SS men and women who had travelled to Trieste with Globocnik, working with Italian fascist militiamen. Everybody on both sides of the Italian and Yugoslav border knew of the camp's existence. But apart from the guards – who weren't talking – it was almost impossible to find out verifiable information about what happened in the camp, as nobody who went in came out alive. Or if they did, it was for onward-shipment to Poland and Austria from Trieste's Central Station.

THE PARTISANS CAPTURE SAN SABBA

In the days before the attack on Trieste that began on 29 April 1945, the Yugoslav partisans were given their orders by their commanders. The commander of the Yugoslav 4th Army, General Petar Drapšin, had several priorities for the capture of Trieste. The liberation of the concentration camp and its inmates was one of them, as soon as the rest of the city had been secured. The importance of the capture of its guards, both Italian and German, was underlined.[1]

The National Liberation Army had raced to occupy Trieste at the same time as it was fighting for the town of Opicina. An entire brigade of some 2,000 men had headed into the city and then split into three. A first detachment headed to the Tribunale building, a second to the Castello di San Giusto, and a third to the Risiera di San Sabba camp. The Yugoslav soldiers, accompanied by a troop of partisans, found the steel doors of the camp closed, but unlocked. Weapons cocked, they pushed them open and dashed into a wide passageway, with high red brick walls rising on either side of them. The first thing that hit them was the smell. Burning human decay, faeces, and rotting life. It blew at them like a warm moving wall. Smoke curled round down the passageway from a wide, sunlit courtyard in front of them. A huge pile of bricks, mortar, wooden beams and something else seemed still to be on fire.[2] The soldiers moved forward. Where were the guards, asked the Yugoslav soldiers, the Germans, Italians? Gone, came the answer from the first inmates questioned. Fled. Last night. Towards the city. On the left of the main entrance, large wooden doors opened into a block containing the cells. The live inmates shared the cramped space with dead bodies stored and stacked there. Piles of people's looted possessions were scattered around. They included combs, some of them tortoiseshell, eye-glasses, make-up compacts, fountain pens, silver tweezers, and a handsome silver fob watch with the numerals in Hebrew.*

The building containing the crematorium had been demolished. Rubble was strewn around. In the piles of brick and ash, the partisans discovered three large sacks, made of strong paper, like those used to hold cement. Inside them human remains, mostly turned to lumpy ash, seemed to be mixed in with building rubble. The Yugoslav fighters also found a metal object that at first glance looked like a small riding whip with a heavy metal head. Then they saw it was a type of hammer. Inmates said the Germans had used it to kill people. And then as the soldiers and partisans moved through the building complex and the separate cell blocks that it held, they noticed the messages scratched on the walls. The last signals from the condemned, the now-dead, and even from survivors. The Yugoslav unit commanders ordered their men to start looking after the living survivors. They ordered a few other men to start writing down every single message they could find that was scratched into the grey and cream flaking plasterwork. They provided vital clues to who had been here, when, and where they might have gone.

* These possessions, stolen from Jewish inmates at San Sabba, and discovered by liberating partisans and Yugoslav soldiers, are preserved in the camp museum today.

6

Death on the Plateau, 2–3 May

On the afternoon of 2 May, the Red Army raised its flag over the Reichstag in Berlin. The war in Europe had only days left to run. In Austria and Italy, nearly a million Germans and Italians were surrendering to the Allies; in Croatia the Germans would hold out for another week. Slovenians, Germans and Croats who had fought against Tito were fleeing westwards into Austria, desperate to surrender to the British or Americans. Tito sent a telegram to his commanders that specified that if these prisoners surrendered to the Yugoslav National People's Army, they were not to mistreat them. Allied officers who saw and read the message were immediately suspicious – it was uncharacteristic for Tito to put such orders in writing. They immediately suspected that he was trying to put into place a series of pre-emptive barriers, in case atrocities took place and any war crimes trials followed. Across Trieste and the eastern Venezia Giulia, the Allies, Germans and Yugoslavs were spinning through a complex, fast-moving chess game of liberation, surrender, last stands and sudden firefights.

After the incident on 3 May where the New Zealand soldier had been killed accidentally by the Yugoslavs, the Allies had pulled back to a line in the western suburbs of Trieste. This was situated between the city and the Castello di Miramare. Sherman tanks guarded road-blocks on the edge of the Gulf of Trieste, and on the road that led up the mountain parallel to the coast. The 28th Maori Battalion had now reinforced their New Zealand colleagues of the 2nd Division. The entire unit's complement of men were more than happy to have got to the end of the war in one piece. There were good looting opportunities to be had too. One New Zealand unit discovered that some German cargo barges that sat in Trieste harbour, half-sunk by Allied fighter-bombers, contained cases of wine, brandy and food. That some of these treasures lay underwater was no obstacle: all it took was a New Zealand soldier attached to a rope, stripped to his shorts, and a case or two of Italian or Dalmatian red wine could be brought to the surface. The antipodean men had already made an instant impression on the Yugoslav forces they had met in Trieste, Udine and Gorizia: Tito's men recognised people like themselves immediately. Hard, enduring country men who knew how to fight and knew how to enjoy themselves. To the enormous surprise of the Yugoslavs, some of the burly, dusty Kiwis could talk to them in Serbo-Croatian. Dalmatian immigration in the 1920s to New Zealand meant that some of the soldiers could speak scatterings of the language spoken by Tito's men.

Meanwhile General Freyberg had established the Allied Headquarters at Castello di Miramare. Five miles behind it was a 'gun line' of artillery. 25-pounders were in position ready to return fire instantly, should the New Zealanders and the British tank men and armoured cars come under attack from either Yugoslavs or die-hard Germans. The 8th Army's eastwards advance had halted on the edge of Trieste. Along with American units, its northwards advance was heading for the Austrian border. The city of Trieste, the town of Opicina above it, and its northern and eastern suburbs were now controlled by the Yugoslavs. The British and American liaison officers from the SOE and the OSS, who had accompanied General Drapšin's men across eastern Yugoslavia, had now returned westwards to the Allied lines. This meant that the British and American 8th and 5th

Armies were tactically and operationally 'blind' to the operations that the Yugoslavs were now carrying out in and around the city.

Before the Yugoslav 4th Army and the Slovenian partisans had advanced into Trieste, they had made an amphibious landing on the Dalmatian coast south-west of the city. German units on the Istrian peninsula had then been cut off, surrounded and outflanked by Drapšin's units, who were simultaneously advancing north-west up the craggy Croatian coastline. They had captured all of it, including its key islands, by 20 April. The port of Fiume–Rijeka was the last city to fall. After advancing from Slovenia and along the coast, Drapšin's men had attacked Trieste on 30 May. It had been a two-pronged assault, along the coast, and from the mountain range north of it.

THE YUGOSLAV REVENGE

Having now taken Trieste and its surrounding territory, Tito and his commanders on the ground had to decide what to do with it, and the people who lived or found themselves trapped there. The options General Drapšin and the other Yugoslav commanders had for these people were threefold, depending on who they were. Put them in front of military tribunals, and possibly sentence them to death. Deport them to work camps, or leave them alone. The options for the territory were simple. Firstly to hold it, then to push brinkmanship with the Allies to the highest possible level, and then make them *think* Tito would fight for it, if necessary with possible backing from the Russians.* This was the geo-political nightmare not just of Churchill, Edward Stettinius and Field Marshal Alexander, but of Stalin as well. If the latter was going to go into World War III, it was not going to be on terms dictated to him by Tito. He saw him as an unreliable and unpredictable ally who happened to be in charge of a large army and some of the most

* The Museum of Contemporary History in the Slovenian capital, Ljubljana, now houses the archives of the Museum of the National Liberation of Slovenia, as does the Arhiv Republike Slovenije, the National State Archives. Much of Josip Broz Tito's operational communications to his commanders in the field from April to July 1945 were predominantly done by word of mouth, but some of those written down survive here.

strategically vital territory in Europe.[2] Tito's men had fought for the territory in Yugoslavia that they controlled, and won it without direct support of troops from the Red Army. The SOE and OSS had supplied Tito with weapons and equipment, and in the last six months of the war the Russians had done the same. But unlike territory in Poland, Romania, Bulgaria or Czechoslovakia that the Red Army had physically fought for, and then occupied, Yugoslavia had been conquered by Tito, not Stalin. The Soviet leader found it much harder to assume any form of political control over land he had not won militarily. So while Tito was clearly a political ally and member of the Comintern* who had welcomed the Red Army into Belgrade, he was proving to be a maverick.

The National Liberation Army and the respective partisans groups fighting with them took their orders direct from Tito. It was a monolinear command structure that encompassed the secret police from OZNA at every level. Odeljene za Zaštitu Naroda, or OZNA, the Yugoslav Department for National Security, had been formed in May 1944 by one of Tito's chiefs of staff, Aleksandar Ranković.† It brought together all the different military and domestic and foreign intelligence apparatuses that were then operating in Yugoslavia within the various partisan and military units. It had four sub-directorates. The first was headed by Maks Milić, born Maksimiljan Baće. It was in charge of intelligence gathering, agent recruitment and agent handling in occupied territories, such as in Trieste, the Friuli Venezia Giulia and Austria. The second concentrated on counter-intelligence in territories liberated from the enemy, such as the area around Istria which had formerly been Italian. The Third Directorate handled intelligence activities within Yugoslav partisan and army units, while the Fourth Directorate handled records, data analysis and logistics. It also contained the sub-department for special technical operations, such as decoding, radio intercepts and electronic surveillance. In spring 1945

* The Comintern (short for Communist International) was the international Communist organisation founded and controlled by the Soviet Union which liaised with communist parties in other countries.

† There are no direct or indirect articles in old Serbo-Croat, nor the more modern Bosanski-Hrvatski-Srpski, so it is just referred to as OZNA.

a fifth directorate was added, which concentrated on operations against foreign intelligence units operating within Yugoslavia, such as the NKVD, OSS, SOE and MI6.

The Yugoslav secret police's first priority was to find, arrest, interrogate and put on trial the Nazi hierarchy who had run the Adriatic Coastal Area. This included Rainer, Globocnik and their senior SS and Gestapo commanders. Along with them were the the Ukrainian, German and Italian guards from the Risiera di San Sabba camp. At the same level of priority were the Italian Fascist government officials from Mussolini's Salo Republic, especially those who had worked for the security apparatuses of his Questura. This functioned as a mix of state security and interior ministry. Alongside them were any members of one of the more unorthodox SS divisions that had been raised during the war.

THE PRINZ EUGEN DIVISION AND THE SS COSSACKS

The 7th SS Volunteer Mountain Division was named 'Prinz Eugen', after Prince Eugene of Savoy. He was a Hapsburg who had liberated parts of Serbia from Ottoman rule in the eighteenth century's Austro-Turkish War. The Prinz Eugen Division first recruited, then forcibly conscripted, men from the *Volksdeutsche.* This was the ethnic German minority who had lived in the Balkans, sometimes for generations. These came predominantly from the Banat, a German-administered autonomous region of northern Serbia established in 1941 after the German invasion of Yugoslavia. But some volunteers came from Romanian and Croatian territory. Tito and his men hated them. The 7th SS loathed them in return and didn't miss a chance to prove it. The Prinz Eugen were trained as mountain troops and specialised in anti-partisan operations. The Balkans *Volksdeutsche* felt mistrusted and let down by the mainstream German administration. Not surprisingly – the head of SS recruitment had reportedly said 'no person cares what we do with our ethnic Germans in the south.'[2] Across the Balkans, the division established a notorious track record for committing atrocities. One operation, against a string of villages near Nikšić in Montenegro in 1943, was typical:

> Whole families were thrown into burning houses in many cases and thus burnt. It has been established from the investigations entered upon that 121 persons, mostly women, and including 30 persons aged 60–92 years and 29 children of ages ranging from 6 months to 14 years, were executed on this occasion.[3]

The SS men were often good combat soldiers, but as was so often the case with the Waffen-SS, were their own worst enemies when it came to alienating the civilian population in the areas in which they were fighting. General Mario Roatta's Italians executed hostages and deported people. The 7th SS went further. They destroyed whole towns. They killed everybody, from babies to old people. So their behaviour made them one of Tito's best recruiting sergeants. By the beginning of May 1945, thousands of them had fought a retreat across central Yugoslavia, and were heading for the country's western border with Italy and Austria. Here they aimed to surrender to the Allies who, they assumed, would treat them better than Tito's men or the Red Army. Units of them had crossed into Trieste as well to try to find Allied units who would take their surrender.

Next on the very long list of groups, units and individuals whom OZNA, Tito and General Drapšin were singling out for detention, trial and sentencing were the commanders of any Italian partisan groups that were overtly allied to Catholicism, or were anti-communist. Then there were the renegade Russian Cossack cavalrymen from the XV SS Cossack Cavalry Corps, volunteers who fought for the Germans. The Russian intelligence officers in Belgrade had requested that Drapšin and his men apprehend any they found for repatriation to the Soviet Union. At best, this meant a trip to a *gulag*. After the atrocities the Cossacks had committed against the Yugoslav civilian population, the partisans and soldiers of Tito's army needed no encouragement to arrest them. A rung down on the ladder of culpability were the collaborators, informers, spies, and women who had slept with German or Italian Fascists for favours or safety. So, when Lieutenant-Colonel Peter Wilkinson lay in his camp bed underneath the Austro-Hungarian portraits in the Castello di Miramare, on the night of 2 May, and asked himself who was shooting whom on the streets of Trieste, the answer was, well, where did he want to start?

As Friedrich Rainer and Odilo Globocnik desperately headed north for Austria, with their cadre of Ukrainian bodyguards, the Yugoslavs had captured many of their subordinates. During the night of the 1–2 May, they had taken over the Tribunale building after British tanks had shelled it at point-blank range. Inside they found a combination of two companies of SS troops, Italian Fascist militiamen and German and Ukrainian guards from the San Sabba camp. There were very roughly 800 men. By dawn, around 200 were led out, according to Italian, Allied and Yugoslav witnesses.[4] Italian civilians also saw trucks being loaded with uniformed bodies for most of the morning, even though a cordon had been put around the Tribunale building. The Yugoslav Army then took away the remaining 200 live prisoners who had been led out of the building.

Around 1,200 Germans surrendered in Opicina to the Yugoslavs, while in the town of Gorizia precisely 1,048 Italians went missing between the liberation of the town and the end of May.[5] Another 500 Italians were arrested and went missing in and around Rijeka–Fiume after 3 May. South of San Sabba, on 1 May, the Yugoslav 9th Corps and partisans captured a half-battalion of German coastal defence troops, including sailors, soldiers, anti-aircraft gunners and artillerymen, part of Kampfgruppe Berger that hadn't made it to safety in the Castello di San Giusto.[6] There were some 700 of them. Partisans discovered around 150 Italian officials from the Questura and two different Fascist militia groups hiding in train storage sheds and warehouses at Trieste's central station.[7] They were trying to walk north-east along the coast road to surrender to the Allies.

Two small German minesweepers and five E-Boats, armed motor boats fitted with torpedoes, sailed from Rijeka. They were heading for

Allied territory around Venice. But air attacks forced them to land in the Gulf of Trieste, where they mistook a group of Yugoslav partisans on one of the jetties for British troops. The partisans, who had marched and fought for most of the preceding five months across western Yugoslavia, had taken off their boots and tunics, and some of them were swimming. Others were barefoot; all were delighted to see the sun, the sea and the end of the war. The German sailors were relieved of weapons, watches, food, schnapps, knives, sunglasses and, in some cases, boots, and led into custody by the laughing partisans.[8] There were around seventy-five E-Boat crew, 100 German soldiers fleeing Fiume–Rijeka who had hitched a ride on the boats, and some 200 German sailors and soldiers on the two other vessels. This made an additional 375 men.

An armed German motor-boat carrying some forty sailors and soldiers who had fled Rijeka–Fiume curved in to land on the northern curve of Trieste's harbour. Through binoculars they spotted Allied soldiers and what they recognised as Allied armoured personnel carriers. They headed for land. What only became apparent, as they were too close to the docks to turn around, was that the Allied troops were with a group of Yugoslav partisans and soldiers. They were New Zealanders. Both they, and the Yugoslavs, appeared to have looted some horses from somewhere. The German boat touched the wall of the dock. Neither the Yugoslavs nor the Slovenians were in the mood for a fight, so they and the New Zealanders liberated the Germans of their Luger and Walther P-38 pistols, MP-40 machine pistols, watches, sunglasses and scarves. Then they told them to head as fast as they could north-west, fly a white flag to prevent air-attack, and head for landfall to the west of the Castello di Miramare. They would, they were told, be guaranteed a reception by Allied troops. They were among the minority of lucky Germans that day. Major Geoffrey Cox, Freyberg's intelligence officer, also noted that a significant number of senior Italian Fascists and several Gestapo officials were lucky enough to make it to Allied lines to surrender. It led him to conclude that General Drapšin's operation to capture Tito's enemies cannot have been that well-coordinated or closely targeted.

Nevertheless, with the estimated 3,800 men from the groups of prisoners already listed, the additional German crewmen and passengers on the E-Boats and minesweepers made an initial total of around 4,175 German, Italian, Ukrainian and other prisoners. This was a rough number of those captured by the various elements of General Drapšin's 4th Yugoslav Army from 1 May onwards, in and around Trieste itself. The numbers on the list would only grow in the coming days of the Yugoslav occupation. And this was before the number of dead bodies found on the streets every day. The fire brigade, the *vigili del fuoco*, partisans and ordinary civilians would find the complex detritus of human revenge each morning. The majority of Trieste's citizens huddled indoors on the nights of 1 and 2 May. The city was full of shouting, shooting, running feet on cobbles, the thuds of human flesh being hit, screams. Some short. Followed by shots. Some that went on and on and then turned to gurgles. And in the morning there was the evidence. The Italian *Camicia Nera*, a hated Black Shirt, tied with wire to a lamp-post, dangling forward, the back of his head a small scarlet cave. Creamy brains on his polished shoes. Female collaborators beaten and shot. The Ukrainian SS man lying on the cobbles in a small lake of his own blood, the pink and scarlet snakes of his intestines flowing down his stomach. And the Jewish man, shot. For whoever was out there hunting in the night, somebody among them didn't like Jews either.[9]

On the afternoon of 2 May, a Slovenian Catholic priest stood in the late spring sun in a field high above Trieste. Basovizza is a village that sits a thousand feet above the Adriatic. It looks down on the city, the port and the sea from the mountainous limestone Karst plateau. The clergyman, a Slovenian called Don Malalan, was there to officiate at a burial service for Slovenian partisans killed in the battle for Opicina.

While preparing for the burial, Malalan noticed a large group of Italian men standing in a group in a field close to him. There were around 150 of them, he would later tell American agents from the Counter Intelligence Corps, and British investigators from an Intelligence Corps Field Security Section. Yugoslav soldiers from the national army – as opposed to local Slovene partisans – were questioning them and giving them an impromptu trial.

Malalan recognised the prisoners as officials from the Questura, the Italian Fascist Interior Ministry, in Trieste. As each man was questioned, four or five local Slovene or Italian women would rush up to him screaming that he had murdered her husband, burned down her house or kidnapped her son. As Malalan watched, soldiers lined all the men up, and shot them in the back of the head or neck, so that they fell forward into the crevasses in front of them. Local villagers told Malalan later that their bodies were also thrown into some of the *foibe* in nearby fields, on the top of the Karst plateau. Some of these natural mineshafts, like those near Basovizza, were 700 feet deep.

On 2 May, another priest in the same village noticed a similar group of 200–300 Italian fascists gathered in a field, being questioned in the same way. Don Virgil Seek saw that there were also about forty disarmed German soldiers with them. All of them were executed in front of him. In some cases, two men were tied together; the first was shot, the second pulled alongside him into the *foiba* by the weight of the other man. For decades, the testimonies of the two priests, two British and American intelligence officers, and a local informant who worked for OZNA (and thus could have been anybody from a local mayor to a cowherd) were almost the only witnesses to these executions that took place above and around Trieste. But the soldiers and partisans who participated, the OZNA agents, the Yugoslav colonels and generals who gave the orders, almost certainly kept their diaries, logged their memos, made their reports. The Yugoslav People's Army was a communist, hierarchical and bureaucratic structure. It kept reports of the contents of each air-drop received from the Americans and British, of the numbers of wounded partisans evacuated to Italy.

It listed and numbered and accounted for and kept records on many of the estimated 800,000 men and women who served in its ranks. OZNA spied on its own people. It listed its enemies, those they were hunting, and those they found.

PART THREE

BRINKMANSHIP ON THE ADRIATIC

7

Who was Marshal Tito?

The Central Intelligence Agency kept a card file in Washington on all its assets. Its allies, its agents, its operations, its vast global collection of 'humint', or 'human intelligence'. In its early days in 1951, one CIA agent found the card entry for the Yugoslav communist leader. 'Name: Tito. First name: not known. Last name: not known.' The OSS was the predecessor to the CIA, and had had liaison officers working with the partisans inside Yugoslavia since 1941. This suggests the card file was out-of-date. Or that the Americans, like everybody else, simply referred to the Yugoslav leader by the adopted *nom de guerre* he had chosen for himself in the 1930s. For reasons he explained himself:

> It was a rule in the Party in those times not to use one's real name, in order to reduce the chances of exposure. For instance, if someone working with me was arrested, and flogged into revealing my real name, the police would easily trace me. But the police never knew the real person hiding behind an assumed name, such as I had in the Party. I adopted first the name of Rudi, but another comrade had the same name and so I was obliged to change it, adopting the name Tito. I hardly ever used Tito at first; I assumed it exclusively in 1938, when I began to sign articles with it. Why did I take this name 'Tito' and has it special significance? Apart from anything else, this name is quite frequent in my native district of Zagorje. The best known

> writer (from there) in the late eighteenth century was called Tito Brezovacki, and the father of Ksaver Sandor Gjalski one of greatest Croatian writers, was also called Tito ...[1]

Josip Broz was born in May 1892 in the Kingdom of the Serbs, Croats and Slovenes, which was then part of Croatian territory in the Austro-Hungarian Empire. The seventh child of a Slovene mother and Croat father, he was a child of his revolutionary, politically turbulent times. He was an extrovert and big-hearted show-off and attention-seeker, who'd known poverty in childhood and was determined never to go back to it.[2] This was tempered with a natural human altruism and sense of grievance at the wrongs he saw around him. Brought up a Catholic, he managed four years of school before his family's straitened circumstances made him decide to become a locksmith's apprentice aged fifteen. By seventeen he was selling socialist newspapers to his worker colleagues and taking part in strike actions. He travelled and worked across Yugoslav and Czech territory, and learned German, fencing and how to dance. He was a politically driven revolutionary at a time in central Europe on the eve of the First World War when such allegiances meant violent imprisonment.

In May 1913 he was conscripted into the Austro-Hungarian Army in a Croatian Home Guard regiment. After basic training, his far-sighted commanding officer immediately sent him on a non-commissioned officers' course. He excelled, was promoted to sergeant, and then fought against Serbia, which sided with Britain and Italy in 1914 against the Austro-Hungarian Empire. Tito's wartime service in the neighbouring Yugoslav province to his own was one he would airbrush from his life-story for as long as he could. In 1915 he and his unit were posted to Galicia on the Eastern Front in Russia. Tito fought and commanded bravely. One night he led a small patrol behind enemy lines, under orders to bring back prisoners for interrogation. He returned from the snow drifts and frozen pine trees with eighty frightened Russians, their arms stretched into the air, desperate not to be shot on the spot. Broz was wounded, captured, and then spent two years as a POW, escaping twice. All the while he still professed allegiance to the Austro-Hungarian Empire. This was the time of the Russian Revolution, and the country was in chaos. He fled to Osmk in Siberia, where an International Brigade of the Red Guard captured and forcibly recruited him. He spent the winter of 1917–18 knee-deep in the snow, guarding the Trans-Siberian Railway. When the anti-Bolshevik Czechoslovak Legion liberated Osmk in May 1918, Tito went into hiding in a rural area about fifty miles away, and met his first wife.

Pelagija 'Polka' Belousova was just thirteen, but already beautiful, when she helped the Yugoslav revolutionary and POW hide out in a Kyrygz village. She was the daughter of a local farmer. When the Red Army re-took Omsk in November 1919, Tito returned there with Pelagija, and the two were married sometime in 1920. She was fourteen or fifteen. For the promiscuous, flirtatious Tito, it was his first wife, but by no means his first Russian girlfriend. His time in Russia during and after the First World War show a man strongly attracted to women, supremely capable of charming them into bed, and then supremely capable of deceiving them. They were qualities he would use both as a military commander and as a communist revolutionary leader.

Tito and his pregnant, teenage bride took a boat from Narva in northern Russia to Stettin in Poland, and thence a train to Vienna. In September 1920 he returned home to his village of Kumrovec in what was still the Kingdom of the Serbs, Croats and Slovenes. He promptly joined the Communist Party in Zagreb. His life was now to become the story of communism in central Europe. Tito spoke at trade union meetings, and campaigned for the Communist Party of Yugoslavia (or Yugoslav Communist Party, the YCP), which became the third-strongest party in the country's elections in 1920. But the communists found it hard to maintain focused unity. One of their number assassinated the country's Interior Minister in 1921, after which the party was banned. As a result, Tito lost his job as a waiter in a small town. He continued working illegally for the YCP, angrily distributing leaflets among factory workers, giving speeches, becoming a member of the party's local committee, getting arrested, and seeing his home searched again and again.

His wife had suffered three miscarriages before having a baby daughter. The couple named her Zlatina, or 'little golden one'. She died aged two. Then in 1924 their son Zarko was born. Tito, devastated by the loss of his daughter, saw a glimmering possibility of normality for his life. But when his boss at a local mill gave him an ultimatum of giving up the Communist Party, or his job, Tito chose the latter. Regular employment and even a semblance of a normal family life were now fast evaporating. He took three different jobs in factories and shipyards, working overtly as a communist trade union representative. Strikes were violent, Tito lost his jobs. Pelagija was also, by now, a full-time member of the YCP, and worked in a furniture factory. By 1927 she was helping imprisoned comrades. She ran an illegal printing press and was promoted to the women's section of the Comintern, or Central Committee of the YCP. Like Tito, she was arrested several times by government militias in Croatia.

And Tito himself? The YCP promoted him. Two more jobs in railways and shipyards followed, two more strikes organised by Tito accompanied them, then arrest, hunger strike, and a final decision to go on the run as a full-time revolutionary. The strikes he encouraged got bigger, the arrests more frequent, and a five-year prison sentence followed. Then Pelagija suddenly returned to Russia without telling him, taking their son with her. She got a job almost immediately with the Comintern in Moscow: if she was hoping that Tito would follow her, and their son, she was to be disappointed. If the Comintern in Moscow thought that by recalling one of their citizens and devoted acolytes back to the home land, they could entice Tito to follow, they were also mistaken. As they were in thinking that Tito might fear that his wife and young son were being held hostage in the Soviet Union. Josip Broz was now alone in Croatia. It was at this point that he assumed his three principal false names – Rudi, Walter and Tito. And along with the rest of the YCP, who were effectively outlaws, he moved to Vienna. He then left for Moscow in 1935.

In Moscow, Tito worked in the Balkans section of the Comintern and joined the NKVD: in 1937 the party sent him back to Yugoslavia to stiffen the resolve of the Communist Party there. He was also active in recruiting Yugoslav volunteers for the Dimitrov Battalion that was fighting in the Spanish Civil War. Stalin, meanwhile, had decided that the chairman of the Communist Party of Yugoslavia, Milan Gorkić, was not sufficiently disciplined or committed. So he invited him to meet in Moscow. Tito had provided a report to the NKVD about Gorkić shortly before he was recalled to Russia. On arrival, he was arrested, accused of being a British spy, and taken to the Lubyanka prison. Two days later NKVD officers shot him in the head. His wife was executed shortly afterwards.

Two separate descriptions give a picture of prisoners' last moments in the Lubyanka in this period:

> The execution chambers were lined with asphalt, with faucets and gutters so that the gore and remains could easily be washed away.[3]

> The condemned person was taken to one of the rooms off the corridors in the basement, where he took off his clothes and put on white underwear. He was then brought to a special cell equipped with a tarpaulin rug to stand on and shot in the back of the head. The tarpaulin was removed for cleaning. A doctor signed a death certificate, which was placed in the prisoner's file but usually not disclosed to relatives. The body was carried off, perhaps to be cremated before burial in an unmarked mass grave.[4]

With Gorkić conveniently now dead, Tito took over the chairmanship of the YCP. By 1 May 1941, less than a month after the Germans had invaded Yugoslavia, the government had collapsed, and the country surrendered. Tito and the Communist Party sent out a call to the population to unite and fight against the German occupation. The party comintern made Tito commander-in-chief of all 'national military liberation forces', a name shortly afterwards changed to the Yugoslav People's National Liberation Army. The revolutionary military leader had come of age.

8

The Allies' Support for Yugoslavia

William Donovan was twenty-seven when he led a troop of cavalry on the Mexican border. It was 1916. He and his platoon of riders from the New York National Guard were taking part in the United States' fight against the Mexican revolutionary Pancho Villa. A child of first-generation Irish immigrants, Donovan grew up in Buffalo, New York, and graduated from Columbia Law School. He earned his nickname 'Wild Bill' on the college football field. From the Mexican border, he moved to the battlefields of the Western Front, commanding a battalion of the New York National Guard. In less than eighteen months, he was promoted to full colonel, and won the Distinguished Service Cross and three Purple Hearts. In 1918 he was awarded America's highest military decoration, the Medal of Honor.*

> Near Landres-et-St. Georges, France, on the 14th – 15th October 1918, Lt. Col. Donovan personally led the assaulting wave in an attack upon a very strongly organized position, and when our troops were suffering heavy casualties he encouraged all near him by his example, moving among his

* The Purple Heart is an American decoration awarded to those wounded or killed while serving with the US military.

> men in exposed positions, reorganizing decimated platoons, and accompanying them forward in attacks. When he was wounded in the leg by machine-gun bullets, he refused to be evacuated and continued with his unit until it withdrew to a less exposed position.[1]

He came home a hero. In the inter-war years, he worked as a lawyer in New York State, and travelled in Europe, meeting Benito Mussolini. He saw World War II coming. The U.S Secretary for the Navy recommended him to the President. As a result, he went to Europe as President Roosevelt's personal emissary, trying to make a balanced evaluation of Great Britain's strategic capabilities to fight 'total war' against Nazi Germany. He met Churchill and his intelligence chiefs. Back in America, he stressed to the President the need to pull together the country's intelligence services into one coordinated effort, as the British had done. Prior to the outbreak of war, the Federal Bureau of Investigation (FBI, the United States domestic intelligence unit), the US Army and Navy had run their own networks and organisations. Donovan changed this. In July 1941 he became Coordinator of Information. Despite ingrained institutional resistance from the different bodies he oversaw, his plan worked. The office of the COI became the Office of Strategic Services in 1942.

Jealousy on the part of J. Edgar Hoover, Director-General of the FBI, saw the OSS prevented from operating in South America. And the Director-General of Britain's MI6, Sir Stewart Menzies, was suspicious of the go-getting, operational adventurism that OSS espoused, and the large budgets it required. A scion of the British aristocracy himself, he felt socially ill at ease with the brash, valiant and successful Donovan, the son of Irish immigrants. He was also particularly sensitive about the secrets of the Enigma encoding machine, how the Allies had broken them, and how they used the intelligence subsequently gained. That Menzies owed much of MI6's operational influence to Enigma was significant. Churchill saw the intelligence gained from breaking Enigma as vital to the war effort. Menzies saw it as vital not just to winning the war, but to preserving the status of MI6, the status quo of the British Empire and the British class system, and thus preserving his own place in it. He was a meticulous planner, a cautious and possessive man who was brave too: he had won the Distinguished Service Order with the Grenadier Guards at Ypres. His father was a dissolute businessman who had squandered the family fortune: his son held on to intelligence the way he did to money – determined not to lose it to anybody else. He was extremely well suited to his position.

Menzies banned Donovan from running OSS operations anywhere in the British Empire. He felt insecure about the coming post-war years, where he foresaw that America's expansion into a global superpower would be in counterpoint to the decline in influence and size of the British Empire. For the Americans, not being able to operate in India or Burma or parts of Africa was no hindrance whatsoever, but Menzies' second edict was an obstacle. He specified that OSS should have no dealings with any of the governments-in-exile based in London. This should have made their operations in Yugoslavia problematic, but Donovan decided to over-ride the instruction anyway. He did not need King Peter II's permission to infiltrate missions into Yugoslavia. He needed Tito, and he needed to agree with the SOE on which side to support.

So he was one of the first Allied officers who went to Belgrade in early 1941 to encourage resistance to the Germans. He wanted to evaluate which Yugoslavian faction would resist the Germans most effectively. The Yugoslavian king was in exile in London. At that point, just before the German invasion in April 1941, the British predominantly supported the Yugoslavian monarchy. Both they and the Americans had sided with the Serb-dominated Chetniks, led by the bearded and bespectacled Colonel Draža Mihailović. This was about to change, as Tito and his partisans became ever more operationally successful. Inside the Soviet Union, Yugoslav partisans were already broadcasting their own propaganda on Radio Free Yugoslavia. Stalin was an emphatic supporter of his protégé, Tito, and an opponent of the monarchy. But the Americans and British were still nervous at this point of supporting any partisan or resistance movements that leaned too strongly towards communism. And so OSS and SOE liaison officers were sent to Yugoslavia to find out which side was fighting the Germans most effectively, and what their political orientations were. And thus who the Allies should supply militarily and support politically. As one OSS officer said, the priority was to back the side who was most effective in fighting the Axis. Concerns about political orientation or Yugoslavia's post-war future came a long second.

Fearing large-scale reprisals against the civilian population, Mihailović's men were often wary of confronting the Germans. Some of his officers advocated open collaboration with the invaders. Enigma intercepts picked up German radio signals that suggested that Mihailović was collaborating. The pro-Tito factions in America and Britain leapt on this. But Churchill and Roosevelt wanted to know for themselves what was happening in the mountains and plains of wartime Yugoslavia.

The officers and men deployed into Yugoslavia by the OSS, and the SOE, were nothing if not idiosyncratic and colourful. And certainly not lacking in resourceful professionalism and bravery. One of the first British officers from the SOE sent to operate with Tito was called Captain William Deakin. A highly intelligent academic, he had worked as one of Churchill's literary researchers. He joined the Queen's Own Oxfordshire Hussars, and then was recruited by SOE. He supported the Prime Minister's approach to Yugoslavia: to see which partisan organisation was most effective in combatting the Germans, and supporting them. To begin with, Churchill was sometimes cautious in this, as he had a close sympathy for the exiled Yugoslav monarchy. Deakin worked closely with Basil Davidson, the head of SOE's Yugoslav Section in Cairo. Davidson was a left-wing former correspondent for the *Economist*, while his deputy, James Klugmann, was a self-professed communist.* These two men had seen decrypted German signals from Yugoslavia which, while they didn't prove

* After Deakin met Davidson in Egypt, he described him as 'like Churchill himself, among those Conservatives who thought that an alliance with the devil far preferable to allowing the Nazis the least advantage'.

Mihailović was collaborating, did show that Tito was running by far the more effective resistance movement. Deakin's time working with Churchill meant that he enjoyed closer access to him than most. So when the Prime Minister visited Cairo in January 1943, Deakin urged him in a memo to support all Yugoslav resistance groups, regardless of their political leaning.

Deakin's reconnaissance work in Yugoslavia began a few months later. On the night of 27–28 May 1943, Deakin and the five other men from the SOE pulled on their parachutes at the airstrip at Bari, in south-eastern Italy. Their mission was codenamed 'Typical'. Deakin's objective was to assess the partisans' operational strengths. A larger mission would then follow. After a two-hour flight, and parachute jump, they landed in the soft grass and wild flowers of a large plateau adjacent to the Durmitor massif in north-west Montenegro. The area was in the middle of a German anti-partisan offensive; around 120,000 Germans had surrounded 20,000 partisans. Deakin moved with Tito's headquarters; at one point they were caught in the open under a stand of birch trees during a low-level German air-strike. Deakin pushed Tito into a small trench, saving his life. Both men were wounded by shrapnel, and a Canadian officer called Bill Stuart was killed. Tito's pet Alsatian, Tiger, died too. Deakin formed a very favourable impression of the partisans, and they worked assiduously to cultivate this. Partly as a result of this, Deakin claimed in reports that Mihailović's collaboration had been increasing constantly since 1941.

'My system of indoctrinating Deakin was to take him to a stream nearby, where we used to bathe,' remembered Vlatko Velebit, later Tito's ambassador to Britain. 'I took captured documents with me to translate for his use. Deakin got more and more convinced that the Mihailović movement was really no good.'[2]

Brigadier Sir Fitzroy Maclean followed Deakin into Yugoslavia, and subsequently the two briefed Churchill on their return to Cairo.

'It was a miserable task,' Deakin recalled. 'As I talked I knew that I was compiling the elements of a hostile brief which would play a decisive part in any future break between Britain and Mihailović'.[3]

Deakin was awarded the Distinguished Service Order, and given control of SOE's Yugoslav mission in Cairo, before being transferred to Italy.* That same year, he married for the second time. His new wife was a Romanian SOE colleague called Livia Stela Nasta from Bucharest, nicknamed 'Pussy'. Born in 1916, she was the daughter of a Romanian journalist. When war broke out, she was working in a Bucharest government ministry. After the Romanians signed an allegiance with the Germans in the Tripartite Pact, Nasta and her father fled. She went first to Athens and thence to Egypt, where she managed to get a job working as a secretary with an RAF unit in a Cairo suburb. Beautiful, patriotic and brave, she was vetted by SOE in October 1942, and joined the organisation. She met Deakin in Cairo.†

British Brigadier Fitzroy Maclean, meanwhile, was a British diplomat of Scottish descent, who had served in Moscow in 1937–39, and spoke Russian. The Soviet Union had left him under no illusions:

> I was deeply and lastingly conscious of the expansionist tendencies of international communism and its intimate connection with Soviet foreign policy. The partisans' ultimate aim would be to establish in Yugoslavia a communist regime closely linked to Moscow.[4]

He joined a Highland regiment in 1939, served with the Special Air Service in North Africa, and then became Churchill's liaison officer with Marshal Tito in Yugoslavia. His brief was straightforward: 'simply to find out who was killing the most Germans and suggest means by which we could help them to kill more.'[5] He alternated his time between Tito's front-line headquarters, and the Yugoslav capital,

* At the end of the war, Deakin was posted to Belgrade as the British ambassador. When Churchill lost the 1945 General Election, an old Yugoslav woman reportedly said to him, 'Oh dear, poor Mr. Churchill, I suppose that now he'll be shot.' This was what happened to Mihailović was after the war, after his eyes had been gouged out.

† Her declassified SOE file at The National Archives in London (Reference Number HS9/409/3) has a name heading that itself is full of mystery: Livia Stella DEAKIN, née Nasta, aka Olga PROCMOZKA, aka Mary Ann Wilson, born 18.08.1916. She was reportedly the inspiration for the James Bond character Pussy Galore.

Belgrade, where he would wear a Scottish kilt on formal military occasions. Together with the Russian Order of Katuzov awarded him in Moscow in 1938, he presented a figure that the NKVD felt was somehow approachable. Into the bargain, he was one of the few western liaison officers with Tito who spoke fluent Russian. So occasionally Maclean found himself conversing with NKVD officers about Tito's possible aims and objectives.[6] In 1943 in Cairo, Maclean briefed British Foreign Secretary Anthony Eden, who was *en route* to the Teheran Summit with Stalin and Roosevelt. Tito, he said, was very firmly under communist leadership, and firmly oriented towards Moscow.

President Roosevelt, meanwhile, had read and been immediately gripped by a report from one OSS agent posted to Yugoslavia. Roosevelt was so convinced by it that he gave a copy to Stalin when they met at the Teheran Conference in November 1943. Stalin was amazed. The Soviet marshal would never have dreamed of handing over a NKVD or GRU report to the Americans; especially one so detailed.

The author of the report was an American OSS officer called Major Linn Farish. He was a geologist who had studied at Stanford, and then been part of the American rugby team at the 1924 Olympics. He had joined the Canadian Royal Engineers before Pearl Harbour, fought with a British commando unit, and then joined the OSS, with whom he had parachuted into Yugoslavia in autumn 1943. He was an American observer attached to the same liaison mission as Maclean, coinciding with a period of heavy fighting between Germans and partisans. His reports painted a fairly accurate, though glamourised picture of Tito as a driven, patriotic and independent leader of national liberation first and foremost, and a communist second. 'If ever a movement had the background of indomitable will and courage with which to build great things, it is to be found in Yugoslavia.'[7]

And it had a leader who was in desperate need of American material help. Farish also explained that it was highly likely that Tito was a far more effective and versatile enemy to the Germans than the recalcitrant Serb Chetniks under Colonel Draža Mihailović. This was the same conclusion reached by MacLean. The American policy of supporting Tito with air-drops of arms and equipment, and backing him up with American OSS liaison officers, followed shortly. Farish even travelled to Washington to brief the President in person. Other OSS officers followed. Some were equally enthralled by Tito, his partisans, and his cult of personality. Major Louis Huot wrote of Tito:

> Compact, broad-shouldered, deep-chested and flat-bellied, there was strength, plain physical stamina implicit in every line of him. No simple warrior, no primitive leader of fighting men...he was much more besides...thinker, statesman, artist...and soldier as well. And there was a light in his face that glowered and flickered and subsided as he talked, but never went away...a light that only comes from long service in the tyranny of dreams. Whatever this man might be and no matter what he signified, here was a force to be reckoned with, a leader men would follow through the gates of hell.[8]

In late spring 1944, Farish went back to Yugoslavia to assess the effect of US support. This time his reports were considerably less supportive of Tito. He explained in some detail, and with considerable accuracy, that the partisans and Serb Chetniks were actually fighting a civil war which was far more important to them than the struggle against the Germans and Italians. He also said that this fight was killing large numbers of civilians. He suggested that the Americans actually cut off supplies of weapons to the Yugoslav partisans. His recommendations were ignored back in the United States. Highly frustrated, he applied for one of the most dangerous postings within the OSS. That of air crew rescue missions: parachuting into Yugoslavia and neighbouring regions to identify possible air-strips where aircraft could land, and pick up American and other Allied pilots who had been shot down. It was incredibly risky. The Germans often captured partisans and tortured them to reveal the location of secret landing strips where the Allies' Dakotas would touch down to bring in supplies. The aircraft were guided in on grass strips in remote valleys and on mountain plateaux by partisans holding large, flaming torches that acted as landing lights. Sometimes the aircraft were only on the ground for as long as it took to unload the aircraft, and load it up with Allied flight crews and partisan wounded. Farish survived two three-month tours of duty, and then on his third was killed in Greece in a plane crash. He was posthumously promoted, and awarded the Distinguished Service Cross.

9

Marshal Tito Plays a Double Hand

In December 1941, Field Marshal Joseph Stalin met in Moscow with the British Secretary of State for Foreign and Commonwealth Affairs, Sir Anthony Eden. The Germans had just abandoned their final full-scale attack on Moscow, only eleven miles from the capital. A large Russian counter-attack was already underway. Stalin was in a confident mood, and already looking to the future. He told Eden categorically that after the war, the borders of Yugoslavia should be returned to their pre-war delineation, with 'slight territorial gains at Italy's expense, with respect to Trieste and Fiume'.[1]

Two-and-a-half years later, the fortunes of war had partly reversed. The Germans were fighting the Allies on three losing fronts, in Russia, Normandy and Italy. Field Marshal Alexander met with Tito, one of the three men whose military operations would have most impact on deciding Yugoslavia's borders. The others were Stalin and himself. They had a summit in July 1944 in Tuscany in Bolsena, which sits on the edge of a volcanic lake of the same name. Alexander's multi-national army was fighting its way up Italy, and next would head north-east towards Trieste and Austria. Both leaders agreed that it was probable that their joint forces would therefore meet somewhere at the head of the Adriatic, and at that point they would both hammer out respective lines of frontier demarcation. They agreed to a rough compromise at the summit in Bolsena. A line would run just north of the port of Fiume–Rijeka into the Adriatic, and Tito would control everything to the east, the Allies Trieste and everything westwards. Alexander was impressed and pleased by Tito's agreement – the latter had already told Stalin that it was unlikely the Yugoslav forces would get to Trieste ahead of the Allies anyway, so a compromise would be necessary.

Meetings continued. On 12 August Tito met Churchill at the Villa Rivalta, overlooking Vesuvius and the Bay of Naples. The former was accompanied by Churchill's then-senior liaison officer in Yugoslavia, Fitzroy Maclean. Tito was wearing a formal gold and blue uniform, described by Churchill as 'singularly unsuited to the blazing heat'. The tunic, Tito explained, had been given to him by the Russians, the gold lace by the Americans.[1] The British Prime Minister was in a white linen suit, what he called 'white ducks'. Tito was in a suspicious mood. At lunch, he demanded that two bodyguards with automatic pistols be present, in case of treachery on the Allies' part. He mistrusted his allies. The British persuaded him the two bodyguards weren't necessary, but the Yugoslav Marshal insisted on having them with him at dinner instead. Churchill briefed him on Allied proposals for Trieste and Istria: Tito 'grumbled'. But he was more interested at that point in guaranteeing a reliable supply of Allied arms and ammunition to his soldiers and partisans. Tito then moved on to the island of Capri, where General Donovan met him. On his return home, the Yugoslav leader then promptly disappeared. His headquarters was on the Dalmatian island of Vis: two Allied officers reported on 24 September that two C-47 Dakotas with red stars on their tails, accompanied by Russian Yak fighters, had landed. When they took off, Tito was on board.

The Allies were furious. Was he going to renege on the assurances he had made to them in Italy? Where was he? Neither SOE nor OSS liaison officers could find him. His chiefs of staff were silent. Tito, in fact, had gone to Moscow to meet Stalin. The two leaders negotiated the entry of the Red Army into Yugoslavia on 29 September. Belgrade was liberated on 20 October. Suddenly OSS and SOE lines of approach to Tito appeared blocked: his chief of staff told the British and Americans, who had formally enjoyed good personal access, that all communications now had to appear in writing. General Donovan then cut off all supplies to Tito's soldiers and partisans, as the two Allied liaison missions were now promptly banned from accompanying Tito's men as they liberated the interior of Yugoslavia. Fitzroy Maclean wondered if Tito was prepared for everything that a close allegiance with the Russians would bring.

'Tito may not be too ready for (that) suffocating embrace of the Russian bear,' he noted succinctly.

The OSS wrote a memo to the President's office shortly afterwards:

> Probably the motive behind Tito's move is his desire to curtail and control American and British military representation in the country, now that he believes the civil war is all but in the bag and now that British and American supplies are no longer needed. He evidently does not wish American and British representatives to observe and report developments of his plans to consolidate his military victory in the political and economic field. The order, significantly enough, was issued at a moment when Tito was almost certainly with the Russian leaders in Bulgaria or Rumania. He has not come back to Vis since he left for an undisclosed destination in Russian planes. There is no way of knowing if the Russians come under the phrase 'allied' personnel.
>
> The Russians have for a long time had the closest possible liaison with Tito and his staff and have probably taken part in his political and military councils.[3]

But at higher levels, contact remained. As World War II progressed, meetings between Tito and the Allies continued. Edward Stettinius met with Anthony Eden on the Mediterranean island of Malta in January 1945. They needed to try to agree on what to tell Tito about the Allies plans' for the situation in the northern Adriatic. The perceptive Stettinius foresaw problems with him, and with Trieste.

So they postponed the issue, explaining that any forthcoming peace conference would have to resolve the issue. The next step saw Alexander and Tito meet again in Belgrade in February 1945. The latter was still in perfect agreement with the Allied Field Marshal about Trieste – he even agreed to the formation of an Allied Military Government to run the port and the area around it. The Allies based their operational planning for their future advance into north-eastern Italy and Austria on these assurances given by Tito in February. At that point Alexander did not foresee any problems arising over Trieste. He was adamant that Allied forces would need to control the port and lines of communication to and from it into Austria. The Italian–Yugoslav border would revert to its pre-war 1939 status. Again, the Yugoslav leader agreed – like Stalin, Alexander was heartily relieved.

The issue was still hanging over the Allies when, on 4 February, they met with Stalin at the Livadia Palace at Yalta, in the Crimea. The aim of the conference between the three powers was to discuss and decide the post-war organisation of Europe. Of all the three Allied leaders, Stalin was in the strongest position: his troops occupied almost all of Poland, and were fighting forty miles from Berlin. In the north, the British and Americans were spreading out across the River Rhine, and the French had just cleared the last German defensive positions west of the river. In southern Europe, a huge multi-national Allied army was still trying to break through the German defensive positions of the Gothic Line in northern Italy. The Americans had just entered the Filipino capital, Manila, and were preparing to land on the island of Iwo Jima. Their battleships were shelling Tokyo and Yokahama. Roosevelt was adamant that the Americans still needed Stalin's support in the war against Japan. One of the American delegates was James F. Byrnes, who would succeed Stettinius. He commented: 'It was not a question of what we would let the Russians do, but what we could get the Russians to do.'[4]

Roosevelt's main priority was securing Russian support for the coming Operation *August Storm*, the invasion of the Japanese mainland. Churchill wanted free elections and democratic governments in central and eastern European countries occupied by the Russians. Most particularly in Poland, where the Allies were desperate to be able to guarantee political self-determination to the hundreds of thousands of Poles who had fought for or taken refuge in Britain. And Stalin? He simply wanted to add the countries in eastern and central Europe that he had conquered and occupied – Poland, Hungary, Czechoslovakia – into a massive security belt of satellite states on Russia's western and southern frontier. What he very much didn't want was unnecessary antagonism with the powerful Western Allies over Trieste and the Adriatic, especially as he knew he was about to fly into the face of confrontation with the Allies over his occupation of Austria. He and the British and the Americans were going to occupy the country, and he knew the division of the country and its capital would be confrontational. He had given Tito a tacit free hand with his territorial expansion but still thought he could control him. He was keen to punish Italy territorially for supporting Hitler, but he didn't want to have to make compromises over Trieste that might affect his powerful bargaining position over Poland. Another factor affected his thinking: his intelligence assets in the United States inside the Manhattan Project – the US atomic programme – told him that the Americans were close to testing an atomic weapon. Stalin's own nuclear programme was at least four years behind theirs.* He felt back-footed. Stalin assumed, erroneously, that Tito would follow his instructions over the tactical and strategic situation on the Adriatic. His last major concern about Trieste was not Tito *per se*, but his huge armies spread across Yugoslavia. Stalin knew he had little direct control over them and he hated to be outnumbered.

By the end of the Yalta Conference, Anthony Eden and Stettinius still had not received any firm assurances from the Russians about Trieste and Austria. The Americans were frustrated. So Stettinius and Eden put their concerns in a letter to the Russian Foreign Minister, Molotov. Would the Soviet Union accept that the borders of both

* The Americans carried out their first successful atomic test, codenamed 'Trinity', on 16 July 1945 in New Mexico; the Russians on 29 August 1949.

Austria and Yugoslavia revert to their pre-war status? Molotov wouldn't say yes or no, nor would he in successive meetings in March with the British Ambassador to Moscow, Sir Archibald Clark Kerr. Notoriously short, at five feet six inches, Stalin stood three inches lower than Truman, himself no giant at five feet nine. 'He's a little squirt,' Truman was to say about him jokingly,[5] adding later that 'I can deal with Stalin. He is honest. But smart as hell.'

For his part, Stalin had been initially surprised by Tito's diplomatic stance over Trieste in summer 1944. At that point he saw no reason to get involved in Tito's territorial claims to the port and surrounding territory. He assumed the Allies would get there first and he preferred not to show his cards before he had to.[6] Thirdly, he assumed he still had strong influence over Tito, and that his vision of a huge area of Europe under Soviet communist control corresponded with Tito's image of a future Yugoslavia. 'I will shake my little finger and there will be no more Tito,' he remarked.[7] On both latter counts, he was to be proved wrong. For Tito was playing a double hand. In January 1945, he had sent an ambassador, Andrija Hebrang, to Moscow. This Yugoslav diplomat was the head of the Croatian Communist Party. He asked for, and received, Stalin's secret and cautious approval for Tito's plan to occupy and control Trieste as the war ended. Stalin gave this approval on one strict condition. That the Yugoslavs did not try and expand their territory into the southern Austrian provinces of Carinthia and Styria. Firstly, Stalin wanted his army to occupy Vienna. Secondly, he knew the British and Americans would never agree to the Yugoslavs controlling vital land that linked Trieste with their forthcoming zones of occupation in Austria. Stalin wanted any confrontation in Austria with the Allies to be his, and not one of his junior and unpredictable proxy allies.

So by spring 1945, the players who sat across the green baize card table of world geo-politics had divergent opinions of each other. President Roosevelt had underestimated Joseph Stalin. He had been trying to achieve the enormous task of pulling the United States out of an isolationist national mindset, to engage in its emerging role as a superpower. Roosevelt hadn't believed that Stalin would try to impose totalitarian occupation on parts of Europe:

> I just have a hunch that Stalin is not that kind of a man. I think that if I give him everything I possibly can and ask for nothing from him in return, 'noblesse oblige', he won't try to annex anything and will work with me for a world of democracy and peace.[8]

Then he had to change his mind. The Russians discovered in March 1945 that the Germans were initiating secret peace talks with the British and Americans in Switzerland. In February and March 1945, a group of German officers led by SS-Obergruppenführer Karl Wolff, the senior SS officer in Italy, had made overtures to the OSS office in Berne. The German officers proposed that in return for a separate peace deal that did not involve the Russians, they would guarantee the surrender of all troops under German command in Italy. The Western Allies wanted to sound out the SS to see if their offer was sincere, before asking the Russians to send a delegate to any talks. But the Russians found out about the plan through their spies in Italy, and took massive diplomatic offence. Stalin and Molotov were furious. The plan, they said, showed how little their Western Allies trusted them. They said they saw not 'just a misunderstanding, but something worse'.[9] Roosevelt's response to Stalin showed that his eyes had been opened: 'I cannot avoid a feeling of bitter resentment towards your informers, whoever they are, for such vile misrepresentations of my actions or those of my trusted subordinates.'

On 12 April, Roosevelt suffered a stroke and died. His successor, Harry S. Truman, was more succinct and forceful. With Stettinius behind him, he saw that Stalin's aim was to expand the influence of Soviet communism so that it controlled a ring of satellite states from the Baltic to the Mediterranean. Truman also saw that the promises Stalin made were like diplomatic and political ice-cream, easily melted.[10] Both Churchill and the Americans were keenly aware of the gargantuan human and infrastructural losses the Soviet Union had taken in fighting the Germans. By spring 1945 they needed the Russians as cooperative allies in the continuing war against Japan. But the Americans saw clearly that their hopes earlier in the war for a cooperative allegiance between them and 'Uncle Joe' Stalin had now evolved into a forthcoming confrontation of superpowers. For Stalin's part, he employed a majesty of understatement when he said to Truman that 'he was grossly misunderstood in the United States'. But by late spring, the fourth player in the game called Trieste was somebody who had a proven habit of playing the wild card. Josip Broz Tito.

TITO REVERSES THE ALLIES' PLANS

Tito was a Croat and Slovene by birth, a communist to boot, and a serving NKVD officer. He was convinced that the territory in the Venezia Giulia, and the city of Trieste itself, rightfully belonged to Yugoslavia. As a lifelong socialist revolutionary, imprisoned repeatedly for his beliefs, he wanted to create a working people's state, where they could have decent lives, while still being committed to socialism. He'd seen Russia and Russian communism, and knew it for the brutal ideological sham it was. He also felt passionately that territory his forces had conquered, and would take in future, belonged to them. He didn't trust the Russians, but knew that he needed them to back him up against the Allies. He foresaw that he and Stalin would disagree, and thus he needed a bargaining chip with the United States and Great Britain. He hated what Mussolini had done to the population of Istria and Slovenia, and as a former citizen of the Austro-Hungarian Empire he despised Italy. Lastly, he knew that if he presented enough of a threat to Trieste, then the Allies would occupy it by force, instead of the loathed Italians.[11] But as a proud Yugoslav, still stinging after 500 years of Ottoman rule several generations before, he loathed being under an invader's or occupier's thumb. He found himself having to sing to the tune of the Russians' or Allies' political and territorial demands, while paying the bill in Yugoslav blood. It was he and his men, he knew, and stressed adamantly, who had fought and defeated the Germans. Not the Russians, not the British, not the Americans. So it would be he, as leader and representative of his men, who would decide Yugoslavia's political and territorial future. Tito was proud, possessive, generous, nationalistic, a curious mix of extrovert and solipsist, a grandiloquent show-off with a big heart and an even bigger army. A man who was determined to create, run and rule his own autocratic benevolent dictatorship.

TITO'S GOLD

Tito felt at a disadvantage to the British and the Americans because of money. They partially controlled access to funds he desperately needed to run his army and partisans, and the post-war state he intended to build and govern. When the Germans invaded Yugoslavia in 1941, they discovered that most of the gold reserves of the National Bank of Yugoslavia had vanished. The country's government had seen the shadows of war gathering. So in 1940 it embarked nearly 1,000 crates containing around 3,400 gold bars onto a Yugoslav destroyer, the *Beograd.* This sailed to Plymouth, where an attaché from the Yugoslav embassy in London waited on the docks. This gold joined another 225 bars of bullion already in London. As the possibility of an invasion of mainland Britain increased, the Yugoslavs decided to move as much of their gold as possible to America. They did this in two ways. Between June and November 1940 five separate shipments of gold arrived in New York by sea, deposited in the Federal Reserve. But by 1941, with invasion looming, Yugoslavia still had at least 131 tons of gold in Belgrade, which it was desperate to move abroad.[12] So they sent twenty-two tons to Argentina and Brazil, seventeen more to America, and the remaining eighty to the Bank of International Settlements at Basel in Switzerland. This was then transferred as US dollar assets. And on 5 April, the day before the Axis invasion of Yugoslavia, $2.7 million was transferred to the Federal Reserve in New York. The twelve tons of gold remaining in Yugoslavia, mostly in the form of coins, was stolen by Croats, Italians and Germans.

The Germans found part of the hoard hidden in the cellars of a Serb Orthodox monastery.

By 1943, however, the government and monarchy in Yugoslavia had fled into exile. King Peter II lived in London along with several other displaced European royal families. The Germans occupied the country, and Tito controlled the army and partisans. Not wanting to be dependent on the Russians or Allies for financial help, he decided he needed to access the country's gold reserves in Buenos Aires, Sao Paolo and New York. King Peter and the Yugoslav monarchist faction controlled the gold reserves in London, and they were still competing with Tito for American and British support. So Tito considered that trying to persuade the British to release funds from the Bank of England would be more trouble than it was worth. This was not the case with the Americans or Argentinians or Brazilians. But before releasing any of the vast funds sitting in their banks, they required external references at governmental level from the Allies that Tito and his Yugoslav National Liberation Army were the *de facto* legitimate government in Yugoslavia. And most importantly the regime supported by the British and Americans. Diplomatic representatives of both countries agreed to take up the case of Yugoslavia's gold. They included Sir Ralph Clarmont Skrine Stevenson, Britain's Envoy Extraordinary and Minister Plenipotentiary to the Kingdom of Yugoslavia, based in Cairo.* By 1944, as the Germans were losing the war across Europe, the Brazilians and the Americans transferred their Yugoslav gold reserves back to the Federal Reserve in New York. The Americans, backed up by the British, agreed that when peace came, Tito should be allowed to access his country's gold reserves. But on the clear understanding that he agreed to all and any treaty settlements undertaken with the Allies. The phrase 'all and any treaty settlements' was the crucial one. So in May 1945, with his forces in a fragile stand-off with the Allies over Trieste, Tito knew there was more at stake than

* A total of 383 files from the section titled Foreign Office 371 / 44305 (1944), dealing with Skrine's communications about Yugoslav gold, are all in the Slovenian National Archives, the Arhiv Republike Slovenije, in Ljubljana.

just land. There was gold and cash in America running into millions and millions of dollars. This was money he wanted for himself, to build his Yugoslav People's State.

By April 1945, the Russians were fighting just outside Berlin, the Allies were approaching Venice, and the war had only weeks to run. Stalin suddenly advised Tito that he wanted Austria to revert to its borders of 1938, and that he fully backed Tito's expansionism into Trieste and the Venezia Giulia. Again, he reiterated that he wanted to punish Italy, and make sure he had a hold over the Allies so they wouldn't interfere in Eastern Europe.[13] He was convinced he could do this via Tito, after all a serving NKVD member and head of the Comintern in his own country. But by the first week of May, with his partisans already occupying Trieste, Tito then reneged on all his previous promises made to the Allies in February. He demanded to be allowed to keep territory he had occupied by force, and in the first week of May issued this communique to the Allies:

> The Yugoslav Army as one of the Allied armies has equal rights with other Allied armies allowing her to remain in the territory she has liberated in the bitter struggle against the common enemy. The Yugoslav Army, in fierce battles whose object was to cut off considerable units of enemy forces and liberate enslaved peoples, has suffered heavy losses and has shown many examples of unprecedented heroism.
>
> The fact that the population of these regions has for two years taken part in the war of liberation, that its overwhelming majority is Yugoslav, and that it has borne enormous sacrifices in the struggle against Italian and German fascism, cannot be an obstacle to our demand to entrust our army with the organization of military administration and to entrust the Peoples Committee of Liberation, chosen from the people, with the organization of civil administration.
>
> The needs of our Allies concerning ports and lines of communication have been completely safeguarded in the spirit of the talks between Marshal Tito and Field Marshal [Sir Harold R. L. G.] Alexander [Supreme Allied Commander in the Mediterranean] during the visit by Field Marshal

> Alexander to Belgrade this winter. The honor of our army and the honor of our country demand the presence of the Yugoslav Army in Istria, Trieste and the Slovene coastline.
>
> The decisions of the peace conference, which will be the final decisions as regards the apportioning of the region concerned, are in no way prejudiced. With regard to this the federation of Yugoslavia is opposed to all unilateral declarations.[14]

When they read this, Churchill's and Stettinius' reactions were the same. The problem had to be solved by negotiated agreement, not violence. So on 8 May, Alexander sent his chief of staff to the Yugoslav capital with a list of Allied terms. Lieutenant-General William Duthie 'Monkey' Morgan was another competent and well-decorated British army officer. He laid down a gauntlet to Tito. Trieste, its port and the surrounding, strategically crucial areas of Italy and Austria belonged to the Allies, he said. Any Yugoslav incursion onto them would be seen as similar 'to the actions of Hitler and Mussolini'. Alexander and he hoped there would be no firefights between the Yugoslavs and the Allies. On the conclusion of Morgan's meetings, Alexander's headquarters issued their own communiqué:

> The territory around Trieste and Gorizia and east of the Isonzo River is part of Italy known as Venezia Giulia. The territory around Villach and Klagenfurt is part of Austria. The above-mentioned Italian and Austrian territory is now claimed by Marshal Tito, who wishes to incorporate it into Yugoslavia. We have no objection to claims being put forward by Marshal Tito to the territory. His claims will be examined and finally settled with fairness and impartiality at the peace conference in exactly the same manner as other disputed areas throughout Europe. Our policy publicly proclaimed is that territorial changes should be made only after thorough study and after full consultation and deliberation between the various Governments concerned.
>
> It is, however, Marshal Tito's apparent intention to establish his claims by force of arms and military occupation. Action of this kind would be all

too reminiscent of Hitler, Mussolini and Japan. It is to prevent such actions that we have been fighting this war.

Within these territories our duty and responsibility is to keep lawful order by our military forces and ensure peaceful and secure life for their peoples through our Allied Military Government. We may be relied upon to act impartially, as we do not covet these territories ourselves. In this situation I tried my best to come to a friendly agreement with Marshal Tito, but did not succeed. The United States and British Governments have therefore taken up the matter directly with Marshal Tito. The Soviet Government has been kept fully informed. We are now waiting to hear whether Marshal Tito is prepared to cooperate in accepting peaceful settlement of his territorial claims or whether he will attempt to establish them by force.[15]

Tito refused to make any concessions. Alexander then demanded that the Yugoslav partisans in areas controlled by the Allies lay down their arms or withdraw. An Allied Military Government would now rule Trieste. Again, Tito refused. The Allies saw force as the only remaining option. Tito then made a speech in Belgrade, pointedly aimed at his former supporters from Russia, America and Britain:

We (Yugoslavia) do not want to be used as a bribe in international bargaining. We do not want to get involved in a policy of spheres of influence.[16]

Stalin's reply was immediate.

If Tito allows once again such an attack on the Soviet Union we shall be forced ... to disavow him.[16]

Tito was now going it alone. The Cold War had begun in earnest.

Yugoslav troops watch New Zealand soldiers arrive in Trieste, 2 May 1945. (Photo by Mondadori Portfolio via Getty Images)

The liberation of Trieste, 2 May1945. (© IRSML, Trieste)

May 1945, Trieste: New Zealand tank officer and Yugoslav soldier with his national flag. (Photo by Keystone-France/Gamma-Keystone via Getty Images)

New Zealand soldiers are greeted by civilians, Trieste, 2 May 1945. (© IRSML, Trieste)

New Zealand tanks arrive in Trieste, 2 May 1945. (Photo by: Universal History Archive/UIG via Getty Images)

Posters in Serbo-Croat and Italian urging ex-combatants to come together in 'Partisans' Week', March 1946. (Photo by Keystone Features/Getty Images)

Selling tobacco on the black market in Italy, 1945: under Allied-implemented rationing, men were allowed four cigarettes per day, women none.
(Photo by FPG/Hulton Archive/Getty Images)

The remains of the crematorium at the Risiera di San Sabba concentration camp. (Photo by Walter Mori/Mondadori Portfolio via Getty Images)

Bodies of prisoners executed by Yugoslav partisans and dumped into *foibe*, or ravines. (Photo by: SeM/UIG via Getty Images)

A village house on the Morgan Line with pro-Tito graffiti which reads 'We want Yugoslavia, we're Slovenian.' (Photo by Nat Farbman/The LIFE Picture Collection/Getty Images)

American Colonel Alfred Connor Bowman at his desk in Trieste. (Photo by Nat Farbman/The LIFE Picture Collection/Getty Images)

Giorgio Jaksetich, Trieste, May 1946. (Photo by Nat Farbman/The LIFE Picture Collection/Getty Images)

The coast road approaching Trieste, May 1946. (Photo by Nat Farbman/The LIFE Picture Collection/Getty Images)

Pro-Yugoslav posters in a war-damaged area of Trieste, May 1946. (Photo by Nat Farbman/The LIFE Picture Collection/Getty Images)

A Yugoslav soldier at a checkpoint on the Morgan Line, May 1946. (Photo by Nat Farbman/The LIFE Picture Collection/ Getty Images)

General William Donovan, Director of the OSS. (Photo by Underwood Archives/ Getty Images)

Italians demonstrate in Trieste to keep the city Italian, 1950. (Bettmann/Getty Images)

10

Dividing Trieste, June 1945

Major-General 'Monkey' Morgan had his work cut out. He had to persuade Marshal Tito to agree that the Allies and the Yugoslavs would divide the area of the Venezia Giulia, the city of Trieste and the Istrian peninsula. The main aim was to prevent both sides coming into open conflict with each other. The second objective was to decide when a peace treaty could be arranged to formalise the agreement. This required both sides to hammer out an operational compromise where the strategic and tactical demands of both were met. What did both sides want?

Tito was still unsure by the end of the first week of May what kind of diplomatic and strategic support he enjoyed from Stalin. Before he could make any overtly aggressive moves and demand control over all the territory he considered rightfully his, he needed to see what kind of backing Stalin would offer him. The Soviet leader had not committed by the time General Morgan travelled to Belgrade on 8 May. So Tito, whose men were in effective operational control of Trieste anyway, was happy to compromise. His objectives were threefold. Firstly, to have enough time to complete his clearing-up operations in and around the port itself, to capture and sentence those German and Italian elements that he and OZNA had ear-marked for arrest. Secondly, while he knew he could not hope to prevent the Allies from occupying part of Trieste and Venezia Giulia, he wanted at least half of it. In that way he could still count upon the support of his soldiers and partisans to whom he had guaranteed, as a war aim, that the territory would be theirs. The last thing he needed was thousands of mutinous troops who felt let down by their leader. Thirdly, he wanted to do a deal with the British generals over territory in southern Austria. He had even considered provisional plans to try and carve out a Yugoslav province there. SOE had operated in that part of Austria intermittently since 1943. They had wanted to see if it was possible to organise an anti-Nazi resistance among native Austrians. But Tito was loathe to have a national partisan force to fight against if he tried to occupy territory there. So OZNA and SOE had disagreed about this bitterly. Peter Wilkinson suspected very strongly that his best friend had been caught in the middle of this disagreement and killed on OZNA's orders.

Meanwhile tens of thousands of Tito's enemies from the Croat Ustashe, the Serb Chetniks and German units were now retreating north-west across Slovenia. They were heading towards south-eastern Austria. Under the command of two Croat generals, this fleeing column wanted to cross the border around Bleiburg and surrender to the British. They feared that if they gave themselves up to Tito's men they could face either death or deportation to a work camp. But Tito wanted to assure the British these people would receive fair treatment: he knew the Allies had enough POWs on their hands already. Tito thought that if he gave assurances to the British that these Croats and Slovenians and Serbs and Germans would be treated according to the Geneva Conventions, the British would let his men take their surrender. For their part, the British and the Americans were still doggedly adamant. They wanted control of Trieste's port facilities, and territory that lay west of the River Isonzo. It was vital for them, they kept reiterating, to maintain clear and reliable lines of control and communication between the Adriatic Sea and their zone of occupation in the southern Austrian provinces of Carinthia and Styria. The thousands of British troops there would need a guaranteed and secure link between the sea at Trieste and their new area of occupation. All the tons of food, ammunition and supplies, the medical evacuations, reinforcements and general logistical support required to keep them operational on a daily basis would have to move by road from the Adriatic up to southern Austria. Secondly, they wanted a tactical buffer zone between them and Tito's troops, controlled by both sides, so the possibilities of armed confrontation could be reduced to a minimum. Thirdly, they badly needed any information possible from the Yugoslav intelligence service, OZNA, as to the possible whereabouts of the German war criminals they were now hunting. Fourthly, they could see that compromise with Tito over Trieste would mean a territorial barrier between them and any zone of Russian influence that might spring up in the east of Yugoslavia.

On 11 May, Allied troops occupied Klagenfurt and Villach in south-eastern Austria, and met the Russians at Voitsberg, west of Graz. Churchill, Truman and Stalin were at loggerheads over Poland. So the meeting in Belgrade that had just taken place assumed additional importance. The Allies did not need another zone of confrontation in Trieste. Both they and the Yugoslavs were aware that firefights could break out at any moment between their troops, so decided to concentrate on achieving their main strategic and political priorities. For now, the confrontation of the Cold War over Trieste and its surrounding territory would mainly be fought by proxy, by their different intelligence agencies. Spy games on the Adriatic were underway, with a vengeance.

THE REALITIES OF THE MORGAN LINE

The line that 'Monkey' Morgan agreed upon with the Yugoslavs in Belgrade was formally called the 'Blue Line'. It was then re-named after the general himself. Allied troops of Lieutenant-General Harding's XIII Corps began moving towards it on 22 May. Tito agreed to the demarcation the following day. The line was some seventy miles long, and began on the coast just south of Trieste, before curving round fifteen miles to the east and heading north. Everybody assumed that its precise demarcation had been hammered out during hours of fraught negotiation between both sides. In fact, while both Yugoslavs and the Allies were discussing where the line should go, an American staff officer called Major Arch Hamblen started doodling idly on a large map with a coloured pencil. He drew an imaginary line from the coast, through Trieste, and then ran it north. While he was inspecting his spur-of-the-moment homework, officers from both sides looked at it, assumed it was the finished product, and agreed to it instantly.

From Trieste the line ran north-west to Gorizia, and along the banks of the River Isonzo until it hit the Austro-Italian border just past the town of Rateče. There were now two halves to the territory around Trieste. The area under Allied control was called Zone A, that under Yugoslav administration Zone B. The port of Pula on the tip of the Istrian peninsula was also placed in Zone A. Both sides immediately erected barbed wire, border posts, barriers and road-blocks, the entire alphabet of boundary demarcation.

This idiosyncratic confrontation fanfared the opening of the Cold War in southern Europe. Therein was every identifying hallmark of the coming struggle between East and West for the next fifty years. It ranged from the sublime to the ridiculous and to the lethal. From a knife-edge of geo-strategic confrontation, the bitter and sometimes hateful compromise of *realpolitik*, from spy wars fought out in nondescript alleyways, to moments of amicable fraternisation. Through the cobbled streets of Trieste's most easterly suburbs, coiled pythons of razor wire were laid down the middle of streets, then up country lanes, mountain paths and along main highways. A population of Italians and Slovenes who had been divided by occupying powers for the whole twentieth century found themselves divided again. The confrontation saw the Russians, Americans, British, Italians and Yugoslavs pitted against each other at governmental level. It saw ordinary soldiers from all sides alternately fraternising and fighting, and it witnessed each side cooperate in the hunt for war criminals and the search for revenge. It saw intelligence agencies used as the front-line shock-troops of *realpolitik* and diplomacy, as each side tried to fathom out what were the other's strategic and geo-political objectives. And it left different intelligence and military factions on all sides asking themselves who was really allied to whom, and who was fighting whom, spying on whom, and for what and why?

Trieste herself, however, had seen it all before. The city's name sprang from a mix of Venetian and Roman words for 'marketplace', *trg*, or *tergestum*. For 3,000 years, since the Phoenicians, there had been an important trading port there. The city had been Roman, Carthaginian, Byzantine, Venetian and more latterly Austro-Hungarian. By the end of the First World War it had become part of Italy, sitting at that country's junction with Austria and Yugoslavia. It was a natural harbour, surrounded by two curving spits of land that protected a deep-water lagoon. And like every market place it had seen trade, money, deception, antagonism, arguments and fights over land and space, the constant historical ebb and flow of goods and money and people. Byzantines, Venetians, Phoenicians, Romans, Carthaginians had fought over it and traded from it. The cobbled lanes had been witness to timeless centuries of skulduggery. The extraordinary *Bora* wind that blew down from the mountains above the port had enervated and baffled occupier and invader. So when, in summer 1945, a new set of conquerors installed themselves on the shores of the Adriatic, Trieste shrugged her shoulders. The dark blue waters in the harbour washed and went as they had done for thousands of years. And the old port watched in that post-war summer of violent liberation as everybody spied on everybody else.

Amicable fraternisation between Yugoslavs and the Allies was not hard to find. An Italian family outside eastern Trieste found their farming land cut in half by the Morgan Line. A platoon of Indian soldiers sat in their garden, pointing their Bren guns directly at a detachment of Yugoslav soldiers sitting 100 yards opposite. The farmer's cherry trees were in Italy, his potatoes in Yugoslavia. Tito's men upped the ante one evening, and the Indians watched fascinated as a dozen Yugoslav soldiers sweated and lumbered in coarse, cheap serge uniforms in the ninety-degree heat. They were pushing and pulling the vast metallic menace of a seven-ton 88mm anti-aircraft gun, captured from the Germans, into position in front of them. The barrel was depressed so that from their positions the Indians could stare straight down it. Not to be outdone, a troop of Sherman tanks reinforced the Allied troops, and lined up 100 metres opposite the Yugoslavs. But the soldiers themselves were having none of this. The New Zealanders and the Indians, in particular, found much in common with the straightforward, hard-bitten countrymen in the Yugoslav ranks. Both sides were sick of fighting. Both sides had watched their comrades die to satisfy the orders of senior officers, and both sides had taken enough bullets during the war that they didn't want to take any during the liberation:

> There were many opportunities for friction in this double occupation: the common use of crowded roads, different curfews – the Yugoslavs being two hours ahead – incessant propaganda in which the Italians participated, an abundance of pretty girls (a quarter of Tito's forces were women) and harsh wines. British commanders refused to allow villages to be searched for Fascists or alleged enemies of the state. On acquaintance both British and Indian troops learned to respect the hardy Yugoslavs who had fought so well ... Tito's forces proved to be cheerful folk, good at games, unvaryingly hospitable ... they carried their drink well, for the local wines were bodiless compared to the wild plum brandy of their homeland. These pleasant characteristics fortified the tendency to leave political questions to those who must settle them, and meanwhile make the best of the impasse.[1]

THE YUGOSLAVS' JUSTICE

But underneath this veneer of cooperation, the Allied troops were often blind to much of the venal, vicious cut-and-slash of revenge that was going on. Tito's forces had found and arrested many of their enemies inside Trieste in the days before the physical construction of the Morgan Line began. The Yugoslavs held these prisoners in their hundreds in farms, school buildings, and *ad hoc* detention centres behind Yugoslav lines. As the testimony of the two priests described earlier shows, they had already killed some of them. They had been shot and dumped in *foibe* or mass graves. Many of the remaining German, Italian and Slovenian fascist prisoners were force-fed through the legal niceties of a Yugoslav military tribunal, or field court. Some would have been sentenced to death, some would have been deported to work and prison camps inside Yugoslavia. What is certain is that hundreds, if not thousands of people went missing in those first weeks after the Yugoslavs occupied Trieste and its surroundings. (See Chapter 22, 'The Numbers.')

The aim of these Yugoslav military field tribunals was two-fold. First, to institute a layer of legality over their judgement of alleged war criminals, collaborators and enemies of the Yugoslav People's National Liberation Army. Secondly, to extract information on the possible whereabouts of high-ranking Germans and Italians, like Friedrich Rainer and Odilo Globocnik. OZNA wanted to get their hands on these men, to put them in front of state war crimes courts in Ljubljana or Belgrade for the crimes they had committed against the Slovenian people. But Colonel Maks Milić from OZNA knew that these men had another value as well: they could be horse-traded for information from the Americans and British on the location of senior Ustashe and Serb Chetnik leaders. Tito's men dearly wanted to get their hands on them. And amongst these, the most-prized was Ante Pavelić, the Croatian fascist dictator who had led the Ustashe.

DEATH AT BLEIBURG

Pavelić and his Ustashe leaders were part of the huge column heading towards the Austrian border. He knew that if he and his men tried to surrender to Tito's men their chances of survival could be low. So at the very beginning of May he ordered the Ustashe and the personnel from the government of the Independent State of Croatia to flee north-west and head into Austria itself. British troops had already occupied the south-eastern province of Carinthia. Pavelić told his forces to walk across the border and give themselves up, *en masse*, to them. Their hopes of survival could only be higher. On 2 May Germany had surrendered, but as they fled towards Austria, isolated Wehrmacht and SS units in Yugoslavia continued attacking partisan positions. And thousands of fleeing German soldiers, many from the SS, mingled in with Croat militias, Serb Chetniks and civilians in the huge column of fleeing humans. There were members of the Croatian Home Guard in it too – in January 1945 Pavelić had ordered them to merge with the Ustashe. Six months later this reduced their chances of survival considerably if they surrendered to the partisans. There were also Russian cavalrymen from the XV SS Cossack Corps in the vast mass of marching people.

The massed gathering of tens of thousands of frightened, desperate, hungry, thirsty and traumatised humans contained every possible permutation of the partisans' enemies. They marched through north-west Slovenia and in early May hit the Austrian border. It was early summer. It was hot. In such a column in such conditions rumour and panic spread fast. If those people are surrounded by enemies who have defeated them after four years of fratricidal civil war, and are impelled by revenge, the kinetic energy of fear is almost alive. So it was as the thousands of people approached the Austrian border near the town of Bleiburg. Estimates of the numbers heading for the frontier at different locations, in different sub-columns, varied. Yugoslav partisans, the Croat militias themselves and the British suggested that they ranged from around 25,000 to as many as 70,000.

On 6 May Ante Pavelić's government had fled from Zagreb, the capital of the Independent State of Croatia. On the 7th they arrived on the Austrian border near Klagenfurt. The Allied units in that area were the British V Corps, and at Bleiburg were the headquarters of the 38th (Irish) Infantry Brigade. This unit was made up of the 1st Battalion Royal Irish Fusiliers, 2nd Battalion London Irish Rifles, and the 2nd Battalion Royal Inniskilling Fusiliers. They had fought through Tunisia, Sicily and the whole of the war in Italy. Like everybody else scattered across the fields, forests, semi-destroyed towns and burned villages of south-eastern Europe that spring, they were overjoyed to be alive.

On 9 May Tito issued a demand through Radio Belgrade calling upon everybody in the fleeing columns to surrender. His specific request was to 'all the sub-units who had collaborated with the Germans'. He threatened a 'merciless response' if they failed to give up. The German Commander of Army Group E, General Alexander Lohr, signed the unconditional surrender of his men on the 9th. Some of the Germans, however, continued to fight as the mixed column of Serbs, Croatian militiamen and civilians arrived near Bleiburg. Five days later, on the 14th, the last major armed confrontation of World War II took place at Poljana, in Slovenia. Partisans attacked the fleeing column of Serbs, Germans and Croats. By the time twenty British tanks arrived at dawn on the 15th, the partisans had killed more than 300 people and wounded 250.[2]

On 14 May, Tito sent a telegram to the headquarters of the Slovene Partisan Army:

> You are to undertake the most energetic measures to prevent at all costs any killing of prisoners of war and of those arrested by military units, state organs or individuals. If there are persons among the prisoners and arrestees who should answer for war crimes, they are to be handed over immediately to military courts pending due process.[3]

Fighters from the NDH (Independent State of Croatia) forces began surrendering to the British on 15 May. The commanding officer of 38th Brigade was Brigadier Patrick Scott. A highly capable and diplomatic officer, he had won the Distinguished Service Order in Tunisia and again in Italy. Some of the Croatian forces in the column reportedly began raising white flags that same afternoon, and military representatives from the NDH reportedly attempted to surrender to the British. Tito's forces withdrew from the province of Carinthia on 21 May. In the intervening six days, the partisans took prisoner thousands of Germans, Russians, Croats, Montenegrins, Serbs and

Slovenians from the different columns heading towards, and just inside, Austria. Thousands more were subsequently imprisoned inside Yugoslavia, and thousands more detained in labour or prison camps. How many people were subsequently killed after being taken prisoner is unclear. The final estimates of the dead and detained varied hugely, and ranged from 17,500 to around 75,000:*

> Considering the nature of the struggle among the various competing forces during the Second World War in Yugoslavia, atrocities against the Serbian population in the territory of the Independent State of Croatia and pro-Partisan or dissident Croats, the fact that the Ustase adhered to the Nazis to the bitter end, and finally the fact that the Ustasa leadership wanted to put its troops at the disposal of the Western Allies for possible use against Yugoslav and other Communists, no mercy on the part of the Yugoslav Partisans toward these troops could have been expected.†[4]

* See Chapter 22.

† Jozo Tomasevich was a veteran Croatian-American economist and military historian, who became a professor emeritus at San Francisco University. Accounts of the actions in and around Bleiburg vary hugely, depending on the objectivity or, more frequently, the bias of the narrator.

Part Four

COLONIALISM ON THE ADRIATIC

11

Spies on the Adriatic, May–August 1945

By summer 1945, five sides faced each other around Trieste. Geopolitical, strategic and diplomatic necessity forced all of them to communicate and negotiate with each other constantly. Anxious fingers needed to be kept off triggers. But nobody trusted the other. There were too many hidden agendas, promises made, assurances broken, vested national interests and covert priorities. At the top of the Adriatic, Great Britain, the United States, Italy, Yugoslavia and Russia circled each other like nervous cats. And each nation's storm-troopers of the Cold War, their intelligence agencies, were in action.

THE AMERICAN OSS

'Wild Bill' Donovan was appointed the Coordinator of Information in July 1941. Prior to the official establishment of the OSS, the COI was heavily influenced by British training methods, expertise and operational assistance, learning a lot from the SOE. In June 1942, President Roosevelt established the OSS with a Presidential Military Order. Under the command of General Donovan, it collected and analysed strategic information and carried out special operations, while acting independently of the FBI and army and naval intelligence branches. The OSS spied, spread propaganda, committed sabotage, and infiltrated agents onto enemy territory, particularly Nazi Germany. Throughout the war in Italy it operated behind German and Italian lines; together with the SOE, the British Special Air Service, Italian partisans and other commando units, the OSS fought with considerable success at a local tactical and national strategic level. By 1945 the OSS employed around 10,400 people, some 5,700 of them overseas. Its annual budget for 1945 – the year in which it was finally disbanded – was $20 million. This was reduced to $10.5 million following the surrender of Japan. It operated worldwide, and it reported constantly to its headquarters. It spied on everybody, regardless of whether they were allies, enemies, or neutral:

> 35mm roll of microfilm with copies of XIIIth Corps monthly intelligence summaries 1–6, for August 1945–January 1946. The transmittal memo states that the summaries 'are of a relatively high level of competence and provide an indispensable fund of material on developments … in Venezia Giulia and Trieste for the period covered'.[1]

This was one of hundreds of entries logged in OSS station reports from around the world. But what makes this stand out is that this one from early 1946 shows the Americans were spying on their British colleagues, at the headquarters of the British Army's XIII Corps in Trieste. Their reports are full of intelligence successes, and failures in identifying agents working directly and indirectly for other countries' agencies in that confused, violent, contradictory first year of post-war liberation.

They were technically adventurous too. Along with their British colleagues, the OSS developed a wide range of electronic devices, weapons, gadgets and off-beat equipment designed to help their agents in the field. Their Research and Development Branch was run by Boston chemist Stanley P. Lovell. His mission was simple, he said, his policy was to consider any method whatever that might aid the war, however unorthodox or untried.[2] These included classic tools of espionage such as silenced pistols, very small 'Beano' hand-grenades that exploded on impact, and explosives disguised as lumps of coal. There were hidden miniature 16mm cameras the size of a matchbox, compasses that looked like buttons, the 'K & L' tasteless poison pills that nobody was sure were effective, and didn't want to try. There were notorious attempts to develop truth-inducing drugs: these included cigarettes laced with tetrahydrocannabinol acetate, a sub-extract of marijuana.

More vital was the communications equipment on which agents in the field depended. Electronic beacons located agents, and one vital development was the air-to-ground portable radio system, codenamed 'Joan-Eleanor'.* This allowed agents on the ground to transmit information to an aircraft overhead from a lightweight handheld VHF radio transceiver ('Joan') to a much larger transceiver ('Eleanor') located in an Allied B-17 or De Havilland Mosquito flying high above them. It used a frequency not monitored by the Germans, so the agent's report from the ground could be made in plain speech and the transmissions were virtually undetectable to the Germans. It was a flawless invention. Prior to this both SOE and OSS units operating in occupied France or Italy had had to rely on Morse transmissions. This was both dangerous and time-consuming for the agent in occupied territory, who had to both encode and de-code all communications with OSS or SOE headquarters.

And the OSS was active almost everywhere. Random pages from an unidentified notebook from 1944 describe projects in Italy, the Near East, Scandinavia, France, Holland and Belgium, Spain, Switzerland, in French Equatorial Africa, Portuguese Guinea, Angola, Cape Verde Islands, Eire [Ireland] Afghanistan, Greece, Hungary, the Southeast Pacific, West Africa, and other countries. Reports from 1945 cover discussions on German V-weapons, politics, industrial production and counter-espionage. One seven-page report from

* The 'Joan-Eleanor' system was developed specifically for the OSS by two American scientists who reportedly named it after one of their wives, and a female friend.

June 1945 lists the pseudonyms for foreign agents in Budapest, Bucharest, Vienna, Belgrade and Tirana. Everything that could be reported worldwide by OSS was being reported. OSS Station Algiers had sightings of suspected UFOs from autumn 1945 onwards: 'They were cigar shaped, possibly with wings, going at a speed appreciably less than that of a shooting star, trailing blue flame, and making a sort of whoosh, entirely unlike that of an aeroplane and just like that of a jet propelled plane.' From November 1945 onwards the OSS launched the Pilgrim's Progress Project, which hoped to acquire better information on the Vatican. by attempting to infiltrate agents into the Catholic Church's Rome headquarters.* One signal wondered, would a Catholic Papal *Nuncio* agree to carry classified mail for the OSS, in and out of the Vatican? [3]

From May 1945 onwards, OSS' operations in and around Trieste ran round the clock. What was Tito going to do about the situation there as the war ended? One opinion was contained in a coded dispatch received from an OSS source in Belgrade who had met with Tito. The message was simple. The Yugoslav leader wanted all of Trieste and the Friuli Venezia Giulia east of the River Isonzo. Information came in thick and fast, much of it completely contradictory. Simultaneously, the Americans were trying to gauge Tito's and Stalin's intentions, listen in and report on their British and Italian allies, assess whether and how the Russians were infiltrating agents into Trieste and Austria, and wage an active counter-intelligence campaign against the increasingly aggressive OZNA. Thousands and thousands of pages of intelligence reports, operational daily summaries, unit logs and covert information began to be generated by the various parties in and around Trieste. One of the highest priorities for the OSS was finding out the precise nature of the relationship between Tito and the Russians. The Americans had deduced by that point that Tito was not being direct and honest with them, but suspected he was still being straight and open with

* The Allies wanted to discover who was running one of the 'Rat-Lines' that were helping SS officers and high-ranking Nazi party members escape to Spain and South America.

Stalin. So when a Yugoslav envoy went to Moscow to meet Stalin in 1944, the OSS reported a meeting that they had with him on his return to Belgrade:

> He said Stalin was very cautious with him when they spoke about diplomatic matters, but.............. Stalin warned him not to try to emulate Soviet Russia. Stalin allegedly said, 'You have not the territory of Russia nor the people of Russia. You are a small country of small landowners in the heart of Europe. You will have to build your state upon democratic principles with equal representation for all the national groups of Yugoslavia. You will have to seek economic assistance from America the way we here in Russia are planning to do after the war is over.' Stalin............., spoke in 'very warm terms about the United States.'[4]

OSS' observations were as follows:

> In foreign affairs, as in internal affairs, Russia is the lodestone governing Tito's policies. In every international issue, whether it is the direct concern of Yugoslavia or not, Tito and his press assiduously follow Moscow's lead. In fact, Tito and his followers exhibit a servility toward the Kremlin which contrasts strangely with their otherwise dynamic individuality. It is enough for Moscow to express a view and the Belgrade press reprints it in toto, adding a few biting words of its own. Under these circumstances it is no small wonder that in Belgrade one finds no evidence of a corps of Russian agents directing the activities of individual ministries or agencies. Should the necessity arise for specific guidance, no doubt a brief message from Stalin to Tito would suffice.[5]

At the beginning of June 1945, an incoming OSS agent arrived in Trieste to take up a new mission. He read a situation report on his arrival in the city. It summarised the situation as follows:

> The Italian government said that the Trieste question is regarded in Italy as the most important single problem of Italian foreign affairs;
>
> The entry of the Yugoslav army into Trieste represents the final

> guarantee for the people of Yugoslavia that this territory is now already annexed, and will remain so;
>
> the current conflict would appear to be due to the fact that while the (Yugoslav) parties have recognized under pressure that 'formal annexation' must wait, they continue to regard Venezia Giulia as an integral part of Yugoslavia over which they have political as well as military jurisdiction;
>
> Several hundred (Italian) political prisoners are being held by partisans, from the CLNAI, as well as from any grouping of Fascist Italians and the clergy. The arrest and detention of the Archbishop of Gorizia was only resolved after Vatican intervention;
>
> In Carinthia, the British had arrived in Klagenfurt three hours ahead of Marshal Tito's men. The latter announced they wanted to run the Austrian provinces they have occupied in tandem with the British, as they have agreed with the Russians in areas which both sides have occupied. Tito said on that date he would continue to hold onto the areas of Austria occupied by his men;
>
> On the 12th and 14th May the State Department sent notes to Tito saying that the Venezia Giulia, Trieste, Gorizia, Pola and Monfalcone, and lines of communications to Austria must be under the control of (Field Marshal) Alexander;
>
> as a result of this agents from both the OSS and SOE have been ordered to leave Yugoslav territory;
>
> on May 19th tension between the Western Allies and Yugoslavia appear to have reached their peak – Radio Belgrade says 'the honour of our army and honour of our country demand the presence of the Yugoslav Army in Istria, Trieste and on the Slovene coastline';
>
> the Soviet Union too may be expected to profit in Yugoslavia from the current impression there that the Yugoslav claims have had Soviet backing;
>
> the further course of Marshal Tito's government will depend in large measure on the attitude of the USSR.[6]

The OSS now had its work cut out. And the situation was growing more tense. By early June 1945, the OSS was running a small, six-person office in Trieste – they had been allocated a couple of rooms at Allied Headquarters at the Casa del Popolo in Trieste. Their area of operations ranged east across the Morgan Line, north-west to the southern Austrian provinces of Styria and Carinthia, and west towards Venice. The agents worked in a combination of US Army fatigues and civilian clothes, and were running both Slovenian and Italian agents inside the city, and 'line-crossers' who travelled backwards and forwards into Yugoslavia. OSS went armed, with Colt .45 automatic pistols, and Thompson sub-machine guns in their cars. Some of them were Americans of Italian descent, so they could speak to the inhabitants without interpreters. Regardless, they were not from Trieste. And therefore like every other new arrival that summer, it was obvious to the Slovenes, Croats and Italians with whom they worked that they were some part of the vast gathering of foreigners in town. They were seen as liberators, occupiers or a combination of the two.

From their base in the old Fascist police station, OSS had begun to identify OZNA agents in Switzerland and in Italy, and were also working on a list of OZNA collaborators in Trieste. Using two 'line-crossing' agents, they started to infiltrate the OZNA headquarters at Fasana, near Pola on the Istrian peninsula. This port, which lay some twenty miles south-east of Trieste, was included in the Allied-controlled Zone A of the Morgan Line agreement. In return, Maks Milić's First Directorate from OZNA was first and foremost spying on the Russians and the Americans. The Russians were the more straightforward target. OZNA assumed correctly that every Russian they approached in Belgrade would repeat each conversation they had, and report they presented, to the GRU or the NKVD. It was a question of pushing through the bars of the cage in the zoo the food the occupant wanted to eat. They knew that Stalin still believed, by summer 1945, that Tito was a loyal ally.

OZNA was aware that the foreign intelligence branch of the NKVD, headed by Pavel Fitin, had a ten-point list of priorities. First and foremost was to find out what Tito intended to do about Trieste. Would he try a lightening 'land grab' and call the Allies' bluff?

Secondly, would the latter, if geo-political push came to tactical shove, open fire on the Yugoslavs? Thirdly, was Tito happy with the land he had acquired under the Morgan compromise, and now in a position to try and negotiate with the Allies? Fourthly, Stalin wanted to know simply if Tito was still truly obedient to him. The Russians also wanted any information on the main battle layout of Allied forces opposing them across the Italian and Austrian borders, and the position of Allied naval units in the central Mediterranean, particularly submarines. They wanted to apprehend German and Italian officers who had commanded units involved in war crimes against Red Army units. Once arrested, they intended to bring them back to Soviet-controlled territory for trial. This often required cutting deals with the Allies, and they knew that the best way to do this was through an OZNA 'cut-out'. Next, they wanted to find out Tito's intentions towards the Soviet Union, and to his regional neighbours. Would the maverick Yugoslav commander try and co-opt Greece, Albania and Bulgaria into joining a regional movement that was neither allied to the British and Americans, nor the Soviet Union? In addition to these imperatives, the Russians wanted to bring back to the Soviet Union any of their agents from the 'Pickaxe' programme who were still alive.

From 1943 onwards, both the SOE and the NKVD had formalised an arrangement for 'mutual assistance' in this programme, whereby the former trained and infiltrated agents from the latter into occupied Europe:

> The principal way in which the agreement operates on our side is the offer, from time to time, by SOE of its facilities for the infiltration of Russian agents into various areas of Europe ... SOE, in carrying out such operations, is executing the policy of HMG under the immediate guidance of the Foreign Office ...[7]

Two Russian agents who had infiltrated Italy in 1943 were Andrei Kaliaiev and Alexandre Filipov. Posing as Italian engineers, they were delivered to Italy, and by mid-1945 were still unaccounted for. They were not alone. Many of the 'Pickaxe' programme agents simply disappeared. But Russia wanted them back, particularly to ensure that they had not been 'turned' as agents by the British. The difficulty for the men from the NKVD was that, because Tito's men controlled Yugoslavia, they had to travel everywhere with OZNA escorts. The soldiers and spies from the Red Army were confined mainly to Belgrade and its surroundings. So consequently they saw only what the Yugoslav secret police wanted them to see.

But not always. In mid-summer 1945, a British SOE officer, Captain Alexander Simitch Stevens, was given a mission on the Morgan Line. A Soviet intelligence-gathering unit was posing undercover as a rehabilitation unit caring for just-released Russian POWs. Stevens was half-Serbian and half-British, and was repeatedly asked to deal with confrontational incidents on the Line: 'I was always getting Yugoslav patrols out of our chaps' hands or our chaps' patrols out of their hands ... there was a lot of friction going on, on the line.'

Stevens' colleagues from the Intelligence Corps Field Security Section then sent him to handle the case of the rehabilitation unit:

> I had got very friendly with the Russian colonel in charge of this unit, but our lads thought it was camouflage for a spying unit. So I had to escort him back to the 'Blue' Line. (Accompanied by six Military Policemen) I went to see him, and found him sitting in shirt-sleeves with a Major and Captains and two or three Ukrainian girls released from POW camps. They were eating strawberries. 'They must be joking,' said the colonel, 'I'm no spy.' As we took him back across the line, he hugged and kissed me and said 'what a pity.'[8]

OZNA, in turn, knew the OSS had the widest and best-funded intelligence-gathering operation in Europe. So one technique they used was to spy on those who were spying on their enemies. Because OZNA knew the Americans would be intercepting Russian communications, running agents inside their territory, and inside their operations, the easiest thing to do was to bug and to intercept the Americans and those who dealt with them. It was a simple bypass to finding out what the Russians were doing. So one of OZNA's first American targets from September 1945 onwards concerned Project Caviar. This was an American operation to penetrate the Russian intelligence service in Austria, to identify its agents, disrupt its networks and monitor its operations. A second priority for the Yugoslavs was to track down senior Croatian Ustashe figures, including Ante Pavelić, who were trying to take refuge in the Vatican or escape to South America with the help of it. So from November 1945, OZNA was trying to 'back-door' into the OSS Pilgrim's Progress Project, which aimed to collect better information on the Vatican.

12

Very British Intelligence

In mid- to late summer 1945, British intelligence operations in Trieste and the Friuli Venezia Giulia were run by SOE, by MI6, and by the army's Intelligence Corps. 412 Field Security Section (FSS) from the British 8th Army was the 'Int Corps' unit assigned to Trieste. They had arrived in May. They were responsible for overseeing the operational and intelligence security of the British units deployed in the area, and running counter-intelligence and information-gathering activities. Their sub-unit responsible for the security of the harbour area of Trieste, 21 Port Security Section, also arrived in the second week of May. They took over a bank in the centre of the city as its first headquarters. Hardly had they arrived in the building, when the telephone on a desk rang:

> A voice, speaking English with obvious difficulty, said 'we know all about you' and continued with a warning that we should be careful. Looking out of the window of the bank, (we) saw a Jugoslav machine-gun mounted in the first floor of the window opposite and trained on the section's sleeping quarters.[1]

The British intelligence section had just had their first brush with OZNA:

> The Jugoslav State Security Police, OZNA, conducted a reign of terror over the Italian population arresting suspected collaborators and exacting summary punishment. The Field Security Section ... realised the need for complete security in dealing with local people in order to protect them from reprisals. OZNA was clearly aware of the function of FSS.[2]

From 1945 to 1946, there were eleven different units from the British Army's Intelligence Corps operating in the Trieste area. They had a huge range of different tasks: one was providing a vetting service for local Italians and Slovenians who wanted to get jobs with the Allied Military Government that had taken over the running of the city. They also looked after the port, and ran general counter-intelligence operations across the whole of the Allied Zone A. They assisted the MI6 detachment in the city – nicknamed the 'Chinese Laundry'. The port section gained information about Russian ports by briefing and debriefing officers of British ships who had docked at Trieste, *en route* to Black Sea ports. The Intelligence Corps had sub-units in Monfalcone, Gorizia, Udine and near the Austrian border. Their daily lives, and daily operations reverberated to the idiosyncratic beat that was Trieste in summer 1945. Part direct confrontation, part friendly and idiosyncratic liaison with their Yugoslav and Allied counterparts, and short, sharp violent moments where it seemed to everybody involved that war could, indeed, start again at any moment.

The FSS also used IFCs, or 'Illegal Frontier Crossers', often refugees who went back into Yugoslavia smuggling goods. Anything from petrol to cigarettes to razor-blades, alcohol, women's hair-grips, food, chocolate, penicillin and clothes was fair smuggling game. The only commodity that neither side needed to traffic was arms and ammunition. The area was awash with them. A top smuggling priority was currency. Inside Yugoslavia the Italian *lira* and the Yugoslav *dinar* were traded one-for-one. In Trieste, the going rate was double for the *lira*. In the first days of the occupation of the city, a confrontational approach was common with more senior-ranking officers, but less so with the common soldiers themselves:

> The Jugoslav soldiers, women as well as men (there seemed to be mixed platoons) sometimes garlanded with bandoliers of ammunition, were almost invariably extremely friendly towards Allied soldiers, saluting them punctiliously, NCOs and officers alike. The men went in for impromptu dance circles, often holding up the traffic. There was a Sunday football match between British and Jugoslav teams in the Trieste stadium. It was a good tempered game won by the Jugoslavs ... between the Western Allies and the partisans there was an undoubted measure of good will and respect. Looking back it seems likely that Jugoslavia was less than totally committed to its claim on the city although solid in its determination to regain neighbouring parts of their country which had fallen under Italian rule.[3]

One British intelligence operative remembers eating lunch in a restaurant with a civilian, when an armed group of Yugoslavs arrived and tried to arrest the latter. The British sergeant-major in the charge of the party stood his ground; the soldiers from the National Liberation Army withdrew. On another occasion a British NCO from the Intelligence Corps disappeared for twenty-four hours: fearing him kidnapped, his colleagues prepared to mount a rescue mission across the Morgan Line. Until he reappeared the following morning with a catastrophic hangover, after a night as a 'guest' of the partisans. But against this faintly celebratory backdrop, a vicious war was being fought in the shadows. The Allied Military Government had instituted restrictions on demonstrations and the publishing of newspapers which spread anti-Allied propaganda. Arms and explosives were illegal: people's homes were full of them. The war against the Germans finally ended on 8 May. After six years of conflict, asked Trieste's population, were they instantaneously to assume all was suddenly secure? And that they could rely upon their American and British liberators to keep them safe? From the perspective of local people, with 20,000 Allied and Yugoslav soldiers facing off over the barbed wire of a demarcation line, with martial law and a curfew in place, and people disappearing by the day, it didn't look like peace. So for many of them, former partisans and otherwise, the Sten gun or

Carcano rifle or captured Walther pistol stayed firmly where it was. Up the chimney, under the floorboards, buried under the damson tree in the garden, just in case.

OZNA had also long planned that groups of Slovenes and former partisans would stay behind inside Trieste. They would hand in their weapons under the Allied Military Government's rulings, then find apartments and houses. Their priority was then to take control – by force if necessary – of the informal network of local agents who controlled the supply of Slovene and Italian interpreters and administrative staff to all the varied Allied offices and bases. These employees would either volunteer or be coerced or intimidated into providing information from their employers' offices. The British FSS knew this, and attempted to put a 'vetting' process in place. But both Italians and Slovenes employed by the British and the Americans could easily circumvent this. OZNA were happy to provide false paperwork. Many of Trieste's inhabitants were more than happy to work for them voluntarily. For a woman whose husband was dead, imprisoned or missing, running a home and providing for her children, with prostitution as one of the few remaining employment options, the benefits were self-evident. The British FSS also searched houses and vehicles and factories for weapons. They tried to infiltrate their own men, or local agents, into the gangs operated by Fascist Italians and Slovenians who were crossing over the Morgan Line on nocturnal missions to kill Yugoslav soldiers or police officers.

In the Intelligence Corps FSS headquarters was a door bearing a sign that said 'Cabinet Office Historical Section'. Run by personnel from the Royal Signals, this office contained everything needed to run telephone and wire-tapping operations. The direct opposite of such covert operations was the work that nobody wanted to do. Maintaining the Trieste Security Office's 'Card Index'. Every single report that came in, went out or was in some way generated had to be filed in a box containing small cards, around A5 size. Everybody took turns in the office, cross referencing every name, address and event:

> So the first step was to search for all the cards containing any previous mention of, say, the people involved. Each of their cards was withdrawn and the new information added. You can imagine how tedious this could be if there was a meeting involving several people where a number of events were discussed. Sometimes the information was important and very interesting but it was – more often – routine. Every new arrival in TSO [the Trieste Security Office] had a spell in Card Index and this was a valuable insight into the need for accurate records but it was not exciting and most prayed for an early rescue. Anyone who could type with more than one finger was well advised to conceal the fact.[4]

Alongside officers from the SOE like Maclean and Peter Wilkinson, the British Secret Intelligence Service (SIS), also known as MI6 (Military Intelligence Section 6), had also deployed its agents into north-eastern Italy. They were answerable to the respective British embassies in Rome and Berne. SIS' remit was long-sighted: it wanted to build up a regional network of informers, agents and contacts among the thousands of Italian, Slovenian, Austrian and German civilians and former soldiers in and around Trieste and southern Austria. The OSS, MI6, SOE and the American Counter Intelligence Corps had several main collective priorities. One of them was to track down and arrest prominent German officers and officials wanted for war crimes. And while looking for war criminals, the Americans were also looking for art.

During the German occupation of Italy for the *Kunstschutz*, the German cultural 'conservation' programme. Working in Trieste from autumn 1943 to spring 1945, they had transported stolen works of art from the city's two main museums, and its largely Jewish art dealers, to caches in nearby Austria guarded by the SS. Among the material stolen were original manuscripts from Petrarch, and Venetian and Phoenician artefacts. By summer 1945, the job of hunting down the art fell to the American Looted Art Intelligence Unit, based in Salzburg in Austria. Working with Italian museum curators, and a handful of survivors from the Jewish community, they were trying to find the city's stolen artistic heritage. But this was Trieste in 1945 at the beginning of the Cold War, where everything was divided, and even the cats seemed to take sides between Allies and Communists. Other Slovenian and Croatian officials, who saw Trieste as belonging to Yugoslavia, considered the city's cultural heritage rightfully theirs. So along with every other one of their complex priorities, all sides were now suddenly engaged in a race to rescue incredibly valuable artefacts that they considered theirs. So hardly had the Morgan Line been established, when seven different intelligence agencies with competing agendas – OZNA, SOE, MI6, the OSS, US Army Intelligence, the British Intelligence Corps and the NKVD – began running operations in and around Trieste. In the first weeks, missions began that saw all sides changing their allegiances in the face of the suddenly shifting sands of *realpolitik* that the end of World War II, and the beginning of the Cold War, involved.

13

The Capture of Friedrich Rainer and Odilo Globocnik, May 1945

The two most-wanted men from Trieste were Gauleiter Friedrich Rainer and SS-Brigadeführer Odilo Globocnik. Of all the German and Italian officials who had operated in the city from 1943 to 1945, the Allies, the Russians, the Italians and the Yugoslavs wanted them more than anybody. Up until the day when he fled Trieste at the end of April, Rainer had been defiant and upbeat. On 18 April he was still telling his political colleagues that 'the situation is still not hopeless. We still have a chance.' Odilo Globocnik was more circumspect. 'It was not a quarter to midnight,' he said. 'But only a few seconds away.'[1]

So when OZNA first questioned the captured German and Ukrainian SS guards from the San Sabba camp, they urgently wanted information. To where, they demanded, had Friedrich Rainer, Odilo Globocnik and their three SS subordinates fled? The former was from Carinthia, the latter had operated there in the 1930s. So it was an obvious assumption for the Yugoslav intelligence agents that the Nazis would head north into the southern Austrian province. It would have been impossible to head into partisan-controlled Slovenian territory.

Maks Milić's operatives knew that if the two men and their entourage were captured, they would want to give themselves an even chance of survival by being able to surrender to the Allies. They couldn't head by sea south-east down the Adriatic coast, as that meant landfall in Yugoslav-occupied territory. Going due west on land would lead them to the Allies. Therefore the road to Udine and the Austrian border it had to be. OZNA kicked and truncheoned their way through the camp guards to get an answer. Which of them knew any possible names or contacts in southern Austria? Globocnik had his three principal SS subordinates with him. One, Ernst Lerch, was from Klagenfurt. Had they or any of the Ukrainian SS men or women mentioned anybody or anything? Any possible hiding places? OZNA interrogations could be brutal. The agency was doing its questioning in a requisitioned school house. The Germans probably knew they were going to die. Then came an answer. A name. An *SS-Unterscharführer.* A sergeant called Siegfried Kummerer. Originally from Villach, on the other side of the Austrian frontier.

This was the precise point at which OZNA knew they'd need Allied help. Their First Directorate leader, Colonel Maks Milić, was a radical and flexible free thinker, a former philosophy student from the Dalmatian coast who routinely questioned the orthodoxy of the Yugoslav Communist Party. Like Tito, 'Milić' was an assumed name. He had been christened Maksimiljan Baće shortly after his birth in 1904. But in the fight against the Germans and Italians on the Dalmatian hinterland in 1943, his subordinates had known him only as 'Milić'. For one whose questioning of the party's existing political tenets was extensive, he ran a very tight ship in his OZNA Directorate. He realised he needed his British friends to help him. There was no way his men would have any chance of pursuing Rainer and Globocnik, nor, in a British zone of occupation in Austria, have any hope of finding them or capturing them. So, a bit of hard bargaining was called for. He decided to go and see a British SOE officer whose name he knew, who had operated with the partisans in 1944; General Drapšin had told him the man was somewhere in or near Trieste. His name? Peter Wilkinson. Milić decided to find him, or at the very least, to get a message passed to him.

Peter Wilkinson from the SOE had given assurances to his wife Theresa Villiers that his deployment to Trieste would be his last active service operation of the war. And so, at the end of April, it had been. But before he could be reunited with her, he was given one last assignment. To go to southern Austria. British troops from Lieutenant-General Harding's XIII Corps had occupied Trieste behind the New Zealanders, and the commanding officer wanted Wilkinson with the leading British troops now advancing northwards into Austria.[2] With the war now over, Wilkinson was aware that the possibility of being shot was considerably diminished. His promise to his young wife from the British Women's Royal Naval Service was sliding onto thin ice, but the SOE lieutenant-colonel reckoned he would be safe.

However, his forthcoming journey northwards worried him. He would be travelling to the valley of the River Drau in the province of Carinthia. His best friend in the SOE, Captain Alfred 'Alfgar' Hesketh-Prichard, had died there in 1944. He had been an officer in the Royal Fusiliers who joined SOE's Czech Section, and had trained the agents who assassinated SS-Obergruppenführer Reinhard Heydrich in Prague in 1942. He had disappeared while on an SOE mission in southern Austria the previous winter. Wilkinson suspected he had been murdered by Slovenian partisans on the orders of one of their OZNA political commissars, possibly with Russian connivance. He had always found OZNA officials 'most unsympathetic to British ideals and most hostile to our work in the Balkans'.[3] He was determined to find out more now Austria was liberated. But with the Cold War now crackling into life, Wilkinson was not going to be one of those 'many components of SOE who marched out of the Second World War into the Cold War without breaking step'.[4] He had thought of recasting SOE in Austria for what he called 'a role in the occupational and post-occupational phase' but the Foreign Office had blocked this. SOE was to be disbanded, some of its operatives subsumed into the ranks of its adversary, the SIS. And like everybody else at the beginning of that May in 1945, Wilkinson was tired:

> After six years of war, most of us were used to order and counter-order from remote staff echelons, and had got into the habit of taking our own decisions and justifying them later if necessary ... whereas in a battle you are hyped up and, so to speak, exceed yourself, seemingly indefatigable, my recollection is that after the German surrender I could no longer call on those reserves of energy; I was literally tired out. You cannot imagine the exhaustion or the sense of relief; you had survived and nothing would ever really matter again.[5]

From December 1943 onwards, Wilkinson had commanded Number 6 Special Force of the SOE, on a deployment codenamed 'Operation *Clowder*'. Their main objective was to penetrate Austria from Yugoslavia and north-east Italy, and organise partisan resistance there against the Germans. This is what Hesketh-Prichard had been doing when he was killed. One of Wilkinson's other men was a former Metropolitan Police officer called Major Alexander Ramsay. He had served in North Africa as an officer in the Parachute Regiment, and had then joined SOE. He served in the Balkans under Peter Wilkinson. In 1945 he had participated in the last airborne combat drop of the war, codenamed 'Operation *Herring*'. A group of 114 paratroopers, all but two of them Italians, had been inserted onto targets behind German lines south of the River Po, and south-east of Ferrara. The operation was part success, part disaster: the Italians' killing of German prisoners had prompted reprisals against civilians. But in return, and with partisan help, they had killed nearly 500 German soldiers, captured 1,100, destroyed vehicles, telephone lines and an ammunition dump, and held three bridges intact. Ramsay had then continued north-east and joined up with Wilkinson in Trieste.

He arrived in the city with the Allies on 3 May. Like OZNA on the other side, and most Allied intelligence officers, he was looking for anybody who had had any form of contact with Friedrich Rainer or

Odilo Globocnik. It is possible that a message from Milić, alerting the British to the name of the *SS-Unterscharführer*, reached Ramsay at Allied Headquarters at the Castello di Miramare sometime after 3 May.

Ramsay and Wilkinson then crossed the border into Austria, and were among the first British troops to liberate Klagenfurt at 10am on 8 May. They were three hours ahead of the Yugoslav partisans. Captured SS men in the city said that SS-Unterscharführer Siegfried Kummerer was believed to be hiding with another group of men from Trieste in Paternion, a small mountain village west of Villach. Ramsay discovered that the SS sergeant had known Globocnik since serving in the Hitler Youth in the 1930s in Carinthia, the province of which Klagenfurt was the capital. So there was a chance that he might know where the SS officer was hiding. After the capture of Klagenfurt, Wilkinson stayed in the town and the surrounding area for a few days, to help with negotiations with the thousands of Yugoslav partisans who had entered Austrian territory. On the 12th he flew back to Rome, and travelled south to Caserta, to be reunited with his wife. Ramsay continued his hunt.

Ramsay was then informally attached to the intelligence staff of the British 78th Division. One of their cavalry units was the 4th Queen's Own Hussars, who had headed north from Italy into Austria. It was this unit that Ramsay joined. Winston Churchill had served with the 4th in the 1890s. On 2 May he sent the regiment a personal telegram of thanks and congratulations. The unit had fought north from Padua, entered the town of Udine just after the Maoris of the 28th New Zealand Battalion, and headed north. The road from Udine crosses the border into Austria in between the small towns of Tarviso and Arnoldstein. Five miles north-east is the town of Villach, and then another ten miles further on the road north-west is the small town of Paternion. This is the Austrian Alps, a landscape of lakes, mountains and high pastures scattered with small farms, chalets and mountain lodges. The Hussars had arrived in Paternion at 2pm on the 11th. The unit had started building a rest camp for its men on the shores of the beautiful Alpine lake, the Weissensee, or White Lake.

The area was full of surrendering German prisoners, refugees on the roads, and a local population that had been predominantly loyal to the Austrian Nazi Party. Yugoslav partisans still lurked in small groups, heading slowly south-east back into their own country.

ODILO GLOBOCNIK'S LAST JOURNEY

There were six vehicles in the convoy carrying Rainer, Globocnik and their SS entourage. They left Trieste on the night of 30 April, and by dawn were heading north towards Udine and the Austrian border. The Ukrainian SS guards and two SS officers were in the trucks, Globocnik and two other SS officers in a staff car, along with a driver. Rainer's vehicle was leading. Just after sunrise, the convoy heard the descending, roaring noise that any vehicle on an open road in enemy territory most feared. Allied aircraft. A low-level attack by fighters saw canon and machine-gun shells tearing into the dusty surface of the road on a low-level attack run. Shards of ripping hot shrapnel tore through the canvas of the trucks' canopies, hitting some of the men in the back. One lorry was put out of action, but the men rushed furiously to transfer the cargo into the remaining vehicles before they set off again. Through the towns of Tolmezzo and Arta, they hit the border. SS men and Wehrmacht soldiers were digging foxholes at the side of the road. They were preparing a last-ditch defence of the Austrian frontier. At the village of Hermagor, Globocnik's convoy halted. Rainer headed off in his staff car towards his family home. Globocnik and his group settled in for several nights at a camp occupied by other German soldiers. He wanted to send men off into the mountains to scout out possible hiding places. His departing superior, however, still had political aspirations.

After he reached safety, Rainer had broadcast over the radio in support of the defence of the Austrian homeland: 'In these hours our first and foremost task is to keep our *Gau* [region] free and pure.' He had urged all patriotic Austrians to defend the borders of their land. To preserve Carinthia he declared on 4 May that Klagenfurt and Villach would not be defended against Anglo-American attacks, essentially declaring them 'open cities'. Since he further believed it was possible that a unified Carinthia would be supported by Britain and the United States, as it had been in 1918 and 1919, he encouraged the preparation of logistics and arms. Trieste was shuddering into its freefall of liberation by the Allies and Yugoslavs. Meanwhile Rainer himself was imagining a loyal state of pure, Aryan aesthetes that would be re-born in Austria. The Allies, he said, would tolerate, if not support him. After all, he stood for everything that was good and strong about a new European front against the encroaching red tide of communism. So he spent the dying days of World War II airing these wistful thoughts.

Rainer's authority as the German Gauleiter of the Adriatic Coastal Lands had included the Slovenian capital, Ljubljana. By the end of April 1945 this city was now solidly occupied by the partisans. But Rainer had very carefully turned over the Ljubljana government to an anti-communist Slovene National Committee. By reinforcing the notion of the Slovenes' right of self-determination, he hoped that Carinthians might use the same principle to their advantage. On 5 May, in a radio address from inside Austria, Rainer stressed that communism was the danger, not the British and Americans. On the same day he began talking with an all-party group about a transfer of power to non-Nazis. The two sides quickly drew up a list of provisional government members, but two days later Rainer reluctantly left office to go into hiding. The Allies were closing in. In his view he resigned, he did not surrender. The struggle for Carinthia was just moving to another phase, he said, and shortly before midnight on 7 May Rainer made a final radio speech. He urged his comrades to 'keep the national honour safe' and exhorted them to 'close your ranks in the struggle for a free and undivided Carinthia'. The first proclamation of the provisional government reinforced these notions of Carinthian unity:

> The new Provincial Government will consider as its primary task the maintenance of a free and indivisible Carinthia. German-speaking and

> Slovene-speaking Carinthians, gather around the Government. Long live democratic Carinthia in free Austria![6]

Meanwhile Odilo Globocnik was being more realistic. He told his faithful Ukrainian guards that this was the end of the road for them all. It had been a long journey from Operation *Reinhard* in Poland, to Trieste, and now to a warm back road in late spring somewhere in southern Austria. If nothing else, he and the senior SS officers had travelled a circuitous route back to their country of birth.

There were now five SS officers in the group. Rainer, Globocnik, and the three *Sturmbannführers,* Ernst Lerch, Hermann Hofle and Georg Michaelsen, who had been chiefs of staff and seconds-in-command in Poland and in Trieste. The Allies wanted to arrest and interrogate all of them. They had one truck still with them. In the back, hidden under a canvas tarpaulin, were the piles of trunks and suitcases that held their loot from Poland and from San Sabba. There were reportedly ten-kilo gold ingots, thousands of gold coins taken off Jews and other prisoners who had originally come from France, Switzerland, Germany, Austria, Poland and Hungary. There were hundreds of gemstones and diamonds. There were several jewel-studded, gold-sheathed old Russian religious icons, and an eighteenth-century silver Jewish Torah case. There was a silver table service bearing the double-headed Polish eagle, and a pair of silver-mounted flintlock pistols from the court of Catherine the Great.[7]

The German officers stayed in and around the camp at Hermagor until 13 May. Globocnik chose two of the more junior SS men who had travelled with them from the Austrian border, and gave them a mission. To find a mountain hideout for him, Rainer and the three SS majors. These two soldiers walked westwards towards the mountains surrounding the place called the Weissensee, the White Lake. One of these men was Siegfried Kummerer. Globocnik went to stay a last night with Rainer and his wife, before heading into the mountains. The following morning, saying goodbye to Frau Rainer, he showed her a small pill box containing a capsule of liquid hydrogen cyanide. If the Allies captured him, he said, he would swallow it. It was for everything he had done wrong in Poland. And Rainer? asked his wife, concerned. Did he too have such a pill? Oh no, said Globocnik, he wouldn't need one. He had never done anything wrong, after all.[8] Then along with his three subordinates, the *SS-Brigadeführer* left for the mountains. Delayed by a bad stomach, he arrived several days after the other men at their final hiding place. On 20 May, he finally climbed up nearly 3,000 feet to a mountain hut set in a stand of pine trees, high above the Weissensee. The place was called the Moslacher-Alm farmstead.

CAPTURING THE SS HIERARCHY FROM TRIESTE

At 10am on 29 May, two Germans in civilian clothes came to the castle in Paternion where the 4th Hussars had their headquarters. They told the British officer who came to meet them that they were members of the SS, and had information about the whereabouts of some of their senior colleagues who were hiding in the mountains nearby. Two British soldiers accompanied them, and found a small hut surrounded by another five SS men, armed with pistols. They had all decided to give information about their commanding officers to the British, in the hope that once they became POWs, they wouldn't be held responsible for any involvement in war crimes. The two British soldiers, accompanied by the seven junior SS men, captured the two occupants of the hut. They were put in an *ad hoc* prison the British were constructing in Paternion. That evening, yet another junior SS man appeared, and said that he too knew where his colleagues were hiding. Searching nearby buildings in Paternion, the British found two men dressed as farm workers. One of them in turn said that, although he had been in the SS for six years, and had twice served at Dachau, he had not been involved in any 'atrocity duties'. He too said that he had information about the whereabouts of a group of very senior SS men hiding nearby, and in return for preferential treatment, he offered to guide the British soldiers to the hiding place. This man was Siegfried Kummerer. The hiding place was on a farm 3,000 feet up in the mountains, he said. There were at least five SS men there, one of whom was a *Gruppenführer*, and three of the others *Sturmbannführers.* Thus a major-general and three majors. The British soldiers passed on the news to their officers. If the information was true, Major Ramsay knew, the arrest of these men was a major priority.

The British decided to go and capture them. They put together an arrest party under Ramsay's command. The raiding group consisted of himself, the Hussars' medical officer, a South African captain from an armoured unit attached to the Hussars, and the assistant adjutant, a lieutenant from the 4th Hussars. Twelve NCOs and troopers were detailed to accompany them, the party armed with .45-calibre Thompson sub-machine guns, Lee Enfield rifles and pistols. The drive and climb up to the mountain hut with their SS guide took five hours, and they reached the Moslacher-Alm as the sun was coming up. The British surrounded it. Ramsay climbed in through a loft window, and slipped down to open the front door, as the back entrance was forced by two other British officers. There were five German men in the house, in a combination of uniforms, pyjamas and underwear. Two of them were together in a small bedroom at the rear of the building. None of them put up any resistance as the British forcibly woke them up. Two German women were asleep with two of the German officers, and subsequently described their role to the British as 'carrying out secretarial duties for the SS'. The British then found two further men in the hut. And the plot thickened.

Ramsay took out a photograph of Rainer, and compared it with the gaunt, acerbic man who now stood in front of him, under the dawn pine trees on an Austrian mountainside. With a long duelling scar on his left cheek, it was obviously the former Gauleiter of Trieste. A British military policeman hustled him forward; Rainer spluttered and protested sharply that he couldn't be treated in this way, as he was, after all, a *Gauleiter.* The British soldier kicked him in the behind, put the muzzle of a .38 pistol into the back of his neck and threatened to execute him there and then.

The British Hussars took the SS men back to nearby Paternion, leaving the women to stay in the hut with orders not to leave. They locked up Rainer in a storage room immediately, and sent a radio message to divisional headquarters signalling his capture. His presence at the imminent Nuremberg trials was vital. Ramsay suspected that one of the other four SS men was Globocnik, but he had no way of proving it. The man he had in mind was thick-set, with swept-back dark hair who claimed that he was a merchant from Klagenfurt called 'Konig'. His papers appeared to back this up. So Ramsay and the British military policemen let him, and the three other suspected SS officers, walk round a small courtyard outside the castle. Ramsay was a fluent German speaker. After some minutes, standing on a small balcony overlooking the courtyard, he took a list of names from his pocket. And without looking at any of the prisoners, began to call out names in a loud voice, starting with 'Globocnik'.

On hearing this, the man himself moved his head slightly, but perceptibly, to the right while he was walking. Ramsay and the British lieutenant who had accompanied him up to the Moslacher-Alm noticed this, and called the German over immediately. An SS informer was standing with the group of British officers and NCOs:

> The SS informer insisted he was Globocnik. Major Ramsay and I decided that he (Ramsay) should sharply shout out the name 'Globocnik' while I watched the captive's reaction very closely. Then the name was called, and Globocnik's step never faltered, but his head moved fractionally. I shouted to him (in German) 'you have given yourself away, you moved your head very slightly' and ordered (Provost Sergeant) Sowler to add him to the gang in the lock-up. I then started to go to my room to have a bath only to hear shouts of 'he's dead, he's dying'. I ran downstairs to find Globocnik lying on the ground between the castle yard and the lock-up. He had held his suicide capsule under his tongue continually since his arrest and until using it about 11.25am.
>
> We had noticed at the time that he refused any form of food or drink. Captain M.M. Leigh RAMC, the Regimental Medical Officer, was quickly

> on the scene and he gave Globocnik two inoculations in the arm and one in the heart, but to no avail.
>
> As soon as they saw his corpse (SS-Sturmbannführers) Lerch, Hofle, Michaelsen and Helletsberger, who had denied their identities, admitted who they were and identified the corpse as their former commanding officer Globocnik. Rainer also identified the corpse as Globocnik.[9]

The British buried his corpse in a grave in a small field, on unconsecrated land. They asked the local priest to bury it in Paternion churchyard, but he refused, so the corpse was put in a hole dug near an outside wall of the cemetery.* As the British did not know about the horde of stolen property that he had brought from Austria, they hadn't asked him nor his four SS colleagues about it. Who knew that less than a few miles away, millions of pounds, dollars and Swiss francs-worth of treasure had just been buried.

* Since Globocnik's death, conspiracy theories have circulated, including one that the British turned him over to the American Counter Intelligence Corps. But all parties present at his capture and death – British Army officers and NCOs, and at least three SS majors, colleagues of Globocnik's – have made clear and unambiguous statements about physically watching him die.

14

A New Enemy for the Allies, June 1945

In the first week of June 1945, the Allies agreed to divide Germany into four different zones of control: British, American, French and Russian. The war in Europe was finally over, but in the Pacific fighting continued. The Americans were in fierce combat on the island of Okinawa, and the Australians were trying to defeat the last Japanese outposts on New Guinea. Close to the Japanese mainland, the American fleet was under aerial attack from aircraft flown by *kamikaze* pilots. Churchill and Truman knew how necessary it was to win Stalin's support in the war against Japan, in case of a land invasion of the country. US military planners had estimated this could cost hundreds of thousands of American lives, as both Japanese soldiers and civilians defended their homeland to the death. So Edward Stettinius urged Truman to try to minimise any further form of confrontation, diplomatic or military, with Russia.

On the ground in southern Europe the atmosphere between Russian and British troops who had met in May at Voitsberg, outside Graz in Austria, was friendly and mutually sympathetic. The soldiers who had fought the war were jubilant and relieved that it had come to an end. But diplomatic and strategic confrontation between the Allies and Russia was escalating by the day over the situation in Poland, and neither side needed Marshal Tito and his soldiers to further inflame tensions in Europe. Unfortunately, Tito was in an increasingly confrontational mood. His partisans and soldiers were still inside Austria, despite repeated calls from Field Marshal Alexander for them to withdraw.

By 10 June, the Morgan Line dividing Trieste had been in place for nearly three weeks. The best the Allies could say was that neither they nor the Yugoslavs had started shooting at each other. OZNA was continuing its operations back and forth across the dividing line, hunting its enemies. The atmosphere in the city was one of incredibly fragile compromise. So with the stage set for confrontation between the Western Allies and the Yugoslavs, with Russia closely involved by proxy, the future geo-political shape of southern Europe was being decided. How, wondered the Russians, Americans and British, would it be settled? By negotiation or by armed force?

They all knew that much would depend on the duplicitous and unpredictable Tito. The uncertain fate of all the assorted Croat and Serb and Slovenian militias, soldiers and civilians after the repatriations at Bleiburg had provided further evidence of this. So by the first half of June, Stalin was also concerned that Tito would try a pre-emptive land-grab into the Allied sector of Trieste. Stettinius and the American chiefs of staff were adamant there would be no shots fired between US troops and Yugoslavs. But they were determined to stand absolutely firm over Allied control of the port, and access routes into Austria. Communist influence would stop firmly at the exact point where stood the most westerly placed communist military boot. In Trieste, that meant on the Morgan Line. Italy would not be allowed to fall under any form of communist political control or influence. Churchill did not trust Stalin's intentions. Not just towards Poland, but to the rest of Europe. So in total secrecy, he was making contingency plans for a massive military strike against the Soviet Union. It was the worst-case scenario. Codenamed 'Operation *Unthinkable*', it highlighted the city of Trieste and the region of the Friuli Venezia Giulia as one of

Europe's most volatile flashpoints. The response of American planners to the operational draft was the same: they thought armed conflict with the Russians could break out there.

OPERATION *UNTHINKABLE* AND TRIESTE

In June, Churchill was still the British Prime Minister. There would be a general election in Great Britain in July. The end of the war was one of his many moments of triumph, and as the leader who had taken Great Britain through its 'darkest hour' he was a national hero.

But the British were exhausted of war. One of the most prolific diarists of the Second World War in Britain was a Lancashire woman called Nella Last. She lived in the shipbuilding town of Barrow-in-Furness, and recorded her daily life from 1939 onwards for the Mass Observation Archive. This was a social research project where thousands of normal people wrote about their daily lives. Last wrote two million words during the Second World War alone. Her entry before VE Day was prescient about the coming Cold War:

> All across the nation people turned on the wireless to find out more. People were out on the streets, hanging bunting and banners and dancing. All the shops had got their rosettes and tri-coloured button-holes in the windows and men putting up lengths of little pennants and flags. Till at three o'clock, the Germans announced it was all over. As if by magic, long ladders appeared, for putting up flags and streamers. A complete stranger to the situation could have felt the tenseness and feeling of expectation. Like myself, Steve [Howson, a wartime friend] has a real fear of Russia. He thinks in, say, 20 years or so, when Nazism has finally gone, Germany and not Russia will be our Allies.[1]

Churchill agreed with Steve Howson, but thought the change in allies would take far less time to materialise. The outgoing Prime Minister himself found that the new peace, which had cost so much in terms of human life, brought with it another enormous threat. Aggressive

Russian expansionism. Russia was now significantly more powerful after the surrender of Germany. At the Yalta Conference Stalin had made a series of promises about Poland which he had since broken. What would he do next? At the beginning of June, one of the Bulgarian Prime Minister's secretaries was arrested by the NKVD and tortured. MI6 reported the incident and Churchill was incensed.

> Wherever these Bolsheviks think you are afraid of them they will do whatever suits their lust and cruelty. But the Soviet Government has no wish to come out into the world smeared with such tales. Let them behave, and obey the ordinary decencies of civilisation.[2]

The continuing war in the Pacific was absorbing huge amounts of American lives and money. It showed no sign of ending without an invasion of the Japanese mainland. Churchill was very concerned that the United States might not remain strategically and politically committed to the post-war future of Europe. If they pulled their armies out, leaving the continent's security to the British, Churchill feared the Russians might try to invade parts of it. So he instructed his chiefs of staff to come up with a plan. He codenamed it 'Operation *Unthinkable*'.

'Russia – Threat to Western Civilisation' was the title of the War Cabinet File that contained the plan. The British War Cabinet Joint Planning Staff dated it 22 May, 8 June, 11 July 1945.[3] It was a plan to attack the Red Army in Poland, Germany and across central Europe if the Russians didn't stand by their agreements about Poland. And if the Americans decided to pull out of Europe, leaving the British exposed and vulnerable. It was the plan for the definitive pre-emptive strike. The most controversial aspect of the plan was that Britain and its allies would co-opt up to 100,000 of the remaining German forces onto their side in the attack:

> Great Britain and the United States have full assistance from the Polish Armed Forces and can count upon the use of German manpower and what remains of German industrial capacity. The date for the opening of

> hostilities is 1st July 1945. The overall or political object is to impose upon Russia the will of the United States and the British Empire. 'The will' of these two countries may be defined as no more than a square deal for Poland, that does not necessarily limit the military commitment. A quick success might induce the Russians to submit to our will at least for the time being – but it might not. If they want total war they are in a position to have it.

The British envisioned a first strike of enormous strength, designed to cripple the Red Armies:

> The only way in which we can achieve our object with certainty and lasting results is by victory in a total war ... apart from the chances of revolution in the USSR and the collapse of the present regime, the elimination of Russia could only be achieved as a result of ... the occupation of such areas of metropolitan Russia that the war-making capacity of the country would be reduced to a point at which further resistance became impossible.

Churchill, understandably, was adamant that the report be kept totally secret, and so only a very small group of generals, admirals and experts in the Cabinet War Office knew about it – twenty people in all. On 8 June, the British chiefs of staff said to Churchill that 'the less put on paper on this subject the better'.

To get round the problem of Russia's vast manpower the Allies would need the resources of the US and the enormously controversial reorganisation and re-equipping of the German armed forces, some 100,000 of them in the first instance. 'The defeat of Russia in a total war would be necessary ... to win it would take us a very long time. We must envisage a world-wide struggle.'

The Red Army was going to be the most formidable foe for the Allies. Its submarines and bombers could not inflict damage on Britain as the Germans had done. But the Russians could occupy Norway up to Trondheim, down to Turkey, and close the Black Sea, with south-eastern Europe the worst hit in terms of a major disruption for Britain's influence and commerce. There was a possibility that they would also lose the Iraqi and Persian oilfields, a major supplier of fuel oil. The Russians had eleven divisions deployed in the region, opposite three different Indian brigade groups deployed by the Allies. But the British didn't think the Russians would go as far as India or Egypt. Instead they would ally with Japan, which would attack China again, and there would be stalemate in the Far East.

The principal theatre of war would be central Europe with probable confrontation in Persia. The Royal Navy and Royal Air Force would have a distinct superiority over Russia at air and sea, and would allow them to control the Baltic. The launching of an offensive against the Russians is described in characteristically understated terms – 'a hazardous undertaking'. The Allies would deploy forty-seven infantry divisions, of which fourteen were armoured, against 170 Russian ones, of which thirty were tank units. The war would be fought in central Europe. There'd be an aggressive reaction from Yugoslavia; the Russians would attack Austria, and the Allies would defend it from Italy and the region on the Italian–Yugoslav border. The Czechs would support the Russians, sabotage in Europe was to be expected by communists, and Trieste would be on the front lines. In the middle of this worldwide strategic upheaval, the Allies would desperately need a port on the Adriatic, and, again, this would be Trieste.

One of the more obviously contentious parts of the plan was to re-equip German units to fight on the Allied side: ten divisions, around 75,000 men, would make up the first contingent of Axis troops to fight alongside British, American and Commonwealth soldiers. The German Heer and the SS had been cut to pieces on the Eastern Front. But not in Italy and Austria. Many of the German soldiers required to fill these first ten divisions would come from units who had surrendered in those two countries. A large detachment of them would be stationed around Trieste, helping the Allies secure the port and communications and supply lines to the southern front in Austria. World War II was over by only a few weeks, and already

Churchill envisaged, even in strategically hypothetical terms, turning former enemies into new allies and vice-versa.

The main aim of the plan was 'total war' against the Soviet Union, designed to cripple the country militarily once and for all. Above all, the Allies wanted 'one great engagement'. But they realised that up against estimates of six million Russian troops and 600,000 NKVD personnel in Europe this would be difficult, and that a longer lasting 'total war' would be the result. However, with the Russians, discipline and drunkenness were a huge problem, and this would worsen with a new war. The British and Americans would cut off all supplies to Russia, including the estimated 50 per cent of aviation fuel the Soviet Union got from the Allies: this would cripple their air capacity unless they could occupy Persian and Iraqi oilfields. 'We should be committed to a protracted war against heavy odds – the odds would become fanciful if the Americans withdrew, distracted by the Pacific.'

The document was signed by Admiral Sir Andrew Cunningham, who was First Sea Lord, General Sir Alan Brooke, Chief of the Imperial General Staff, and Air Chief Marshal Sir Douglas Evill. Churchill's reply to the three on 9 June, having looked at their assessment, was that he had had a study made about 'how we could defend our islands if the Americans move to the Pacific and US, this remains a precautionary study of what, I hope, is still a purely hypothetical contingency.'

General Sir Alan Brooke, Chief of the Imperial General Staff, had one reaction when he looked at the planned attack on the Soviet Union: 'Oh dear, Winston gives me the feeling of already longing for another war,' he noted in his diary.[5]

The Chief of the British Joint Staff Mission in Washington was Sir Henry Maitland Wilson, who had previously commanded Allied forces in the Mediterranean. He had lunch with his American counterparts, to gauge their response to the plans for Operation *Unthinkable*. Their answer was simple. They identified the area around Trieste and the Venezia Giulia as the most dangerous flashpoint in Europe. It had the capacity, they said, to be the site of new general conflict in Europe, with Russia as the main aggressor.

THE ALLIES ESTABLISH A GOVERNMENT IN TRIESTE

The Allies' policy towards Trieste was now clearly dictated by two strategic and operational threats. One was present and real, with Tito and his unknown intentions constituting the main opposition. The second was based on hypothesis about the very near future, centred on the contingency planning of Operation *Unthinkable*. So the Allies had to maintain a credible, real, and effective deterrent against Tito, and they had to use their intelligence networks to try to work out what he might be going to do. They had to control the port of Trieste, and the roads to Austria. They had to keep the fragile peace while being instantly ready for a new war with new enemies and new allies. They had to mould and maintain the dominant political establishment in north-eastern Italy to their benefit and Tito's detriment. They had to disarm and demobilise the vast partisan infrastructure, and not back down for one second in the face of Stalin and Tito. They had to be ready to fight to keep the peace.

Almost all of the main city of Trieste, and all of the crucial port and the strategic roads leading north to Austria, were fair-square in the Allied sector. The Morgan Line made no allowances for the fact that a large percentage of Trieste's population was Slovenian, nor that tens of thousands of Italians caught on the Yugoslav side of the line now had become displaced persons. They had begun to return to live on the Italian–Allied side as *de facto* refugees. Some were even accommodated in the ghostly cells and corridors of the old San Sabba camp. Both Italians and Yugoslavs were desperate that when the final geographical reckoning was made, Trieste should be in their respective country.

The Allies had established provisional and temporary military authority across the rest of Italy: like Germany, the country was run by an Allied Military Government for Occupied Territories. Germany was divided amongst British, Russian, American and French zones of control. Italy was run by the British and Americans only, under one single Allied Control Commission. Following the establishment of the Morgan Line, Field Marshal Alexander decided that the Allied-controlled part of Trieste should follow suit, and have its own separate Allied Military Government. 'In as much as the basic law of the area is and must continue to be Italian,' he wrote, 'the Italian administrative system must in its essentials be continued.'[5]

This meant that thousands of Slovenians and Croats in Trieste would be governed by Italians, overseen by the British and Americans. The Council for the Liberation of Northern Italy, the Comitato di Liberazione Nazionale Alta Italia or CLNAI, was the umbrella body of Italian partisan groups that the Allies had supported after their armistice with the Italians in 1943. By June 1945 they had become the political forum with which the Allies consulted over decisions regarding their administration of northern Italy. It was made up of representatives of each political party, almost all of whom had fought as partisans. There were Communists, Catholics, Christian Democrats, Social Democrats, Liberals and the Action Party. They disagreed constantly. The Allies' main priority was to keep the influence of the Communists to a minimum.

The main priority of each Italian faction was accessing political power, and maintaining it until such time as the Allies would inevitably depart. In practice, this meant that the Italians said one thing to the Allies, and consistently did another. Italy was, by June 1945, at peace, in as much as there was an absence of fighting. The one place where all sides feared that fighting could break out was of course Trieste. Compared to the rest of Italy, starving, half-destroyed and economically bankrupt though it was, Trieste was a live hand-grenade with the pin pulled out. Only the Allies holding the lever safely in place prevented it exploding.

The CLNAI had an immediate priority. That local government administrators in Trieste be chosen by them, from cadres of political appointees who had fought against the Germans and Italian Fascists, and were naturally sympathetic to the Allied aims. Before announcing the formation of the Allied Military Government (AMG), and the officials who would run it, the British and Americans told the CLNAI their intentions at a meeting in early June. Regardless of which side they had fought on or been allied with – Allied, German, Yugoslav or Italian Fascist – local municipal administrators would re-take positions they had occupied before the war. So parts of Trieste and surrounding territory that had been overseen by Fascist municipal counsellors before the 1943 Armistice would in some cases see them returned to power.[6] As a counter-balance the Allies also planned to establish a 'Purge Commission' which gave them and the citizens of Trieste and its surroundings the power and ability to vet and investigate any clear abuses of this plan. They were to receive thousands of cases to examine.

The CLNAI, naturally, were astounded and horrified. To the list of problems the Americans and British had with Yugoslavs and Russians, they had now added the Italians. The Allies were staring straight across the Morgan Line at Marshal Tito and his unspecified and aggressive intentions, looking into the future at possible war with Stalin, and simultaneously managing to antagonise their former Italian allies to the maximum. They needed a good Allied governor for Trieste. From the thousands of highly capable men and women in their diplomatic and military armouries that six years of war had produced, they wanted one of the cleverest, most resourceful, toughest and most experienced. They chose an American lieutenant-colonel, who on being informed of his new appointment, had one reaction:

> We knew very little about Trieste in those days ... I had heard that Field-Marshal Alexander and Marshal Tito had, earlier in the year, had a talk about Venezia Giulia, which I knew dimly to be the portion of the pre-World War II Italy which prior to the treaty following World War I, was part of Austria.[7]

The stage was set for the imposition of Allied colonialism.

15

A New American Sheriff in Trieste, June 1945

Alfred Connor Bowman was a forty-one-year-old lawyer from Detroit, who before the war had been the Deputy City Attorney for Los Angeles. After Pearl Harbor, he was put on the list of reserve officers to be called up as needed by the Judge Advocate General's Department. The JAG was the department of the US Army that provided every possible form of legal advice to the military. It prosecuted and defended in court-martials, adjudicated in claims by the civilian population of any given country, and advised commanders on operational law. Senior JAG officers had advised Allied commanders, for instance, on the legality of the bombing of the Benedictine monastery at Monte Cassino in April 1944. JAG officers had prosecuted two American soldiers accused of the unlawful killings of seventy-three Italian and German prisoners at the Biscari airfield on Sicily in July 1943.* They had acted for and against US soldiers accused of rape, desertion and

* An American army captain and a sergeant were both charged with the unlawful killings of two different groups of seventy-three Italian and German prisoners, after the US 180th Infantry Regiment had taken the Biscari airfield in southern Sicily on 14 July, 1943. The officer was acquitted, later to be killed in action. The NCO received a sentence of life imprisonment, but the sentence was remitted four months later. The Biscari airfield killing was one of the two largest killings of German and Italian prisoners in World War II by American soldiers. The other was the execution of Waffen-SS camp guards in Dachau after it was liberated in April 1945.

theft from the Italian civilian population. They were uniformed representatives of United States military and civil law. The motto of the JAG was 'soldier first, lawyer always'.

Bowman assumed full-time active duty as a major in January 1942, attended the US School of Military Government in Charlottesville, Virginia, and left for Italy in late September 1943. He arrived via North Africa, and was posted to the main Allied Headquarters in Italy, at the Palazzo Reale at Caserta. Following the September 1943 Armistice, the Allied Commission oversaw the military government of all Italian territory then under the control of the British and the Americans. As the Allies advanced up Italy, province by province and region by region, military government followed them the moment fighting had ceased and the Germans withdrawn, been killed or taken prisoner. American and British officers like Bowman waited several stages behind the front line, ready to deploy. The enormous German defensive positions on the Gothic Line gridlocked the Allied advance from September 1944 to late March 1945. But the Allies broke through it that spring and occupied northern Italy, advancing towards Switzerland, Austria and Yugoslavia.

In September 1944 Bowman became one of the Allied military governors of the region of Emilia Romagna. This lies along the valley of the River Po, with its capital in the city of Bologna. His sector of the region was in the east and included the city of Rimini. The opening British assault on the Gothic Line in August 1944 had been directed right at it, and the city was partly in ruins. The surrounding countryside was covered with the battle-smashed hulls of British, Canadian and German tanks. Half-tracks, jeeps and lorries lay scattered across the flat plains and ridges outside Rimini. The immediate remainder of war is something created by the gods of disorder. The physical infrastructure of land – fields, earth, trees, bushes, stone, rivers – is smashed and interfered with and thrown around by high-explosive artillery shells. Splintered German half-track personnel carriers slumped broken on dirt roads; red-hot shrapnel had cut in half and beheaded the horses towing Wehrmacht artillery. Where Allied artillery or fighter bombers had hit a German convoy, great patches of dirt road were stained with gluey pools of the dried blood of dead horses. Parts of their meaty carcasses hung splattered in the lime trees by the roads. Flies buzzed and hummed in vast orchestras as they flicked and fed on the corpses that lay everywhere. Allied Sherman tanks sat by the roads in lines of three or four, destroyed or disabled by German anti-tank guns. The smell in the vineyards and fields days after battles was of hot, rural summer, of trees and grass and flowers and leaves, overlaid with cordite, petrol and smoke. On the warm breeze wafted the sweet, grilled faecal smell of decaying flesh. Battle is anything but tidy.

Hardly, though, had the Allied tanks, artillery and infantry stopped firing, and moved forward to the next battle, than military–civilian administrators like Bowman arrived. They were there to set up, administer and oversee *ad hoc* governments that ran every aspect of the lives of the Italian civilians and Allied troops in the zones under their control. The lawyer from Michigan proved adept at this. He was good at administering some form of rule-of-law and infrastructural management to a politically divided, heavily armed, and constantly disagreeing network of partisan–politicians. Sometimes only days after the last battles had finished. Bowman's administrative mantra was simple: 'preventing disease and unrest, in short to maintain the status quo, or something close to it. Until the fate of the territory can be determined.'[1]

As well as governing territory occupied by Allied soldiers, the military–civilian administration had to look after and manage the civil and political affairs of the civilian population. In autumn 1944 in north-eastern Italy, civilians were frequently starving, always frightened, often wounded, sick and displaced from their homes, which all too often were destroyed by the retreating Germans, or in many cases by Allied bombing and artillery bombardments.

Three Americans and two Britons governed northern Italy for the Allied Commission based in Rome. On the Mediterranean coast west of Genoa, a British brigadier ran the region of Liguria. Piemonte, with its capital in Turin, was the fiefdom of a former businessman from New York. Around Milan, an ex-governor of New York City ran the region of Lombardy. Venice and its environs was under the jurisdiction of another British brigadier. Bowman ran the AMG in the Rimini province of the Emilia Romagna region. The key area in question was that dubbed 'Italia Irredenta', Italy Unredeemed. The land of the Venezia Giulia given to Italy after its service and sacrifice in the First World War, which it saw as rightfully its own.

The AMG in each region would normally comprise 125–150 British and American officers, and another 150 NCOs and other ranks. The respective military governments in each region reported to the senior civil affairs officer at the Allied Commission in Rome, who was an American admiral. Bowman and his co-governors were dubbed 'The Barons of the North' by colleagues. Bowman later wrote:

> The exercise of power by military government is virtually unlimited. The persons governed have no rights as that word is understood under any of the constitutional systems of western countries. The only restraints on the man who holds the job ... are those imposed by military government or superiors.[2]

Because the partisans and hence politicians in Emilia Romagna were predominantly communist, the region's capital in Bologna was nick-named 'the Kremlin of Italy'.

In Rimini, the AMG's headquarters was in a large villa by the sea, in the suburb of Riccione. It was the former headquarters of Field Marshal Albert Kesselring, the supreme German commander in Italy. Rimini was a popular seaside resort, and in the weeks after its liberation in September 1944, it had quickly tried to rebuild itself and revert to its former maritime glory. It was a hard job. Each morning a queue of Italian civilians would form around 6am outside the military government's main office in the town. We don't have any coal and my baby is freezing, would say the first housewife in the queue. The Germans took my husband as a hostage because he was a partisan, and I don't know where he is, said another. There's an SS officer and two men hiding in the church crypt in this or that village, they burned our houses down and shot my son. Soldiers from the Himalayas stole my donkey. Greek infantrymen told us to come here to ask for penicillin. Can we have some soap, petrol, electricity and food? Is it permissible for my two small sons to help the American soldiers on the nearby airfield peel their potatoes in return for scraps of food? The neighbour of the mayor in our village is obviously working as a prostitute – we've known it for years. She smiles at the Canadian soldiers. The list was endless. And every day Bowman and his combined military and civilian staff had to deal with the requests and the complaints, while trying to govern an entire Italian province.[3]

Although winter on the Adriatic was a far cry from its summer warmth, Bowman's British deputy tried to take advantage of the sporting opportunities to be had. Major Percival Hubert Graham Horton-Smith-Hartley was a former housemaster at Eton who had been commissioned into the Coldstream Guards on the outbreak of war. He had rowed for his college at Cambridge. Each morning he liked to go and bathe in the Adriatic, 'and he used to swim east out of sight every day,' remembered Bowman.[4] One day even he discovered the sea was too cold, and when asked by Bowman why he wasn't swimming that day, answered, 'Colonel, I started to, but found that the pain would have exceeded the pleasure.'

Bowman was awarded the US Legion of Merit for 'exceptionally meritorious conduct' in execution of his duties both at Caserta and in Emilia Romagna, and promoted from major to lieutenant-colonel. Winter 1944 became the spring of 1945, itself the last season of war. The spring sun was about to shine on new days of liberation and peace, when Bowman heard about his new posting. On 10 April he and the other 'Barons of the North' travelled to Florence. They went to meet senior American commanders including General Mark Clark, then commanding the 15th Army Group, which comprised all Allied forces in Italy. The trip was a chance for the governors not just to meet the senior Allied generalship, but also to enjoy a social day out in Florence and the Tuscan city of Lucca, and then to return to Rome. The war had less than a month to run, but an incident that night in Rome reminded Bowman how tenuous was the security situation in Allied-occupied Italy. His executive officer, an American, was returning from a night at the Allied officers' club. He climbed into a taxi to take him back to headquarters. For an unspecified reason, an invisible gunman in the rear seat shot him in the back of the neck.*

The Acting President of the Allied Commission was the British politician and government minister Harold Macmillan. He visited Rimini on 21 April for a staff meeting. He invited Bowman to accompany him to Bologna the following day for another, larger meeting, and to brief the American lawyer about the details of his next posting. Bowman met the English minister early the following morning in the town of Forli and they climbed into his Willis jeep. So they could talk face to face, Macmillan insisted that both of them sat in the small metal seats in the rear of the four-wheel drive vehicle. This required both men to sit with their knees under their chins, holding on as tightly as possible to metal handles and the edge of the tailgate to avoid falling out. Macmillan was wearing a large tweed hunting coat, Bowman tired and worn-out military fatigues. As the jeep swerved and splashed through roads of spring mud and endless Allied convoys, Macmillan told Bowman how worried he and other senior Allied officials were about another city, one Bowman didn't know much about, in a region he'd only dimly heard of. Trieste.

Travelling to Bologna that April, Bowman tried to listen as hard as possible to the moustachioed British aristocrat. It was difficult – the small vehicle was constantly bumping onto the verge of the road to overtake slow lorries filled with troops or supplies heading for the capital of Emilia Romagna. Mud leapt into the air from deep puddles. The suspension under the metal seats bounced the two men in the air. American and Indian and Polish soldiers marching down the sides of the road smiled and waved at them. The soldiers' eyes were tired, the men smoking, mud splashed up to their knees, Bren guns and Browning Automatic Rifles balanced on their marching shoulders as the formation line swayed

* He survived.

forward to another battle. The Allies were at that moment in the middle of the fight for Bologna, the crucial central hinge of the Gothic Line. Within hours they would be rushing forward onto the flatlands in the valley of the River Po.

The Friuli Venezia Giulia, said Macmillan, was more than just a piece of territory to the Italians – it was a badge of honour, a sort of Mecca and Holy Grail. The Italians had sacrificed over half a million lives for this piece of territory in battles on the River Isonzo in the First World War. The *ad hoc* briefing in the jeep continued, slightly vague and unspecific about what had happened in Trieste for the preceding two months, and when Bowman wrote that the 'port of Trieste wasn't worth a nickel or a dime to both sides (Italians or Yugoslavs)' he feared he was in danger of missing the strategic point. It mattered to the Allies, and they didn't want the Yugoslavs or Russians there. And that was why he was speeding bumpily along roads clogged with refugees, displaced people, Allied soldiers, returning Italian POWs and civilians trying to restore their life to some semblance of order.

The cleaners at the City Hall in Bologna had not yet wiped the blood off the walls in the lobby when Bowman and Macmillan walked in a few hours later. The bodies of two well-known partisans were lying in coffins in the centre of the huge entrance, surrounded by bouquets of flowers. It was their blood that was sprayed up the walls. Just before they fled two days earlier, Italian fascist troops had executed them in the hall of the building. Within hours Bowman was told that he was temporarily posted as an assistant governor in Bologna, pending his later posting to Trieste.

In those two months his job was identical to that in Rimini, except that he was in a bigger city with bigger politics. The municipal counsel, the partisan leaders, the leading politicians in Bologna were all communists. Bowman's superiors in Caserta and Rome were adamant that he and his colleagues from the AMG should do everything in their power to prevent the return to any form of any political power of anybody who was a communist. Bowman disagreed. His argument was that if the Allies were going to promote supposedly fair and democratic government that was the diametric opposite of Mussolini's

Fascism or Stalin's communism, they had to let the Italian population choose for themselves. There was a world of difference, he argued, between mainstream Moscow-style communism, and a broader left-wing socialism that preferred to be described as 'communist' simply to differentiate it from Fascism.

Reminders of the fighting were everywhere. Bowman noticed in Bologna that on the outside of the town hall where he had his office, there was a red and white flag, the national banner of Poland. The first troops into Bologna in April 1945 had been from that country. On arrival in the city, one of their soldiers had found an Italian flag, with its vertical green, white and red stripes. Tearing off the green portion of the flag he had then turned it horizontally, producing an *ad hoc* Polish national symbol.

While based in Bologna, Bowman bought a shiny Buick sedan from an Italian who had kept it hidden from the Germans under a haystack. The shiny, new American vehicle was fast, and swung like a galleon in a gale when overtaking; its body was also set low on its wheels, making it completely unsuitable for muddy, pot-holed Italian roads. But Bowman loved it.

So, on the afternoon of 4 July, with two suitcases and a rucksack in the car's boot, a holstered Colt .45 automatic pistol on the seat beside him, and a head full of scrambled information about Trieste, Lieutenant-Colonel Alfred Connor Bowman drove north-east. Around dusk he saw Trieste for the first time. He drove round the headland on which the Castello di Miramare was built, and headed down the coast road. It is the point at which travellers arriving by road or train get their first proper view of the city, its port, and the bay on which it sits.

'Trieste is fairyland,' he wrote in his diary about the moment he rounded the headland. 'The stuff dreams are made of. It is possible at that moment to imagine that everyone living in such a place would be so happy to be there, that he would be filled with love for his neighbour, and all about him.'

Part Five

WAR IN THE SHADOWS

16

Hidden Conflict, July 1945

It was 16 July, and Bowman had been in Trieste for twelve days. He was giving a press conference. He was trying to explain what the Allies had done in Trieste since their arrival two-and-a-half months before.[1] It was hard to realize, he said, but Tito had marched into Trieste and taken possession of it, and then continued right on to the Isonzo river. The British and New Zealand troops went into Trieste as well, but the Yugoslavs were allowed to maintain administrative control for forty days. He explained about the Morgan Line, and the different contingents of troops, both Allied and Yugoslav, and where they were stationed, and how.

In the audience in front of him were at least twenty foreign newspaper and radio correspondents. They had been flown in especially for the press conference, on a Dakota DC-3 arranged by the Allied Commission in Rome.[2] There were another twenty Italian and Slovenian journalists too. Bowman was impressed to see that in the audience in front of him were not just C. L. 'Cy' Sulzberger from the *New York Times*, but also the well-known Phil Hamburger from the *New Yorker* magazine. Bowman was wearing sunglasses. His residence was now at the Villa Ina, a large house on the Via Romagna overlooking the city, with one of the best views across Trieste and the Adriatic. There were three floors, and one of the bedrooms was equipped as a gym. There was a sunlamp in it, and Bowman had been trying it out. Unfamiliar with its dials and settings, he had overdone the UV rays and burned the edge of one of his corneas. The result was not only painful, but required him to wear what he called 'smoked glasses' almost all the time. To the Italians, Slovenians and Croatians, not to mention the run-of-the-mill Allied soldiers, the glasses did nothing to lessen their curiosity about this strange civilian–military hybrid who had come to govern them.

Meanwhile the foreign correspondents had a pressing question. What, they wanted to know, were the Allies doing about communists in Trieste? Bowman issued the line that Allied Headquarters wanted him to stress at every opportunity, about the creation of the Allied Military Government, and his position within it. He then continued to brief the journalists about the laws that were now in effect in Trieste and the Venezia Giulia: essentially they were the same as the Italian Constitutional System in effect since the end of the First World War, with some additions made by Mussolini's government. The arriving Yugoslavs had obviously refused to accept this, and had held their own elections on May 18th, abolishing the old forms of government. They also elected and appointed a new revolutionary government, called The Council of Liberation, which the Allied Military Government then promptly refused to recognize. The events of that morning of the press conference bore witness to this.

Dawn comes early on the Adriatic in mid-summer. So the sun was already up when American and British soldiers kicked in the doors and raided thirty-three different apartments, houses and farms across Trieste and its surrounding villages and suburbs.* Despite Allied attempts to disarm them, several different Italian and Slovenian partisan factions were still armed to the teeth and hell-bent on revenge. Ten weeks after the end of the war, when it came to ensuring their security, neither side trusted the Allies an inch. There had been a variety of posters pasted up around the city, Allied soldiers were

* The arrests were widely reported, including by the Associated Press in London on 17 July 1945.

patrolling everywhere, and messages broadcast on the AMG radio network told all parts of the local population that security and peace had come to stay. Nobody believed it. In Trieste that summer, the language of revenge was spoken in the vocabulary of the night, when Allied soldiers were almost all in their barracks, a curfew in force. Following three partially successful operations to disarm partisan groups, the AMG had decided that possession of weapons was now a criminal offence, and had passed a bylaw to this effect. Amid this seething city, the Allies then made a huge blunder.

One of the people they arrested that morning was a popular Trieste figure, an Italian communist leader called Giorgio Jaksetic. He was the editor of the communist newspaper *Il Lavoratore*, 'The Worker'. During the forty-day Yugoslav occupation of the city he had been an assistant chief of staff to one of the Yugoslav Army chiefs of staff, despite the fact that he claimed that he had never visited Yugoslavia. When the Military Police from the 56th London Division burst into his apartment with Sten guns at their shoulder, they couldn't at first find him. Then they heard noises coming from the bedroom. Jaksetic was there with his girlfriend. Things had reached a crucial and sensitive point in the bed when the British soldiers kicked open the door. The naked couple were on the bed, clothes scattered across the floor. A handgun was lying next to them. It was enough for the MPs. They pulled Jaksetic off the bed, his girlfriend tried to cover herself with a sheet, they told him why he was being arrested, allowed him to get dressed, then handcuffed him. All he said was: 'I was *in orgasmo,* so of course I was in no position to know whether the gun on the floor was mine.'*

The Allies told international, Italian and Slovenian journalists that they had captured a dangerous Slovene communist rebel: Jaksetic was appalled. As was much of Trieste, regardless of ethnicity or nationality. He was from Trieste, had never visited Yugoslavia, didn't speak Slovenian, and was totally Italian. The Allies had just started alienating themselves from both sides.

* The transcripts, documentation on, and court reports of the trial of Giorgio Jaksetic held in the IRSML in Trieste extend to over 2,000 pages.

And Yugoslavia's *de facto* dictator had scored another victory. For in his newspaper editorials, Jaksetic had made a huge enemy. Marshal Josip Broz Tito. The journalist had argued that Moscow should be the ones to negotiate with the Allies over the future of Trieste and the Venezia Giulia. The future of Europe was a huge, vital matter to be decided by the Great Powers. Not by the Yugoslavs. As an Italian of Slovenian ancestry, albeit a communist, his forebears and intellectual standing in Trieste were the antithesis of what Tito and his militaristic proletarianism stood for. Jaksetic's message in his editorials had been clear. Moscow's communism is the real thing; Tito's is just village moonshine. So OZNA were given the job of getting the wrong information to the right people. Ten days later the newspaper editor was in an Allied cell at the Coroneo prison. The blood on the walls and the sweaty fear hanging in the summer air had hardly had time to dry or dissipate since Odilo Globocnik's SS men had left in a hurry ten weeks earlier.

Two weeks into his tour of duty in Trieste, Bowman realised that the media were going to be his ally, his enemy and a petard by which he constantly risked hanging himself. He noted repeatedly in his diary about this: 'Throughout my incumbency ... the local and international press, day to day, week to week, year to year was possibly the most powerful single force I had to deal with.'[3]

Because the American, British and Commonwealth military was largely blind to, and ignorant of the revenge killings, kidnappings, assassinations and routine violence taking place yards from their barracks, then so by extension were Bowman and his governmental headquarters staff. He relied upon his assistants, chiefs of staff and military liaison officers with both the British and American divisions to keep him informed. Without them he knew nothing about the ebb and flow of violence taking place in the city streets that lay below the gardens of the Villa Ina. And if they knew nothing, then neither did he. In an eight-month period when people of four different nationalities – Yugoslav, Italian, German and Austrian – disappeared and were killed in the most sudden and violent ways on a daily basis under the Allies' noses, in their operational area of responsibility, Bowman absolved the Allies' collective ignorance thus. He described the summer of 1945 as 'relatively peaceful' and said that 'virtually every murder when thoroughly investigated ... proved to be motivated by love, hate, greed, jealousy or one of the other deadly sins than by political considerations'.[4] Bowman was about to learn that when it came to anything to do with the Balkans, the seven deadly sins, ethnicity, revenge and political considerations were all the same.

The arrest of Giorgio Jaksetic was the first incident that caused the Allies to be seen as overbearing occupiers rather than enlightened liberators. A much larger problem was that of missing persons, and what to do with the thousands of refugees, deportees, prisoners of war and Holocaust survivors who were now pouring back into the city. The Allied government had by now made a list of around 3,000 people.[5] Those who had allegedly been forcibly disappeared or gone missing from their homes or elsewhere since the Germans had arrived in 1943. This had taken a considerable amount of effort. But given that it was likely that more than this number had gone missing during the 'Forty Days of Trieste' alone, the Allied investigators had only touched the surface. And both sides, in Zone A and Zone B, Italians and Yugoslavs, saw this immediately. Everybody knew that an accurate estimate of missing persons was completely dependent on relatives or friends reporting an individual's fate. But problems started when a family or person with a missing relative went to the AMG headquarters. These were now located at the former Fascist police headquarters at Casa del Popolo, and were always a stressful location to visit. This was because the perpetrators of the murder or disappearance in question had probably been based in or used this building. And because the missing person might well have spent some of their last days in the building's basement cells.

The Allied investigators were a mix of military policemen and civilian staff officers working for their *ad hoc* government. As the AMG was firmly forbidden by its headquarters in Rome and Caserta from doing anything more than 'administering and governing Trieste', the problem of missing persons was deemed to be a political one, and therefore not to be handled by Bowman and his teams. Having gone to the considerable, highly laudable, and contentious effort of compiling the list of 3,000, the staff in Trieste had to pass it upwards to Rome. They couldn't take substantive investigative action themselves. So all the personnel in the lumpen former police building could do was tell the distraught relative that their individual case was being dealt with by higher authorities. It did nothing to inspire confidence in the Allied authorities at all. 'Our inability to act positively or produce concrete results caused much disillusionment among the local people and cost us considerable loss of credit,' Bowman later wrote.[6]

In the middle of July 1945, a group of British and American military agents from the Field Security Sections and Counter Intelligence Corps drove to the top of the mountain above Trieste to the village of Basovizza. They conducted interviews with the two priests who had witnessed the killings on 3 May, both of whom received exactly the same description in subsequent reports. 'Fanatically pro-Slav,' and 'bitterly anti-Italian' summed up their passionate lack of objectivity. They talked to villagers. From interviewing German POWs at the wire cage that sat westwards down the coast at Sistiana, the MPs had a very rough idea of how many Germans could have been taken prisoner by the Yugoslavs when they occupied the city. The floor of the Basovizza mineshaft was described as comprising a bottom layer of Gestapo officers, with Italian Questura officials on top of it. Both were decomposing so rapidly in the summer heat as to be almost unrecognisable without proper laboratory or forensic equipment. This British and American visit, and the rough assessment report of the number of missing persons forwarded to Allied Commission Headquarters in Rome and Caserta, was to be the sum total of the efforts made by the AMG and Allied forces to deal with the question of missing persons in Trieste up until September 1945.

The British in particular were keen to appear politically even-handed to all sides in Zone A. They also wanted to maintain as much sympathy as possible among the Yugoslav soldiers and partisans whom

An Italian anti-communist protester is arrested by a British Army officer, and an Italian officer of the local Trieste Police Force, dressed in British uniform, 1952. (Photo by Hulton-Deutsch/Hulton-Deutsch Collection/Corbis via Getty Images)

Two men in the all-Slovenian village of Smarje, in Zone B outside Trieste, May 1952. (Photo by Archivio Cameraphoto Epoche/Getty Images)

An American soldier kisses goodbye to his Italian girlfriend, Trieste 1953. (Bettmann/Getty Images)

Communist politician Vittorio Vidali seated underneath a portrait of Stalin. (Photo by Walter Sanders/The LIFE Picture Collection/Getty Images)

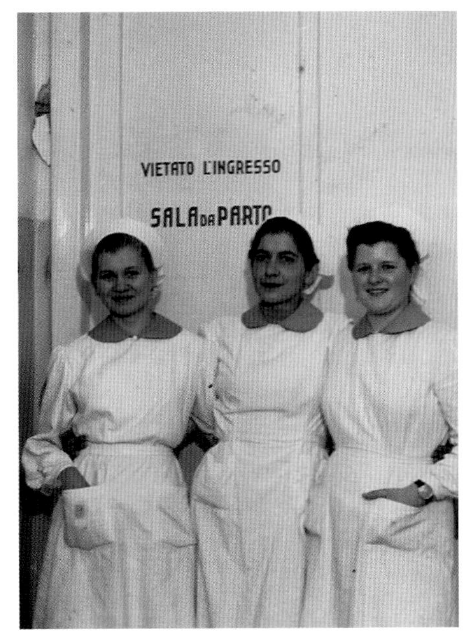

Ondina Peteani working as a midwife, Trieste 1955. (© Gianni Peteani)

Ondina Peteani and her dog, Trieste 1958. (© Gianni Peteani)

Ondina Peteani, Trieste, 1959. (© Gianni Peteani)

In September 1953 at Okroglica, Slovenia, a mother holds up a picture of her four sons, all Slovenian partisans killed by the Germans. (Photo by Archivio Cameraphoto Epoche/Getty Images)

Former SS General Karl Wolff appearing in court during a war crimes trial in Munich in July 1964. (Photo by Keystone Features/Hulton Archive/Getty Images)

President Josip Broz Tito at Buckingham Palace in November 1971 with, left to right, Princess Margaret, Queen Elizabeth II, Tito's wife Jovanka Broz, and Prince Philip. (Photo by Keystone-France/Gamma-Rapho via Getty Images)

A chapel near the entrance to the Huda Jama mine in Slovenia, where the remains of more than 700 people were found in 2009. (JURE MAKOVEC/AFP/Getty Images)

The offices of the Free Territory of Trieste organisation, Piazza della Borsa, Trieste, 2016. (Author's collection)

The city of Trieste and the Adriatic, seen from the Castello di Miramare, March 2016. (Author's collection)

Looking westwards from the Castello di Miramare, towards Monfalcone, March 2016. (Author's collection)

The Canal Grande in Trieste, March 2016. (Author's collection)

Piazza dell'Unità d'Italia, Trieste, March 2016. (Author's collection)

they had supported militarily and politically during the war. On 5 July there was a general election in Great Britain, whose results were announced on 26 July. Winston Churchill, the standing British Prime Minister, lost. A Labour government was elected, with Clement Attlee as Prime Minister. In both Russia and Yugoslavia the communist parties expected that Britain's foreign policy would swing in their favour. In and around Trieste this hope was obviously particularly strong among the various communist factions in Italy and across the Morgan Line in Zone B of Trieste. Bowman noted that:

> The number one hero of the late war was defeated and replaced by a Labour government headed by an unimpressive and unpicturesque lawyer/teacher/social worker/politician named Clement Richard Attlee. This development was ecstatically hailed by the communists, not only in our administrative zone but in Yugoslavia and the USSR, as 'the communist victory in England'. The press and all pro-Yugoslav and pro-Russian political and propaganda bodies prophesised great changes in British foreign policy. They were soon set right.

When Ernest Bevin, the new Secretary of State for Foreign Affairs, gave his inaugural speech, it was evident that Great Britain was not going to adopt any substantial policy alterations with regard to either the Soviet Union or Yugoslavia. It was business as usual, and the Russians and Yugoslavs realised that some sort of pro-communist rapprochement by Great Britain was impossible. In effect Churchill's foreign policy still stood. In the Trieste media on both sides of the divide, anti-Allied, and anti- British propaganda simply increased.

Bowman found himself caught in the middle, accused of substantial political and nationalistic bias towards both parties. One way in which both Yugoslavs and Italians explained this apparent sense of preference to the 'other side' was by claiming that Bowman's extra-professional love life was to blame. They said he was strongly influenced by an alleged mistress. Two different AMG intelligence reports from summer 1945 illustrated this:

From a pro-Italian source:

The supposed love-life of Colonel Bowman is still one of the most-discussed subjects in town. 'The Slav Mistress' has been projected into a Hungarian secretary with the additional function of a mistress, who is in reality a Slav and an OZNA agent. This would explain the alleged pro-Slav sympathies of the Colonel. The name of a Mrs. Mandic is often used as one of the Slav lovers.

From a pro-Slovenian/Slav source:

A frequent subject of conversation in Slav circles and in pro-Tito groups are claims that the Colonel has an Italian mistress of the Trieste aristocracy, and this would explain his pro-Italian and pro-reactionary attitude. The names of Cosulich and Parisi are frequently mentioned. The entire Tito group is positive that the Colonel has an Italian girlfriend named Mara, who is a SIM* agent.[7]

THE ALLIED PROPAGANDA MACHINE

The Allied Military Government decided that a dedicated press operation and positive propaganda campaign was now necessary. Its objective being to persuade the populations on both sides of the Morgan Line of the economic, political and psycho-social benefits of the AMG. And that its fundamental aim was the improvement of the general well-being of those it governed, regardless of nationality, ethnicity, political orientation or geographical location. So the AIS, the Allied Information Service, was born. It was run by British and American intelligence. An early psy-ops campaign, the AIS was set up in 1945 to 'inform, educate and supply propaganda to the local Italian and Slovenian population'. The main aim was in fact simple – to explain the perils and pitfalls of Russia, Yugoslavia, communism and Stalin. And then to extol British, American, Italian and 'western' values as being essentially beneficial to political economic growth and stability, peace and security, personal quality of life and a happy

* Servizio Informazioni Militare, the wartime Italian military intelligence branch.

future. The AIS put on films, poster displays, had a reading room and library, distributed British and American newspapers, and showed early documentaries in public viewings. Its headquarters was in an old villa overlooking the central railway station. By late summer 1945, its staff constituted around twenty-four people. They were a mixture of British and American officers and NCOs, and Italian and Slovenian staff.

The AIS' daily updates and summaries paint a picture of a Trieste under Allied government, where the incumbent occupiers are engaged in a perpetual battle of wills and influence with their more resourceful and cunning national staff. [107] The centre of the AIS' facilities at the villa was a public reading-room, made out of a large converted dining-room. Copies of *The Times* and the *Daily Express* were laid out on a table; there was a coal fire for the winter, and a fan in summer. A tea-urn dispensed well-stewed British Army Indian tea, ready-mixed with sugar and tinned condensed milk. One daily AIS summary simply notes that the Italians had a tendency to avoid the tea urn. Another says that two of the Italian female staff tend to entertain 'gentlemen visitors' in the reading-room, often on the very table where *The Times* and *Daily Express* are set out. The British newspapers go missing, replaced with Italian communist ones. The Allied government staff are buying some of their technical supplies, such as electrical generator parts, from Italian suppliers. Random over-pricing is the order of the day – the brother of one of the AIS Italian employees promises to supply a number of simple valves for a radio set. The only problem, he explains, is that they have to come from his family in Salerno, on the other side of the country. The cost will be at least 800,000 *lire,* then the rough equivalent of about $US 5,000. Are we being over-charged, wonders one American officer?

One of the AIS' aims was to help persuade the inhabitants of Trieste and the Venezia Giulia that America, Britain and the West represented a triumph of proper values and morality, and was the direct opposite of communism. To this end, a regular programme of twenty-minute films was chosen for public broadcast in Trieste and the town of Gorizia. All were British or American government-produced, and were short feature-length productions of newsreels illustrating various aspects of life in America, Great Britain and across the Empire. The head of the AIS approved the choice of films. The following was the list proposed for his approval, a month in advance, for three days in the coming winter months:

> *Piazza Della Borsa, Trieste.*
> Film 1: Penicillin (Great Britain)
> Film 2: Types of Men and Women (United States) [This portrayed the perils of prostitution and the men who took advantage of it.]
> Film 3: Rolls Royce (Great Britain)
> *Gorizia.*
> Film 1: Native Life in West Africa (Great Britain)
> Film 2: Woman, as the Artist sees her (United States and Great Britain)
> Film 3: Grimsby Trawlers (Great Britain)[9]

In the orientation lectures given to arriving Allied troops, officers issued warnings. Soldiers were told to stay away from two things which constituted 'malign influences'. These were communists, and so-called 'Bad Women'. The post-war atmosphere in Trieste had not changed noticeably by 1952, when one US soldier arrived:

> Our officers stressed the need to stay away from communists and bad women, and warned us that we might meet women who were both communists and bad. To avoid these perils we should stay away from bars and other buildings – i.e. brothels – which were marked with an 'X' in a circle and the words 'Off-Limits'.[10]

Meanwhile, the men of the 88th Division had been in heavy combat in Italy. They were nicknamed the 'Blue Devils' by the Germans because the blue quatrefoil of their shoulder patch reminded the Germans of their own SS *Totenkopf* insignia. On the Gothic Line south of Bologna in September 1944, the division had fought for, occupied and then held for seven days the strategic heights of Mount Battaglia. From the early attacks on Monte Cassino in January 1944 to the end of the war in Italy, the unit had been in action for 344 days, and taken over 15,000 casualties. By the time they got to Trieste in summer 1945, they were in the mood to meet some bad women. American soldiers found Trieste interesting and lively, but worn, and poor. The country's recovery from the war was just beginning, and the GIs watched Italians picking up cigarette butts from the streets, beg for food from Allied soldiers, and sweep the streets with brooms made out of twigs. In café bathrooms, the toilet paper was torn newspapers. The American soldier mentioned above listened to a Slovenian woman, from a village on the Karst plateau above Trieste, as she talked about the differences between German soldiers as occupiers and American soldiers as liberators:

> She compared the American soldiers she saw around her village after World War Two with the German ones who had been stationed there during the war. When Americans entered a bar or restaurant they were noisy, and might even put their feet on a chair or table. The Germans, on the other hand, though they had burned her village to the ground, had been polite. When they walked inside a restaurant they said 'hello' and hung their helmets on the coat-racks.[*11]

What American soldiers remembered about Trieste, though, was simple. The women. The city and villages around it abounded in attractive girls:

> In a tram I saw the prettiest girl I've ever seen, her hair so black that it seemed faintly tinged with blue. Of course the 'good' girls avoided us: to be seen in the company of a soldier would destroy her reputation. On one occasion when another GI and I had 'double dates' the girls insisted we take them to the movies not in Trieste but in Gorizia, so we drove there.

* The American soldier from the 88th Division worked for its unit newspaper, *The Blue Devil*, in Trieste, and married the woman in question on his return to the United States in summer 1953.

> Once X was walking with a respectable young secretary, and a woman shouted at her 'Vacca!' (Cow). And of course some of the young Americans ignored the advice the officers gave us at our orientation to avoid 'bad women'. It wasn't hard to find these girls on the streets, at bars not far from barracks, in night clubs, and in Trieste's eleven 'case di tolleranza'.[12]

ONDINA PETEANI AND POST-WAR TRIESTE

Ondina Peteani returned to Trieste in July 1945. After her deportation in March 1944, she had been taken to Auschwitz, and tattooed with the serial number 81672. Next came the women's concentration camp at Ravensbruck. As she was young, relatively healthy, and had previously been employed in a shipyard, she was made to work, instead of being gassed. Another thing kept her going as she stood in her concentration camp pyjamas: the thought that the moon she saw from her accommodation block in Auschwitz was the same one shining down on the Adriatic. In October 1944, she was transferred to a factory in Eberswalde, near Berlin. In the plant she managed to slow down the production cycle, thanks to continuous and repeated tampering with the machinery. In mid-April 1945, during a five-day forced march in a snowstorm back to Ravensbrück, Ondina escaped from the column of prisoners. She began to walk back to Italy, a roundabout journey of nearly 700 miles from Berlin to Trieste.

The roads were clogged and flooded with some of the millions of refugees from every European nationality. They'd survived the war: now they had to make it through the liberation. Her long walk home took her across the heart of central Europe. Through bombed-out towns and villages newly garrisoned by American GIs, she headed south. Her priorities? To avoid rape, capture or violence at the hands of drunken soldiers, released prisoners, vengeful Russians, resentful Germans and Austrians, partisans, anybody. Passing by farms and small villages she begged enough to eat each day. She offered to work in return for meals. She rejected offers of food in return for her body – unlike tens of thousands of women across Europe who didn't have the luxury of such choice. She spent twelve weeks on the road, and walked an estimated thousand miles, waiting for the moment when she would finally see the Adriatic.

Ondina arrived home in Trieste in late July, to a reception as a local heroine. To her astonishment, she found the Allied Military Government running her city. Their emblem was on the stamps. She was required to get a new identity card. British soldiers at the Casa Popolo headquarters asked her if she was Italian or Slovenian. The visit to the former fascist police headquarters at Casa Popolo was more ironic than painful: she and partisan colleagues from the Garibaldi Brigade had made plans to blow it up in late 1943. Other Holocaust survivors like herself had drifted like broken ghosts back to Trieste. From Mauthausen–Gusen, Dachau and Ravensbruck. Not everybody in Trieste wanted to believe their stories.Typical exaggeration, said many Italians, particularly the surviving Fascists. They'll do anything to attract attention, these people. But those who knew, those who had been anywhere near the San Sabba camp, understood and believed her. And these people were mainly all former partisans, disarmed weeks before.

They were now engaged across the board at every level in every way. From humanitarianism, to trying to get Trieste back on its feet, to local politics and crime. To the lucrative business of providing sympathetic English-speaking staff – in other words, trusted friends and relatives – to the American and British army units and government offices. Of course these people, grateful for the job, were happy to pass on any information they happened to come across in the course of their daily work. Ondina was lucky – her extended family were in Monfalcone, and her parents were still alive, and overjoyed to see her. It was high summer on the Adriatic and she was alive. And yes, the moon over the Adriatic was the same as the one that had looked down on her as she stood freezing in the slushy excrement-stained snow in the extermination camp.

With a cautious but adoring suitor, a journalist called Gianluigi Brusadin, she threw herself back into the life of her city. She decided to train as a midwife, while working for a women's group and setting up a library centre. And she was desperate to try and have children too. But the malnutrition, beatings and lung infections she had suffered in Poland meant that she couldn't.

Meanwhile, under the eye of the Allies, black marketeering, assassinations, riots about politics and lack of food were the order of the day. Trieste's infant mortality rate was huge, and hundreds and hundreds of prostitutes had flooded into the city to attend to the international military personnel. For many hungry families facing starvation, having a female family member was the only source of income. The Allies arrested dozens of women a month for having sex below the walls of the Castello san Giusto, on the far end of the jetty that led into the Adriatic, behind the marshalling yards on the station, and underneath broken cranes by the docks. There were semi-sunken or half-destroyed ships in and around the entire area of Trieste harbour by July 1945, mostly riddled with canon fire, or hit by the rockets and bombs of the Spitfires and Beaufighters of the Allied Air Force. These ships included the 28,000-ton battleship *Conte di Cavour*, at Monfalcone, and the 45,000-ton *Impero*. That summer a lot of Italian women, and American and British and New Zealand men, would have seen this maritime graveyard as a backdrop to their illegal, hurried sexual exchange. The going price was negotiable on the client. Americans paid over the odds in dollars, cigarettes, tins of K-Ration food and even army-issue mattress covers. These were used to make clothes. The problem was that they were stamped with the insignia of the US Department of Defence, which needed careful removal. Some women accepted no more than a tin or two of army ration food. Unwanted pregnancies rocketed.

17

OZNA Sve Dozna (OZNA Can Find Out Anything), August–September 1945

On 17 July, the three Allied powers met at Potsdam in occupied Germany. Their aim was to decide how to administer a defeated Germany, and to bring order to the European continent. The war had finished eight weeks earlier on 8 May, Victory in Europe Day. The need for Allied unity in the face of a common enemy was now replaced by the vital necessity of hammering out a workable relationship between two emerging superpowers, American and the Soviet Union. The latter now controlled Russia, the Baltic States, Romania, Hungary, Bulgaria, Czechoslovakia and Poland. Stalin had installed a communist government in the latter. The United States had a new President, Harry S. Truman, now highly concerned and suspicious about Stalin's plans for Soviet expansionism, and his obvious readiness to break promises made at the Yalta Conference nine months earlier. There had been a general election in Great Britain. While they both awaited the outcome of the vote, the Labour leader Clement Attlee accompanied Prime Minister Winston Churchill to the meeting at the Cecilienhof Castle. It lasted from 17 July to 2 August.

The leaders agreed on a number of main objectives. Germany would be subject to the 'Five Ds'. Denazification, decentralisation, democratisation, decartelisation, and demilitarisation. The Russians, French, Americans and British would each have a zone of control in Germany and Austria. Germany itself was divided into east and west, along the Oder–Neisse Line. The Allied and Russian leaders would prosecute Nazi war criminals. An 'orderly and humane' expulsion of Germans from Poland, Czechoslovakia and Hungary would take place, but not from Yugoslavia. Truman also told Stalin that he had an unspecified 'powerful new weapon of unusual destructive force'. Stalin's intelligence agents inside the United States' Manhattan Project had already informed him that the Americans were ready to stage their first test of an atomic bomb. He urged his own chief of atomic development to try to speed up the Soviet Union's nuclear programme. Towards the end of the conference the three leaders gave Japan an ultimatum to surrender, or face utter destruction. The Japanese Prime Minister did not respond.

Stalin felt at a tremendous disadvantage knowing the Americans had tested their new atomic weapon. At the Yalta Conference in February he had agreed to join in the fight against Japan three months after the defeat of Germany.* With the atom bomb at their disposal the Allies did not now need Stalin's assistance in the Pacific campaign as they had five months before. Stalin didn't need further, potentially violent disagreements with the Allies over Trieste and Yugoslavia. And he wanted Tito to follow his example on this. Stalin wanted Yugoslavia to be part of a geographical string of southern European countries that were either Soviet satellite states or firmly allied to Moscow. He did not want an independent Yugoslavia that refused to bow to the Soviet decree. But Tito had other ideas.

* The dropping of two atomic bombs on 6 and 9 August made academic this question of support from Stalin.

YUGOSLAVIA AFTER THE WAR

By July 1945, the Allies were face to face with Marshal Tito across the Morgan Line in and around Trieste. The Americans and the British wanted Tito and the National Liberation Army to reunite with the other factions in Yugoslavia. Both with the Yugoslav royal family, who wanted to return from exile in London and New York, and with the Serb monarchists loyal to them. The Yugoslav royal family, with King Peter II at its head, had been evacuated from Belgrade in April 1941 just before the Germans invaded. It had fled to Greece, Palestine, Cairo and then London. The family lived in Suite 212 of Claridge's Hotel in London for the entire duration of the war from mid-1941 to November 1945. In March 1945, the King disbanded the *de jure* Yugoslav government, as well as its disparate armed forces. These included all the opposing factions like the Serb Chetniks who were not part of Tito's army. King Peter II then declared that Tito's partisan army was the only legitimate form of government and military force in the country. Tito was delighted. It meant he now had formalised and legitimate backing from the royal family of Yugoslavia to be recognised as sole ruler. The bankers in Brazil, Argentina and, most importantly, at the United States Federal Reserve, would have no choice but to release the Yugoslav gold and dollar assets.

Tito also knew that any ideas the Allies had about allowing officials from the Independent State of Croatia, or the Serb monarchists, to become part of any future Yugoslavian government were just fantasies. Tito and his commanders had already arrested or murdered many of the armed components of these two factions, the Ustashe militia and Chetnik partisans. So Tito announced that in the coming November of 1945 he would hold elections. He would stand as Prime Minister. In the interim, his communist National Party, backed up by 800,000 partisans and soldiers, would run the country. The Allies had no choice but to agree. There was nothing else they could do. They had had two forms of leverage over Marshal Tito until near the end of the war. The guarantee of continued military support to his armed forces was one. Control over the release of the gold reserves in New York and London was the second. With the war now over, and the King backing Tito, these two forms of Allied leverage ceased to exist. Tito could now do much as he wanted.

But he was aware that the post-war era could herald very significant changes and developments in international justice. Following the declarations made at Potsdam, he knew the Allies and Russians intended to put Nazi war criminals on trial. But he was astute enough to realise that this remit could be extended to leaders of other nationalities who were alleged to have committed war crimes. The Italian General Roatta and Croatian Ustashe leader Ante Pavelić were just two amongst these. So by August 1945, what were Marshal Josip Broz Tito's aims and objectives, and how was he going to achieve them? He wanted to establish and run his own National People's State, run by a communist government, owing no allegiance to Moscow, London or New York. He wanted to guarantee a safe and secure homeland and workable socio-economic future for the million-odd men and women who had fought as his partisans and in his army. He was determined to resist Stalin's interference, and any attempts made by the Soviet leader to influence this form of government. He was determined to hold the Americans and British in strategic check over Trieste until such time as he was the legitimately elected ruler of Yugoslavia. If it required armed clashes to reinforce this point, he was prepared to risk this eventuality. He was gambling that with Churchill now out of power, a war-weary Britain would have no stomach for taking casualties in a gunfight with a former ally. Their generals might, but their troops? That was another matter. He needed the country's gold reserves returned. He wanted to continue taking revenge on his former Serb, Nazi and Croat enemies. He wanted to form a non-aligned strip of countries across southern Europe, to include Bulgaria, Greece and Albania, that would provide a geo-strategic buffer zone between Soviet territory and the Mediterranean. And lastly, he was not intimidated by Stalin, and was not afraid to demonstrate this.

Tito's natural reaction to externally imposed authority was confrontational: his decade of strikes, street-fights and imprisonment in the 1920s and 30s showed this. He was manipulative, in his dealings with both his military subordinates and the Soviet and Allied political leadership. And in his dealings with a succession of women. By summer 1945 his Russian teen bride, Pelagija Belousova, was long gone. In 1936 he had reportedly married an Austrian woman, Lucia Bauer; in 1940 he had married a German, Herta Haas, who had a son in 1941. By this time Tito was fighting with the partisans in the rural interior of the country. He was simultaneously sleeping with a Bosnian woman, Davorjanka Paunovic, a partisan courier who became his personal secretary.

He had seen Russia and its communism and was determined not to replicate it. He had fought for and liberated Yugoslavia with his own army, reliant on precious little external assistance from the Red Army. His was the only communist country in Europe where the Red Army's military triumphs had not led to the imposition of Soviet political will. This meant that when the Germans were defeated in Yugoslavia, Tito and his army and government had an almost free hand in deciding how the country should be run and under what style of communism. He was certainly brave, he was courteous and very charming, he was determined, and he was a show-off. A man who lunches with Churchill in 100 degrees but insists on wearing a heavy, full-dress uniform is not one for modesty. He was a communist who lived and acted like a capitalist dictator, but his heart and best intentions seemed to remain with his people. He and they, he felt, had spent too long in the mud and blood and trenches of two world wars, under successive autocratic regimes and invaders. SS-Reichsführer Heinrich Himmler was to say of him: 'I wish we had a dozen Marshal Titos in Germany, leaders with such determination and such good nerves, that even though they were forever encircled, they would never give in.'[1]

By summer 1945, it was time for some self-determination. And when it came to self-determination at home and abroad, the people

Tito turned to for help were from OZNA. The American Office of Strategic Services, the OSS, had said that 'OZNA is well on its way to rival the Russian NKVD police in notoriety ... as long as OZNA remains, the Communist Party will rule Yugoslavia.'[2]

OZNA: SPYING, AND BEING SPIED ON

The British SOE and MI6 were happy to cooperate with the Yugoslavs over the exchange of information about Stalin's intentions towards Trieste, the Venezia Giulia and Yugoslavia. In return for this they were prepared to help the Yugoslavs reclaim the portion of their national gold reserves and American dollars from both New York and Brazil. OZNA knew that securing these assurances about gold bullion and currency were utterly vital to the new country that their boss, Marshal Tito, would be building. The Americans were chasing Nazis who were trying to escape from Trieste and Croatia towards Italy and South America. The Italian Communist Party wanted to make a deal with Tito, but Stalin had new cold feet about further expansionism into western Europe. Increasingly, the Italians, Americans, British and Russians were discovering that by autumn 1945, the constant unknown quantity was the Yugoslavs, and Marshal Tito. Who was benefiting from the current gridlock in Yugoslavia? Who seemed to be pulling the intelligence strings? They all agreed it was Tito.

18

A Gurkha Beheading, October–December 1945

On 6 and 9 August, the US Air Force dropped two atomic bombs on Hiroshima and Nagasaki. At least 130,000 people died in the first twenty-four hours from the effects of the strikes. On the 8th Stalin declared war on Japan, and by 2 September the Japanese were signing an instrument of surrender on board the USS *Missouri* in Tokyo Bay. In Vietnam the OSS provided Ho Chi Minh with a copy of the American Declaration of Independence and, drawing heavily on it, he issued his own proclamation of independence. The British liberated Singapore and Hong Kong.

And across Europe the winter months of peace were freezing and bitter. There was a famine in Holland. By November 1945, the first winter of liberation had also come to Trieste. Suddenly it seemed difficult to remember the endless hot march of summer days that had stretched from May to October. Autumn arrived sharp and chill, and then winter exploded. The *Bora* wind blew ferociously on the Allied and Italian ships in the harbour, knocking white-caps over the end of the jetty. The palm trees huddled against the wind. Grey clouds knocked across the top of the Karst plateau. Trieste shivered in its threadbare winter clothes. Coal was rationed, heating fuel restricted, and 40 per cent of the city's immediate needs of food, fuel and medicine was being provided by the Allied Military Government.

Lieutenant-Colonel Bowman had realised that the *Bora* wind was a natural force of which the Triestini were fearful and respectful. A military statistician and researcher from the AMG applied himself to the question of verifying some of the unique claims made about the powers of this wind. He tried to source, reliably, two separate stories. The first was about an incident where a tram had been blown on its side by the gusting wind. The second concerned another where a tram had been blown into the Adriatic. Neither proved verifiable. That local inhabitants put large stones on their roofs to prevent the tiles being blown off, and strung chains alongside pavements to prevent people being blown into the street was, however, true. So Bowman decided that an early-warning system should be devised to warn of the oncoming wind. Sentries would be posted on tops of hills, and at entrances to the town, and a series of whistles would announce when the wind was on its way. The local inhabitants were respectful of the wind. But in the words of Bowman himself they found this idea 'hysterically ridiculous'.

Meanwhile American President Harry S. Truman and the new British Prime Minister Clement Attlee were determined to present a determined and tough military threat to Stalin, from occupied Berlin to the streets of Trieste. Yugoslavia held elections on 30 November. The Yugoslav People's Front took 90 per cent of the vote, after the opposition boycotted the elections. As Prime Minister, Tito declared the elections the 'most democratic Yugoslavia had ever had'. Voters made their choice at the polls with rubber balls held in each hand. They approached the two ballot boxes representing each party, put their hands into both boxes, and then dropped one ball into their box of choice. Tito's party denounced the King, declared a republic, and adopted a new constitution based upon the Soviet model. The parliament declared itself the People's Assembly of the Federal People's Republic of Yugoslavia.

Tito's landslide victory was of huge concern to Britain and the United States. The Allies were desperate that the battle of the Cold

War in Trieste's piazzas should not lead to Allied servicemen's deaths. The British 4th Queen's Own Hussars arrived from Austria to take up occupation duties in Trieste in October 1945, and they found riots about lack of food, and about the fate of the thousands of people who had disappeared across the city and surrounding region since 1945. Alfred Bowman's Allied Military Government was blamed for both. The ban on weapons and explosives sat firmly in place; the Risiera di San Sabba camp was being used to house refugees; and prostitution had reached an epidemic scale.

In July 1945 two refugee camps were set up in Trieste, one in Pola and one in Gorizia. A total of 1,800 refugees registered in July, 11,000 in August and another 5,000 in September. They were made up of Italian soldiers returning from POW camps, Holocaust survivors, and displaced Italians from Yugoslavia who wanted to be as close as possible to their homes across the border when the time came to return. The AMG also registered the formal arrival of close to 10,000 Italians who came to live in Trieste. These were not necessarily all people who required any form of economic or social assistance, but simply some had arrived in the city encouraged by friends, relatives and politicians. They had come to swell the Italian population of the city and its surroundings, in preparation for an eventual vote on its future. Unofficial figures collected by AMG officials suggested the figure could be as high as to 30–40,000. This amounted to a substantial 10 per cent of the population of a city whose pre-war population had been around 350,000.

A full-scale intelligence war was underway between both sides, across the Morgan Line. And among those returning home were Jews from concentration camps in Poland and Germany. A British corporal from the 4th Hussars was invited to supper one evening by an Italian family. Afterwards he walked a female guest back to her house after the curfew. Leaving her at her door, he heard a muffled, thudding impact on a nearby pavement. Neighbours gathered and quickly told the story. A Jewish man, newly returned home from a concentration camp, had just committed suicide by throwing himself off a roof. The

Hussars were on standby to go into action should the moment arise. The Allies suspected that the Red Army and the Yugoslav People's Army would go into battle again, this time against the Allies, without questioning orders. Would the Americans and the British do the same? The events of one winter night outside Trieste suddenly provided a very clear answer.

Sergeant Tom Norton from the British Intelligence Corps was fast asleep at 4am one mid-November morning in a small village outside Gorizia. Suddenly, there was a screech of brakes outside and heavy knocking on the front door of the Slovenian cottage where he was billeted. He thought it was a false alarm, so tried to go back to sleep. Then screams joined in the hammering on the door. He got up and went downstairs, shivering in the winter cold. The teenage daughter of the household was terrified because standing in the doorway was a huge, bearded Indian Sikh soldier.

'Major Khan says you must come with me, hurry up, rush!' the Sikh told Norton. Thinking that Tito's men had stormed across the Morgan Line into Trieste, the sergeant from the British Field Security Section grabbed a pre-prepared bag of equipment, and jumped into a jeep with the Indian driver. The icy road, the Sikh's crashing gear changes and the sense of urgency rapidly dispelled his hangover. The two Allied soldiers sped along the edge of the River Vipaco, which in that sector divided the Allied and Yugoslav areas of control. A Bailey bridge, built by British Army engineers, crossed it. What, asked Norton, was going on?

'Plenty trouble, Sahib,' answered his Sikh driver.

As they approached the bridge, Norton could see the figures of Yugoslav soldiers splashing about in the river, some of them submerged, looking for something. On the bridge was a young and panicking British subaltern, being screamed at by Yugoslav soldiers who were on the opposite side of the bridge. A barrier that cut across it marked the demarcation line between Zones A and B. The young lieutenant looked distastefully at Norton, dressed in corduroy trousers, leather jacket and his own boots. What on earth was happening, demanded the Intelligence Corps sergeant.

'We've had a spot of bother,' said the officer. 'One of my Gurkhas has beheaded one of their chaps.'

Norton said nothing. He immediately saw that this was going to escalate fast and viciously.

'Yes,' said the officer, 'one of my Gurkhas has beheaded one of their chaps. They've removed the fellow's body, and they're looking for his head now. In the river.'

The officer shrugged his shoulders.

'It's all right, Sergeant. My chap did it in self-defence. You can ask him – he's over there.'

Standing, grim-faced and shaken, with his back to a sentry box by the river was a young Gurkha soldier. It had, he said, started in a friendly enough way. A few partisans on their way back from a local bar had stopped and offered him a sip of their plum brandy. *Slivovic.* The Gurkha, not liking to be offered drink while on duty, had taken offence. When one of the partisans had tried to take the Gurkha's *kukhri* knife off him by force, he had reacted. And cut the man's head off.

The lieutenant showed Sergeant Norton a blood-stained astrakhan hat, a red star on its front, lying near the side of the bridge. A line of red traced its way between two of the bridge supports.

'That,' said the British officer, 'is where his head rolled ... unfortunate, eh?'

To Norton, this spelled complete disaster. It was exactly the kind of incident both sides feared could provoke a much larger confrontation. Then, with a huge shout, one of the partisans clambered up the river bank holding his comrade's severed head. Suddenly, his partisan colleagues charged forward over the bridge, and began prodding the British Army lieutenant with the muzzles of their rifles. He stepped back. They advanced. Norton looked behind him. A group of Gurkhas was approaching, their hands hovering over the hilts of their *kukhris*. Please

God, he thought, don't let any one of these Yugoslavs do anything stupid.

As he imagined what could happen, a Volkswagen drove onto the bridge, a red star painted on its door. A hefty man in a blue suit got out, looked at Norton, raised his arm in a clenched fist salute, and shouted '*Smrt Fascismu.*'

'Death to Fascism!' replied the Intelligence Corps sergeant.

The Yugoslav man was a party political commissar from OZNA, attached to the 2nd Serbian Brigade. He ordered all the troops to back off the bridge and called the British sergeant over to sit with him in his car, out of the freezing cold wind. By a huge chance, the two men knew each other. The commissar had arrived one evening in the tiny mountain hamlet where Norton was based, ostensibly to borrow a map. In fact he was extremely curious to see why a single British NCO was living by himself with a Slovenian family away from any other British unit. When he met Norton the answer was obvious – here was an Intelligence Corps sergeant who had set himself up in an *ad hoc* reconnaissance position. The two men looked at the map, and drank a fair amount of Norton's whisky. The visits repeated themselves. Norton's hangover, as he sat in the Volkswagen, was the result of a drinking session the night before. But now the Yugoslav political officer was anything but friendly.

'Our brigade,' he stated very firmly, 'has been ordered to take immediate action to avenge our comrade's death, the murder of a brave anti-fascist fighter.'

It was a dreadful mistake, insisted Norton. He explained the ritual about Gurkha soldiers and their *kukhris*. How the Nepalese soldiers would not see their curved weapons unsheathed without drawing blood. Norton told the Yugoslav officer how he himself had offered to let a Gurkha cut him, and draw some blood, so he could see the man's fighting knife. The commissar seemed impressed.

'Do you remember,' he asked, 'how one shot from Gavrilo Princip in Sarajevo started World War I? We wouldn't, really, want that to happen again here.'

Norton sighed with relief. He got out of the car, which reversed off the bridge and drove away, the commissar stating firmly that he would be back. Despite his words, he was in a mood to take action to avenge the beheading. Then, as he drove away, the young British subaltern intervened, as the older and more experienced Norton listened horrified. The officer had contacted the headquarters of the British XIII Corps to inform them of the situation, and the American military at Gorizia had been ordered to move up instantly in support. With tanks. The situation was fast escalating. On one side, Norton knew, was a victorious Allied force in absolutely no mood to let any more European territory fall under communist control. On the other was a jubilant partisan army that had just defeated the Wehrmacht. And to make things worse, the Red Army was only a few hundred miles away. Sergeant Norton could see how the next war would start.

'Fucking hell,' he thought. 'Just one shot from a stupid gunner. A single shell. And World War III here we come.'

Suddenly the noise of roaring engines made both him and the subaltern look sharply over at the other side of the bridge. It was, he said, seething with activity. Soldiers were spilling out of lorries, a column of armoured cars was approaching and Yugoslav soldiers were manhandling and hauling an assortment of captured artillery into place. The Indian soldiers around him were, he thought with relief, superbly disciplined. They wouldn't open fire first. And, luckily, no units of gung-ho Texans from the 88th Infantry Division, the 'Blue Devils', had yet arrived to up the ante. But there was distinct menace on the Allied side of the river, too. The Gurkhas were sitting quietly on a grassy bank sharpening their *kukhris*, while further upstream, a group of Sikhs had removed their turbans and were combing their long, black locks like ancient Greeks preparing for battle. A sudden bugle call brought the whole British company moving at the double into position. Machine guns and mortars were set up behind outcropping rocks. Belts of .303 ammunition were laid with clicking precision through machine-gun feed-trays. Mortar tubes angled for the correct trajectory of fire. Norton, meanwhile, could do nothing but pace up and down the icy surface of the metal Bailey bridge.

Then the Yugoslav commissar returned. This time he was in an impressive staff car, accompanied by a three-star general and two colonels. The three officers lined up and saluted perfectly. Norton stood there in corduroys and leather jacket and replied with a theatrical bow. One of the two colonels then started to read out a statement.

'One of our brave freedom fighters has been barbarically butchered by the colonial lackeys of the pro-Italian, Allied forces.'

Then, saw Norton, came the gut-wrenching threat.

'The news of this brutal murder has reached our allies, the glorious Red Army, which is prepared to assist us in avenging ....'

Norton saw it all. World War III. Then his thoughts and the colonel's reading were interrupted by a heavy, distant rumbling. Was it American Sherman tanks, thought Norton, coming to assist? The Yugoslav colonel had paused, so the British sergeant started to repeat his side of the story. The drunken Yugoslavs, the grab for the knife, the Gurkha's honour, an unfortunate action ...

'So, you will apologise?' asked the commissar of the 2nd Brigade suddenly.

Norton saw a way out.

'I give you my solemn word,' he said, 'that we sincerely regret this unfortunate incident and I can assure you that if you, Comrade General, withdraw your gallant partisan forces, I will guarantee that our forces will do the same.'

The absurdity of a twenty-two-year-old sergeant making such a grandiose gesture on behalf of the Anglo-American Command never occurred to him. But it seemed to impress the general. They solemnly shook hands. The staff car drove off and Norton sprinted towards the British Royal Signals truck parked near the bridge. The transmission he sent was as fast as he could make it.

'URGENT GHQ 13 CORPS INCIDENT SETTLED. AGREED JUGS WITHDRAW ALL FORCES.'

There followed another half hour of anxious bridge pacing. Then the first signs of partisans climbing back into their vehicles. Then, Norton said, like the passing of a thunder storm, he heard the rumble of the Shermans slowly fading away. The Gurkhas were grinning again but their young officer sounded disappointed.

'Pity we didn't get the chance to teach those cocky bastards a lesson,' he said sadly.

Norton stared at him without replying. The officer was, he thought, probably the same age as himself, but beside him, he felt like a seasoned veteran. He and the Sikh then returned to Norton's house in the jeep, the Indian soldier elated and chatty. He had been fighting since the days of 1941 in the Western Desert. He had a wife and child waiting for him at home in the Punjab.

'Last night you did a very, very good job, Sahib,' he shouted over the sound of the grinding gears. 'Maybe you stop another big war.'[1]

This time the quick-thinking of one British NCO had. But on the next occasion it would be Tito who would decide whether or not to escalate matters. And he wouldn't hesitate.

Part Six

THE NEW EUROPE

19

Bloody Compromise, February–April 1946

Winter had sat on Trieste like a cold and suffocating bear. The best anybody could say about the situation in the city was that war had not returned. Slovenes, Italians, Croats, returning Jews, celebrated the first New Year without armed conflict. Nearly 20,000 Allied and Yugoslav soldiers faced each other across the Morgan Line. Zones A and B were firmly in place. The city was as divided as ever, and there didn't seem to be any hope of breaking the deadlock. In March 1946, war had been over for ten months, and both the British and Americans were keen to demobilise their armies, air forces and navies as quickly as possible. Unemployment on both sides of the Morgan Line was severe: 48 per cent of both populations depended on aid either from the Allies, or from the new United Nations Relief and Rehabilitation Administration.

The roll-call of characters who had dominated Trieste in the summer of 1945 had changed, too. The New Zealanders had long sailed for home, and the SOE had departed. MI6 had assumed many of their roles, and along with the American Counter Intelligence Corps and the British Field Security Sections, were hunting Nazi war criminals across south-eastern Europe. The Ustashe leader Ante Pavelić had entered Italy disguised as a priest, arriving in Rome in spring 1946. He had taken shelter in a series of residences owned by the Vatican, sheltered by Croatian Catholic clergy. The former Gauleiter of Trieste, Friedrich Rainer, was in custody and giving evidence in the Nuremberg trials, which had begun in November 1945. Odilo Globocnik was dead, his treasure still lying undisturbed. The American 88th Division, the 'Blue Devils', was one of the Allied units holding the Morgan Line. Lieutenant-Colonel Bowman was still the Allied military governor of Zone A.

Along with British and American help, he had set up the new Venezia Giulia Police Force. It absorbed 5,000 men, many of whom had been partisans. Before it became part of the AMG's civilian administration, a British lieutenant-colonel ran it. He proposed his idea for the emblem of the new police force, and submitted it to Bowman for approval. It was the heraldic coat-of-arms of his own English family. The American governor's answer was negative. On 1 April 1946, the force became part of the AMG administration, and was then run by a former member of the London Metropolitan Police. The first choice of uniform for the force was American army uniforms dyed black, topped with a white helmet. The Italian population of Trieste nicknamed these police officers *cerini*, or matchsticks, from the Italian name for black waxed matches with a white tip. The AMG then introduced a blue uniform with a blue helmet, modelled on the traditional British 'bobby'. This then led to the force being dubbed 'the British Police', much to the chagrin of the American trainers. Bowman also recruited female police officers.

He called himself 'a little lame boy born not long after the death of Queen Victoria'. And one of the reasons why his quixotic and idiosyncratic administration functioned as well as it did was that he liked both Italians and Slovenians, and got on very well with the British. This was partly because of his mixed Irish and British parentage: as he said, he 'liked these characters from the start'. From the time of his arrival on 4 July, onwards into 1946, his routine was full and varied. He recorded that it consisted of meetings with politicians, military leaders and visiting diplomats, including meeting the American General Mark Clark, confidently chewing gum in a military receiving line, as well as Field Marshal Montgomery.

There were visiting American and British politicians, foreign and local journalists, Slovenian businessmen, Italian labour leaders, the officers of Royal Navy or US Navy ships, local fishermen, and visits to Allied units based in and around Trieste. He would have a brief siesta when the weather was warm, and then ride after lunch in the hills above the city. And the citizens of Trieste wrote to Bowman about every conceivable subject. Italians and Slovenians accused at work of being former Fascists claimed they weren't.* An Italian–Slovenian nobleman claimed sovereignty over three large Dalmatian islands dating back to 1433, saying it gave him the right to print and sell postage stamps in Trieste. One letter that arrived purported to be from a group of dead people buried in a mine in Istria, which Bowman was asked to forward on to their living relatives, giving the whereabouts of their final resting place. Communications were sent to him to be forwarded to President Harry S. Truman. Residents of a local village wanted a military bridge built so that lorries carrying building materials could reach their war-damaged community. There were letters about industry, public works, food education and public safety.

'As a practical matter,' he wrote, 'nonetheless, after some difficulties during the early months, I did indeed exercise all the primary powers of a totally unrestrained monarch.'[1]

Major-General 'Monkey' Morgan, who oversaw the implementation of the Morgan Line, called him 'King Bowman I of Trieste'. And all of this authority had come from Harold Alexander's Proclamation No. 1, of 13 June 1945, which designated his government and position.

Back in the United States, Edward Stettinius was now the first American Ambassador to the new United Nations. And across Zones A and B in the Venezia Giulia, fierce propaganda continued. Bowman

* The controversial Purge Commission was designed to identify former fascist officials and sympathisers, and bar them or remove them from any form of administrative power. It heard 40,059 cases in Trieste. 94 per cent, or 37,787, were dismissed without adjudication. Yugoslavs and Italian communists were naturally furiously critical of this.

had been joined by another Allied officer, who took up the position of his de facto deputy. Lieutenant-Colonel John Christopher Smuts was originally from South Africa. Educated at Oxford, he became a barrister, and stood for election as a member of parliament for the British Liberal Party in 1935. He firmly believed in the notion of international collective security and peacekeeping, as espoused by the United Nations. After serving in the 8th Army in Italy, he was made an Area Commissioner of Trieste, with responsibility for the town of Gorizia, in early 1946. Along with Bowman, his was the complex task of implementing an idiosyncratic mixture of military policing, peacekeeping, nation-state building and colonial administration. He was dealing with political riots, border security with Yugoslavia, the enormous American and British military presence, and viciously conflicting territorial claims from Slovenia and Italy.

But the overarching military and intelligence threat was from neighbouring communist Yugoslavia. Many of the British and Americans feared that Marshal Tito's main foreign policy directives were still partly coming straight from Moscow, via the NKVD bureau in Belgrade. Inside Italy the Communist Party, led by veteran pro-Russian Palmiro Togliatti, was a threat. Many former partisans now swore allegiance to him. Lieutenant-Colonel Smuts was one tip of the Allies' ideological spear: he stood for what Field Marshal Alexander called 'every reason for which we fought this war'. The fight for democracy, liberty and egalitarianism versus oppressive and murderous totalitarianism. Many Italians thought Smuts was a type of last ambassador for the old British Empire. Slovenians thought he could help Trieste return to them.

The Americans' priorities were still to keep their strategic access to the Adriatic and Mediterranean safe, and to keep communism at bay. While also implementing the Marshall Plan, to help save those Europeans now on the post-war breadline. Smuts found himself trying to steer a middle course between all these conflicting currents. And in the middle of this conflicting policy, Tito was taking full advantage. He had won his war, won his elections, defeated the Wehrmacht, the

SS, the Chetniks, the Ustashe, murdered or imprisoned thousands of his enemies and kept himself autonomous of Stalin, without the other's knowledge. Now, Balkans strongman that at heart he essentially was, it was time to antagonise the neighbours.

So when he gave a speech in March 1946 to the Yugoslav parliament, entitled 'Yugoslavia's Foreign Policy', Venezia Giulia featured highly in it. Population makeup, he said, gave Yugoslavia the strongest claim to the area: 'Not only to politicians but to the whole world it is known that the areas demanded by Yugoslavia are inhabited in great majority by Croats and Slovenes, despite many years of denationalisation and terror against the Slav population.'[2]

A foreign ministers' conference in London in October 1945 had begun to discuss the question of Trieste, and then had postponed it to the future, to 1947. The conference had had time, though, to refuse Tito's demands that the area of Venezia Giulia be divided on ethnic lines, that the city become a Federal Unit of the Yugoslav Republic, and that the port be internationalised in a free-trade zone. So in Belgrade in March 1946, Tito simply turned to propaganda, aggressive rhetoric and provocative invention.

The Allied Military Government, he stated, were helping Fascist 'bandits' infiltrate both Zones A and B. There was accurate data, he told his faithful members of parliament. In the last week, he thundered to the chamber, with the tacit help of the AMG, about twelve full trains and seventy lorries full of bandits had arrived in Trieste and Zone A from the rest of Italy. Those in the chamber who disagreed with Tito, or saw through his claims, were keeping quiet. The new regime in Yugoslavia had been in power for five months. But already everybody knew what happened to those who spoke out, criticised Tito, opposed him, or stood up to him and the all-powerful OZNA. A trip to Goli Otok awaited.

The two-square mile island, completely barren and uninhabited, was becoming Tito's personal *gulag*. It sat in the northern Adriatic, south of the port of Rijeka, just next to the island of Rab. In the First World War, Russian prisoners had been sent there by the Austro-

Hungarians. It was a perfect prison. Uninhabited apart from by sheep, the climate was unforgiving. Mid-summer in southern Croatia can see temperatures rise to 115 degrees Fahrenheit; in winter freezing winds and maritime storms make life miserable. Prisoners worked in a quarry, digging out vast slabs of limestone which they moved predominantly by hand, and on small barrows, up and down the ragged slopes that sat above the prison buildings. While the guards beat and humiliated the prisoners, they didn't kill them. They encouraged the prisoners to do this to each other.

Meanwhile, claimed Tito in his parliament address, the Fascist bandits in Trieste were breaking into property. 'They break into the dwellings of anti-Fascists and citizens of Slav origin and demolish everything,' claimed Tito. 'These Fascist bands, quietly watched by the Allied military organs, are insulting our country, our peoples, our most responsible personalities.'[3]

These infiltrators were also responsible for attacks on Yugoslav army officers, he added. But the greatest provocation to Yugoslav sovereignty, he said, were Allied 'overflights' of the country's national air-space. There had been 223 such flights in one month alone, he said. Tito was correct in principle if not in precise figures. To intimidate Tito, the US Air Force had started a programme of provocative overflights of Yugoslav territory. In one week in April 1946, American pilots flew 32 such missions.

In the same week, the American Political Adviser to Allied Force Headquarters in Trieste made a report to the Secretary of State. There was unrest and a noticeable drop in the morale of the population of Zone A, he noted. There was a run on the banks and a mass evacuation by the Italian population. Yugoslav forces were being strengthened in Zone B. Both the British and the Americans reiterated their intention to fight the Yugoslav Army if it advanced across the Morgan Line. As the political temperature in Trieste rose, another meeting of the Council of Foreign Ministers began in April in Paris. Trieste was high on the agenda. The Americans were worried that their humanitarian and relief aid to Yugoslavia was being misdirected.

The Council of Foreign Ministers ordered five separate studies into the situation in north-eastern Italy. They reached a compromise decision in June. Italy would cede to Yugoslavia 3,000 square miles of territory which included the Isonzo valley, Istria and Pola. The population of this region was estimated to be 225,000 Slavs and 128,000 Italians. Trieste was to remain under international control. The Yugoslavs were furious, despite gaining a large amount of territory. They said that they wanted more of the Venezia Giulia. It was a necessary measure for the security of the Yugoslavs against future attacks from Italy or Germany. They also claimed this region as rightfully part of Yugoslavia by virtue of its population. Yugoslavia could not, they said, agree to the main city of the Venezia Giulia, Trieste, being torn away from the rest of the province; nor could it accept to be cut off, at only a few miles from the sea, from the only adequate port it possessed. So Yugoslavia, they said, would not sign, nor give its agreement in any form whatsoever to any peace treaty in which its just claims would be ignored.[4]

Military tension between both sides escalated. On 12 July three Yugoslav soldiers crossed illegally into Zone A. An American patrol was sent to investigate. The Yugoslavs opened fire. The Americans shot back, and one Yugoslav was killed. The Allies sent a second American patrol to reinforce their first unit, and it ran straight into another Yugoslav patrol of ten to fifteen men, but before either side could shoot, Tito's men withdrew. The Americans immediately lodged a protest against this unprovoked firing by Yugoslav troops upon the American military and the illegal crossing of Yugoslav troops into Zone A. Things then deteriorated further.

THE YUGOSLAVS OPEN FIRE ON ALLIED AIRCRAFT

On 9 August, Pilot Officer Dragomir Zecevic was on patrol over Slovenia in a Yakovlev Yak-3 of the Yugoslav Air Force. He and his wingman observed a US Army C-47 Dakota flying below them. Contacting his base, he was given orders to engage, open fire and try to force the aircraft to land. The American aircraft was flying from Vienna to Udine, in north-eastern Italy, and when the Yugoslav aircraft made visual contact it was circling the airport at Ljubljana, the regional capital of Slovenia. They chased the plane, and rocked their wings up and down, the internationally recognised signal to land. The Dakota ignored these instructions, so Zecevic opened fire. 20mm shells from his Berezin B-20 cannon tore into the aircraft. Trailing smoke, the Dakota landed in a field. There were four American crew members and six passengers on board. They consisted of three Americans, two Hungarians and one Turkish officer. Everybody on board survived.

Ten days later, it happened again. This time Pilot Officer Vladimir Vodopivec, again flying a Yak-3, shot down another Dakota, again over Slovenia. This time the five-man crew, all American, were killed. War between the Allies and Yugoslavia was closer than at any other time.

The American chargé d'affaires in Belgrade instantly sent a telegram to the Secretary of State in Washington. An immediate investigation was ordered. But before the United States could issue its reaction to Tito's government, the Yugoslav authorities protested vehemently against the continual violation of Yugoslav airspace by Allied aircraft, especially American ones. They claimed that between 16 July and 8 August 172 aircraft had made unauthorised flights over Yugoslav territory. These included eighty-seven bombers, forty fighters and forty-five transport aircraft, all American. These flights were allegedly made over north-western Yugoslavia and Zone B of the Venezia Giulia. They also stated that American planes had been guilty of repeated violations of Yugoslav territory in spite of government warnings to the United States military attaché in Belgrade.

On the same days that Yugoslavia was justifying its actions to the United States and the rest of the Allies, other nations joined the United States in its outrage over the incident. This had been the first reported European armed aggression against a US aircraft since the end of World War II. The British embassy stated that though no such incidents had occurred involving British and Yugoslav planes, this was because in the past officials in Vienna had given strict orders that British aircraft were not to enter Yugoslav territory. On 11 August, the American commander of the Capodichino airbase near Naples had told the media that negotiations were in progress for the release of the passengers and crew taken from the first, downed C-47. Yugoslav officials were holding the occupants of the plane hostage at an undisclosed location.

When a US State Department representative asked to see the passengers and crew, the Yugoslav officer in charge at the scene of the crash refused to tell him where they were. Harold Shantz, the chargé d'affaires in Belgrade, later stated that the Yugoslav government had given no indication as to when the hostages would be released. The Russians were overjoyed. Their foreign minister, Vyacheslav Molotov, 'almost embraced' the leader of the Yugoslav delegation in Paris, Foreign Minister Edvard Kardelj. 'Though he cautioned him against shooting down a third,' noted Tito's chief of staff Milovan Djilas in a subsequent report. A former partisan officer who had helped liberate Belgrade from the Wehrmacht, Djilas was also then heading an OZNA operation to try and persuade Italians to leave the Istrian peninsula.*

The American Under-Secretary of State Dean Acheson immediately stated that Yugoslavia had never told the United States that it would shoot down American aircraft within its borders. His statement about both incidents was to-the-point:

> The deliberate firing without warning on the unarmed passenger planes of a friendly nation is in the judgment of the United States an offense against the law of nations and the principles of humanity.[5]

* Djilas travelled to Moscow several times from 1944 to 1948, meeting Stalin and Molotov. After the split between Tito and Stalin, Djilas took an increasingly anti-authoritarian and anti-communist stand in Yugoslavia. He criticised Tito's policy of rewarding high-ranking military officers and politicians with property and large salaries and allowances. His increasing criticism of the regime saw him sentenced to a total of ten years in prison. One of his many literary achievements while incarcerated was to translate John Milton's *Paradise Lost* into Serbo-Croat, written on toilet paper.

The Americans then put forward two demands: the immediate release of US passengers and crew in custody of the Yugoslav government; and that permission be given to US representatives to communicate with any member of the crews of the two planes still alive.

If the demands were met within the 48-hour limit, the United States would seek appropriate resolution to the conflicts with Yugoslavia. If the demands were not met, however, the United States proposed calling a meeting of the Security Council of the United Nations to take immediate action against the Yugoslavs.

The die was cast. Meanwhile, on 19 August, a Yugoslav army officer called Major Vlado Despot, and three other Yugoslav soldiers, had driven a jeep into the middle of an anti-Yugoslav demonstration in Trieste. Made up of Italian protesters, the demonstration had been given the go-ahead by the Allied Military Government. The four men detonated two hand-grenades. Furious Italians surrounded their car and tried to kill them, but an Allied military vehicle rescued the Yugoslavs, only to find more ammunition and hand-grenades inside the jeep. Along with the tensions over the downed aircraft, this incident pushed Trieste onto the top of the United States' foreign agenda.

A US Navy carrier battle-group was ordered to take up position off the Dalmatian coast. A US infantry division was posted to Gorizia as reinforcements to the 10,000 men of the 88th 'Blue Devils'. These men paraded in full battle equipment in front of the Morgan Line on 20 August. But the bell of warning and protest the Americans were clanging so loudly was a curiously hollow one. On 21 August, Acheson called a meeting of the Joint Chiefs of Staff. Their discussion of how to provide armed escort for planes on the Austrian–Italian route near Yugoslavia brought up the whole question of what resources they had at their disposal to back up their protests to Tito. Aircraft were thought to be a particular problem – rapid demobilisation of the US Air Force, Marines and Army Air Force meant that of 460 fighter aircraft available in Europe, only 175 of them were crewed by properly trained, first-line pilots.

There were twelve million men and women serving in the American armed forces in May 1945; by June 1947 this was reduced to 1,566,000. This was a fast and efficient operation, given the trans-Atlantic logistics and huge numbers involved. But for many US servicemen it was not swift enough. Since late 1945, the perceived slow progress of demobilisation had been the cause of mass demonstrations across countries occupied by the US Marines, Army, Navy and Air Force. In Manila, 4,000 soldiers had protested against the cancellation of a repatriation ship around Christmas Day, 1945. On 6 January, 20,000 more soldiers marched on the US Army's headquarters there. The protests spread worldwide, and involved tens of thousands of soldiers in Guam, Hawaii, Japan, France, Germany, Austria, India, Korea, the United States, and England. The army, said one report, was reduced 'to a state of near impotency ... it weakened the prestige of our national policy, and endangered the security of the Nation.'[6]

The US Army, with 10,000 men on the Morgan Line, three further divisions in Italy and Austria, and the assets of the 7th Fleet, would have been well capable of stemming any military aggression into the Venezia Giulia by Tito's army. The Allies' total dominance of tactical airspace alone would have guaranteed this. But the predominant factor affecting American diplomatic and military thinking was that if war with Yugoslavia broke out, threatening to escalate into a confrontation with Russia, America would be totally overstretched in Europe. If their strategic commitments in Asia were taken into account, they were blocked.

'In other words,' said Acheson, 'the United States could not stand another war at this time. It was entirely unthinkable – militarily, economically and politically.'

And then, just at the moment when all sides thought Tito held the cards, and was calling the deals across the table, a surprising ally intervened on the side of the Allies.

Marshal Joseph Stalin.

20

The Free Territory of Trieste, March–August 1947

To Tito's horror, and complete surprise, Stalin refused to back him over the incidents with the American aircraft. He made Tito issue a public apology. For Stalin, this was his way of putting the recalcitrant and truculent Yugoslavia in its place. For Tito, it felt as though the rampaging robber baron in his big castle had decided to rein in a particularly difficult village headman. Tito had, understandably, always felt outnumbered and intimidated by the Allies. He also felt very sensitive about Moscow's overbearing political bullying. The behaviour of the Red Army in Yugoslavia since 1944 had made it few friends and thousands of enemies. The incidences of rape of Yugoslav civilians by Soviet troops, and looting of property, had been nowhere near as horrific as in Poland or Germany, but it was still a substantial issue. The Yugoslavs had really started to see the Russians for who they were. When Tito's chief of cabinet Milorad Djilas went to Moscow, Stalin kissed his Serbian wife in front of him, and then criticised him for showing ingratitude. 'Every crime was possible to Stalin,' Djilas was to write:

> For there was not one he had not committed. For in him was joined the criminal senselessness of a Caligula with the refinement of a Borgia and the

> brutality of a Czar Ivan the Terrible. I was more interested, and am more interested, in how such a dark, cunning and cruel individual could ever have led one of the greatest and most powerful states, not just for a day or a year, but for thirty years. He was one of those rare terrible dogmatists capable of destroying nine-tenths of the human race to 'make happy' the one-tenth.[1]

Stalin's humiliation of Tito was not yet complete. He went one step further. At the Foreign Ministers' Conference in Paris in 1946, Stalin also refused to support Tito's position over Trieste. For Tito this was the beginning of the end – on no other issue did the Yugoslav leader so completely define himself in terms of foreign policy and national self-determinism than over the Adriatic port and the surrounding Venezia Giulia. Russian and Yugoslavian relations were starting to crumble.

At this point, in mid-summer 1946, the United States and Great Britain chose the moment to announce they would, by 1948, return all of Yugoslavia's pre-war gold reserves to Marshal Tito. Tensions between him and the Allies started to ease, while relations with Stalin worsened. The Russian leader feared that Tito wanted to absorb Bulgaria, Greece and Albania into a non-aligned bloc, independent of any form of control from Moscow, thus creating a barrier of non-Soviet, independent states all across southern Europe. Stalin was right – this is what Tito proposed to do. But over Trieste, he would have to wait.

TITO AND STALIN SPLIT

The central disagreement between the two leaders was the fact that Marshal Tito simply wouldn't do as he was told to by Stalin. He felt he had fought for and won his country's independence, against the numerically and economically superior Third Reich, and the Red Army had offered little help. Nor had Tito needed it – he had been extremely cautious in accepting excessive amounts of Russian arms or equipment, or training teams, when he knew he could be given them on much more favourable terms by the British and Americans. He also refused to accept Moscow's position as the world leader of communism. But fundamentally, he disliked and disapproved of Stalin. Tito was a killer, but Stalin was a murderer. Tito felt that, ultimately, his hardline yet benevolent leadership would benefit the people of Yugoslavia most directly. Stalin, he knew, had no interest in anything but the perpetual stoking of the fires of his own power. In addition, Tito had sent his army into Albania to stop the ongoing civil war in Greece from spreading into Yugoslavia. Stalin was furious about this: there was nothing he could do about the civil war, as it was a matter, he believed, that was engineered by the British. He had given his word to Churchill – whom he admired – that he would leave it to continue to be a problem for the British Empire. But he could vent his fury on Tito, who also wanted to annex Bulgaria into Yugoslavia. So he asked two of Tito's closest aides, Edvard Kardelj (who had headed the Yugoslav delegation at the Foreign Ministers' Conference) and Milovan Djilas to come to Moscow. The result was impasse. Meanwhile, the situation in Trieste came to a head. The Foreign Ministers' Conference made their judgement.

Trieste was never to become part of Slovenia or Yugoslavia, and never to be returned to Austrian territory. It was to remain part of Italy, until the United Nations (UN), in 1947, in turn adjudicated. The Americans and the British had been extremely keen that the newly formed UN should be seen to make decisions that were globally binding and of international geo-strategic importance. So in March 1947 the UN Security Council declared Trieste an independent city state under the protection of the United Nations. For the foreseeable future, until such time as another international peace conference adjudicated, it would be called the Free Territory of Trieste. The Morgan Line continued to divide it into Zones A and B. The Allied Military Government still ran Zone A. Lieutenant-Colonel Bowman left Trieste in June 1947, his mission over. Another American would follow him in the position. Bowman left Trieste on a note of confident happiness. His final words to the people of the city where he had spent two years were simple.

'I love you – all of you – and wish you well.'

The Yugoslav media were not quite so easily placated. One local newspaper, the *Primorski Dnevnik,* was to say that 'the balance of two years has not been a happy one. We are not to be blamed for the fact that these same (Allied) tanks which were used during the war against Fascists … are now used against anti-Fascists. We will never sell our anti-Fascist creed for a plate of lentils.'[2]

The occupying troops were divided between the American contingent, called Trieste United States Troops, and the British Element Trieste Force. Confrontations continued, but following the split between Tito and Stalin no actual shots were fired along the Morgan Line. Tito knew he was out on a limb. But frontier disagreements continued, and in one incident Yugoslav soldiers physically moved entire sections of border-posts overnight.

The British foreign correspondent Richard West was a national serviceman in the Intelligence Corps in Trieste in 1947. He talked to Milovan Djilas about Tito's intentions at that point, after the split with Stalin. 'Tito was ready to go into Trieste, fire on the Italians, and take on the Americans and the British,' answered the veteran revolutionary and aide of Tito.[3]

Captain Robert Andrew was a Field Security officer in the Intelligence Corps in Trieste in 1947. He remembers the period when Tito broke from the Cominform in 1948:

> When the news came through no-one knew what the implications would be and there was much speculation and excitement in Trieste Security Office. Would the Red Army move into Jugoslavia to restore Moscow's authority? How would the local communist party in Trieste react? We were despatched in our jeeps to the border checkpoints, not knowing whether to expect to see Soviet tanks or a flow of refugees. In fact, at my particular checkpoint nothing appeared all day, except for an old woman in black with a donkey and some goats. [4]

Tito and Stalin then decided to exchange letters between the Communist Party of Yugoslavia and the Soviet Communist Party.

The first was sent on 27 March, 1948, and in it the Soviets accused the Yugoslavs of denigrating Soviet socialism by making such statements as 'socialism in the Soviet Union has ceased to be revolutionary'. In a sublime piece of unintentional irony, the Soviet Communist Party also claimed that the CPY was not 'democratic enough', and that it was not acting as 'a vanguard that would lead the country to socialism.' Stalin commented disparagingly, 'We cannot consider this kind of organization of the Communist Party as truly Marxist-Leninist or Bolshevik. One does not feel any policy of class struggle in the Yugoslav Party.'[5]

Tito replied: he still had a high opinion of the Soviet Union, he said through a party spokesman. However, the Yugoslav Party also noted that 'No matter how much each of us loves the land of socialism, the USSR, he can in no case love his own country less.'[6] The Soviet answer on 4 May bore the answer that the Yugoslavs had always suspected was behind much of Stalin's resentment and antagonism towards its southern European little brother. It accused the Communist Party of Yugoslavia (CPY) of being too proud of its successes against the SS and the Wehrmacht: the Red Army, said Moscow, had saved them from destruction. This was blatantly untrue. The Russians admonished the CPY for failing to admit and correct its mistakes, and went on to accuse the CPY again of being too proud of their successes against the Germans, still maintaining in another statement that the Red Army had 'saved them from destruction'. Belgrade's answer to this was ferocious denial. Both sides then agreed to meet at the next session of the Communist Information Bureau that June. Tito didn't even go. All the other member countries then expelled Yugoslavia, saying that the leadership of the party had been taken over by 'nationalist elements'. Their last comment was, from the perspective of Soviet communism, the nail in the ideological coffin. Yugoslavia was back on the path to bourgeois capitalism. Tito didn't care. He was going it alone against both East and West. And Stalin? His reported reaction to the Yugoslav Marshal's disrespectful position was characteristic. Tito had to die.

21

Killing Tito and Dividing Trieste

Stalin reportedly decided to liquidate Tito after the humiliation of the split between the Yugoslav and Soviet communist parties in 1947 and 1948. The decision brought into direct confrontation two different kinds of human absolutism – the ruthless dictator who never fails to impose his will through whatever means necessary, and the tough military leader and eternal survivor. Did it happen? Was it true? Did Stalin really give an order to assassinate a head of state of a fellow communist country, albeit one that was trying to leave the Soviet fold? Because Tito left no record of many parts of his operational intelligence activities, the only Yugoslav reports are second-hand, at best. The material from the Soviet Union, by contrast, is considerably more authoritative and convincing.

First comes the story of Josip Kopinič. He was a Slovenian who fought in the Spanish Civil War, and then afterwards worked for the Russian Communist Party. He headed the Soviet intelligence office in Zagreb during World War II. He was under orders from Moscow to try to establish a parallel communist party in Yugoslavia to dilute Tito's influence. From 1946 to 1949 he worked as an intelligence officer in Turkey, providing information both to the Russians and to Tito. After the split between Stalin and the Yugoslavs, Kopinič returned home to live and work on the Dalmatian coast. He wrote to Tito in April 1948 and told him to 'beware their [i.e. the NKVD's] man in Zagreb, he has been ordered to kill you'. Replying via the Yugoslav ambassador in Ankara, Tito reportedly told Kopinič not to get involved in 'intrigues'. In tandem with this warning, a Croatian revolutionary and founding member of the country's Communist Party, called Ivan Krajačić Stevo, told Tito he had been ordered to kill him by the Russian intelligence services. These loosely sourced claims and counter-claims were reported by a Croatian author and journalist Vjenceslav Cenčić, who published a book in 1983 about Josip Kopinič, written with him. Called *The Kopinič Enigma*, the book was widely criticised by both the media in Zagreb and Belgrade for being distorted, loosely sourced, exaggerated and even made up.

The second source about attempts on Tito's life by the Russians is, however, perfectly credible, and much more strongly grounded in fact. In 1993, a Russian historian and former Soviet colonel-general called Dmitri Volkogonov wrote an article in the Russian daily newspaper *Izvestia.* He was a former head of the Soviet Army's Department of Special Propaganda in the 1970s. His father had been shot during Stalin's purges, his mother had died in a labour camp during World War II. He was no great admirer of Stalin. He had developed a keenly questioning approach to the accounts of Soviet history that the Communist Party disseminated. In the early 1990s he became the Chair of the Parliamentary Committee for KGB* and Communist Party Archives. While working in these, he discovered more and more about the actual, truthful workings of the Soviet Union and its leaders under Stalin and Lenin. He wrote biographies of Lenin, Trotsky and Stalin: the last of these was highly critical. From the 1960s to the 1990s he was probably one of the best-informed and most objective critics and documenters of the inside workings of Soviet history. He said in his article in *Izvestia* that while conducting

* KGB stands for Komitet Gosudarstvennoy Bezopasnosti, or State Security Committee. It was the Soviet Union's main security agency between 1954 and 1991.

extensive research in Soviet archives, he discovered that Stalin had decided to liquidate Tito following the split between the two in 1948. Lavrenty Beria, head of the KGB, resisted the idea but did not want to disagree with Stalin. So in Vienna in 1952 a group of Soviet intelligence officers decided on a plot codenamed 'Scavenger'.[1] The details of the operation were reported to Stalin in a report by the Ministry of State Security, or MGB.*

The report from the MGB recommended that a Soviet citizen called Iosif Grigulevich be chosen for the job. Their choice of killer brought developments into a circle returning upon itself. For if the split between Stalin and Tito had several of its principal origins in Trieste and the war in Yugoslavia, then the man chosen to kill Tito on Stalin's behalf had strong links to the Adriatic port too. Iosif Grigulevich was an intelligence operative and assassin who operated on behalf of the Soviet Communist Party, without diplomatic cover, from about 1936 to 1953. He specialised in murdering leading communists and left-wingers who had proved disloyal to Stalin. He acted under a false identity as the Ambassador of Costa Rica for Yugoslavia and Italy, based in Rome. The name he used was Teodoro B. Castro.

Originally Lithuanian, his family had emigrated to Argentina, and Yosif was then sent back to Europe to go to university. He joined the Polish Communist Party, studied at the Sorbonne, and was recruited by the NKVD in 1935. They sent him to Spain during the Civil War to work under an NKVD general who ran a group that killed suspected Trotskyists. While working with this group, he operated with an Italian communist called Vittorio Vidali – who was from the small port of Muggia, not far from a city he saw as being rightfully Italian. Trieste.

Under orders from Moscow, he and Vidali travelled to Mexico in 1940, where they both took part in the first, failed, attempt to kill Trotsky. Grigulievich was then sent to Argentina for the duration of

* MGB stands for Ministerstvo Gosudarstvennoy Bezopasnosti, or Ministry of State Security. It was the Soviet Union's main security agency until Stalin's death in 1953.

World War II, running anti-Nazi operations. He married a Mexican woman, Laura Aguilar, who was also an NKVD agent. In 1949, he obtained a fake Costa Rican passport, and settled in Rome. He tunnelled his way into a position as a diplomat at the Costa Rican embassy in Rome, becoming a chargé d'affaires. He was then also granted Soviet citizenship, while meanwhile becoming promoted to Costa Rican Ambassador to Italy and Yugoslavia. Vidali, meanwhile, returned to Trieste to take up a position as the head of the Communist Party of the Free Territory of Trieste. He followed Moscow's direction and immediately started to pull the Trieste party away from Tito's influence, while directing a violent regime against any of his political allies in both Zones A and B, as well as the surrounding territory.

After the MGB meeting in Vienna, the Soviet intelligence officers officially assigned the 'Scavenger' plot to Grigulievich. The latter had met Tito several times at diplomatic functions in Belgrade. How was Tito to die? The answer was that the fake 'Costa Rican' diplomat would gas him. Initially, the MGB officers thought that at a meeting with Tito, he could shoot a poison dart into Tito from a tiny launcher hidden in his suit – a pen, a lighter – or even from a briefcase. Then they changed their mind, and suggested that he could follow Tito on a trip to London, and shoot him, while throwing tear-gas grenades to distract other diplomatic guests. Finally, they decided that Grigulievich, or 'Max' as he was codenamed, would give Marshal Tito a present. A small and beautiful jewellery box which, when opened, would squirt a poison into Tito's face. It would be laced with the *Yersinia Pestia* bacteria, taken from infected fleas. It was more commonly known as Bubonic plague. Volkogonov described this mission as 'the authentic thinking' of the MGB. 'Max' would then leave a fake letter claiming to have killed Tito because of his own personal disappointment at the split with Moscow. This, it was thought, would cover up any suspicion of direct involvement from the Soviets. Stalin had initial reservations. After all, Max had bungled his first assassination job with Trotsky. He'd missed Trotsky and his wife, and only managed to shoot their grandson in the ankle. But then his MGB officers persuaded Stalin, and he approved the plot. Planning went ahead. According to the MGB memo:

> The death of Tito and every other person in the room would be guaranteed. Max himself would not know anything about the nature of the substance. To save his life, Max would be immunized against plague beforehand.[2]

But the operation never went ahead. As Stalin approached death in 1953, the head of the MGB, Lavrenti Beria, cancelled it. After his death in March 1953 from a cerebral haemorrhage, a letter was found in Stalin's desk. From Marshal Tito. It said:

> Stop sending people to kill me. We've already captured five of them, one of them with a bomb and another with a rifle... If you don't stop sending killers, I'll send one to Moscow, and I won't have to send a second.

The final word on Stalin's attempts to kill Tito belongs to Nikita Khrushchev, who visited Belgrade in 1955, and apologised to the Yugoslav leader for the assassination attempts. He said:

> You did well in protecting yourself. You had good guards and good informants who informed you about everything Stalin was planning for you.

Tito responded:

> Stalin knew that I was very well guarded. After many warnings that it was enough sending assassins, he evidently got a bit scared.[4]

THE FREE TERRITORY OF TRIESTE, COMMUNISM AND THE CIA

Vittorio Vidali was born in the Dalmatian seaside town of Muggia, on the Istrian peninsula some three miles south of Trieste. He joined the socialist movement in Trieste while he was still a teenager, and when

Mussolini came to power in the early 1920s, he was expelled from Italy. He travelled to Moscow and joined the NKVD in the 1930s. The Soviet Comintern then sent him to Mexico to monitor the activities of the Mexican Communist Party. The Spanish Civil War followed, where he and Iosif Grigulevich, as previously mentioned, participated in the joint killings of several Trotskyists. In Mexico afterwards he took part in the failed attempt to kill Leon Trotsky in Mexico City. He returned to Trieste in 1947, as it became an official 'Free Territory'. His brief from his Russian handlers in the MGB was to take the political direction of the administration of Zone B as far away as was possible from Tito. To this end, Moscow suggested that he form as close ties as possible with Italian communists from the Italian Communist Party, or PCI, headed by Palmiro Togliatti. The party was about to go head to head with the Christian Democrats in the 1948 general elections in Italy, the first since the war. The Americans, seeing the PCI as a communist threat, were strongly influential in helping the Democrats campaign against it. So when they saw that the head of the Communist Party in Zone B was not only pro-PCI, but anti-Tito, and pro-Moscow, they had him earmarked as trouble. Which made him a prime target for attention from the bureau in Trieste that had replaced the OSS. The new CIA, or Central Intelligence Agency.

RICHARD STOLZ AND THE CIA IN TRIESTE

When Richard Stolz joined the Central Intelligence Agency in 1950, his first position was working in the Central Registry. It contained thousands of 3-inch x 5-inch cards with names on them, all of the fledgling agency's 'human intelligence' it had inherited from the OSS. One of Stolz's favourites was the card that bore the wording 'Name "TITO"'. The remainder of it was empty of any detail, except the words 'first name not known, last name not known.'[5] He and his wife Betty left for Trieste in May 1951 – they sailed to France as first class passengers on the liner *Ile de France.* For the young case officer, then making $3,824 per annum, it was a change from when he had last made the trans-Atlantic crossing. He had fought in France during the war, and both crossings to and from Great Britain had been made on a troopship. Unlike his earlier intelligence and military counterparts, who arrived in Trieste on foot, in combat boots, by C-47 Dakota on the end of a parachute, or on an army lorry, Stolz and his wife arrived in Trieste in style. On the Venice–Simplon Orient Express. Italy had gone to the polls three years before, and the Christian Democrats had won. In a coalition, the Communist Party had taken 31 per cent of the vote. Zone B of Trieste was naturally still dominated by the Yugoslav Communist Party. Zone A now had an Italian Christian Democrat majority, but its Communist Party was run by Vittorio Vidali. Another, smaller Communist Party also existed, pro-Tito, so socialism's bases were well covered. The CIA had its work cut out. Refugees were pouring into Trieste. Some of them were being sheltered in the ghostly buildings of the San Sabba camp. 'Line-crossers' were being infiltrated by both sides across the Morgan Line divide. Vidali's Communist Party apparatus controlled much of the black-marketeering and organised crime in Zone A, with close links to Yugoslavs in Zone B. The pro-Moscow and pro-Tito communist parties were fighting each other not just politically but also for control of criminal turf. The British had their hands full as well:

> In late 1953, a lot of young men were going AWOL from the (refugee) camps ... I was able to bust a recruiting unit from the French Foreign Legion. At that time the French were losing their war in French Indo-China, now Vietnam. ... I've often wondered how many young men from our camps died in places like Dien Bien Phu.[6]

Being an agent for the British brought few rewards and many dangers. Agents were paid little, and often in cigarettes – Players, or Lucky Strike – which they would then sell or barter on the black market. In January 1953 one of the British Security Office's regular agents disappeared: contact with him was normally weekly. So when a month elapsed, and the Istrian exile, who was a member of the Committee for the National Liberation of Istria, hadn't reappeared, the British were very concerned. He worked as a freelance journalist. About three weeks after his disappearance, a local newspaper, the *Giornale di Trieste,* included a very specific story. A group of fishermen from the Slovene town of Koper, five miles south of Trieste, had found a half-submerged human body. It was drifting near a wrecked ship in the bay. Eyewitnesses, including the fishermen, reported that the hands and feet had been bound with wire. The fishermen took the body back to their port, where it was seized by the Yugoslav State Security Service, UDBA, which in March 1946 had replaced OZNA. The secret police put a name to the body. Almost as soon as the body was landed on the dockside it was seized and taken away by them. The name of the 'disappeared' journalist from Zone A was the name of the corpse reported in the newspaper.

Stolz meanwhile was assigned to the 17th Detachment of the US Army's Counter Intelligence Corps (17th CIC). His chief of station was running under cover, and had made a deal with the Counter Intelligence Corps that three or four of his agents would work out of their headquarters and provide liaison with them. The Counter Intelligence Corps detachment was based in a large building in the centre of Trieste. There was a large square inner *cortile*, an internal courtyard, with stairs climbing up around it. There was a balcony on the second floor, with metal railings. Ten faded and dried memorial wreaths were still hanging on them. These marked the points at which Italian partisans had been hung from the balcony by Fascist police during the war. When Stolz first arrived, his chief of operations at the 17th CIC said to him:

> I do not want to see you for ten days. Spend it getting to know this city, public transportation, bars, cafes, Communist Party Headquarters, and the harbor, and find a place to live. When you come back, I will see how much you have learned. Then we can put you to work.[7]

The detachment's mission was fourfold: providing basic counter-intelligence support for the US military mission, and running cross-border operations into Zone B. They were doing some intelligence-gathering work against the Yugoslav military mission in Zone B, debriefing East European refugees in the camps, and vetting prospective Italian and Slovenian 'war brides', who in those days required security and health checks before marriage to US soldiers was permitted. These soldiers were all, it went without saying, white. Coloured soldiers in the American military were not allowed to marry white civilian women of any nationality until 1967, when inter-racial marriage became legal in all American states.

A blanket suspicion of communism, and its intentions, was also prevalent. In 1951 the CIA's special projects arm, which carried out covert action in the way the OSS had, was called the Office of Policy Coordination. Stolz's office at the CIC was tipped off that on a regular basis a cargo ship from Albania, called the *Queen Teuta*, would sail from the port of Durrës on the Albanian Adriatic coast up to Trieste. What, wondered the CIA, was an Albanian ship doing sailing regularly from its home berth to a port in another country? Something was clearly not right. Action had to be taken. So Stolz and two of his colleagues were given the task of planning how the Office of Policy Coordination might sink it with limpet mines when it next docked in Trieste. They then discovered from talking to the harbour master in the port that the *Queen Teuta* was a wooden-hulled tramp steamer that hauled building sand up and down the Adriatic. The ship was spared.

Of equal concern were the activities of the two official communist parties active in the Free Territory of Trieste. For a year, by complete chance, Stolz and his wife ended up living in the same apartment building as Vittorio Vidali. Stolz on one occasion found himself on the stairs sandwiched between the Italian communist politician and his huge Slovene bodyguard, who moved aggressively in on the CIA agent. In an amiable mood, Vidali waved him away.

In 1953 and 1954 the struggle between Italy and Yugoslavia over the future of the Free Territory of Trieste intensified. The Americans and the British were fully occupied in keeping the situation from boiling over. Both sides insisted that both Zone A and Zone B belonged to them. A number of people were killed in Zone A in the rioting which occurred during this period, some by the local police force, which had been trained by and supervised by the British authorities. To get people off the streets, these police frequently used a successful tactic invented by the then Italian Ministry of Interior. They would drive a convoy of jeeps very slowly, in four-wheel drive, down the narrow streets and rhythmically and loudly beat the sides of the jeeps with rubber hoses. Anyone who did not duck into a doorway or run away down the street got hit. 'I can still remember the sounds of those jeep motors and the sharp thud of the hoses on both metal and people,' said Stolz.

On another occasion, in 1954, several hundred members of the pro-Fascist Movimento Sociale Italiano party marched on the Allied Military Government building. Stolz was marching with them on the sidelines to report on what was happening. Just as the demonstrators reached the AMG building and were confronted by police armed only with clubs and shields, there was an explosion about twenty yards in front of him. One man in the crowd fell to the ground. He had been about to hurl a hand-grenade at the police, but he had pulled the pin too soon and had blown off his own leg. He was later elected to the Italian Assembly as a member of parliament. He thus escaped trial.

Meanwhile, although neither Stolz, his station chief nor his British colleagues were aware of it, the Italians, British, Americans and Yugoslavs were in the middle of four-power negotiations in London and Vienna. Trieste was about to be divided equally between Italy and Yugoslavia. So in the late autumn of 1953, all British and American dependants were ordered out of the territory on short notice.

Definition, when it came for Trieste, was far more simple and less controversial than anybody had expected. The city which had been the scene of an intelligence and diplomatic battle was to be divided. On 5 October 1954 the Memorandum of London was signed. The vast majority of Zone A, including the city of Trieste, was given as a civil administration to Italy. Zone B was given as a civil administration to Yugoslavia. All five main parties to the first battle of the Cold War – Italians, Yugoslavs, Americans, British and Russians – were expecting huge trouble and probable armed confrontations when the announcement was made. All sides were waiting for the others to react. But the result was accepting silence. Trieste, it seemed, had had a long, and well-spotlighted run on the world stage, seeing the first shots of the Cold War and its very protracted aftermath. But this very Cold War had now spun onwards entropically, across the globe. Other things were happening far away from the idiosyncratic, mysterious and ancient sea port at the top of the Adriatic.

Stalin had died the year before; the world breathed a sigh of relief and hoped his successor, Nikita Khrushchev, could only be more enlightened. Dwight D. Eisenhower was American President, and the United States had launched the first nuclear submarine, USS *Nautilus*. Tito had become President for Life of Yugoslavia. In the North Vietnamese mountain valley of Dien Bien Phu, the French colonial forces had been beaten in open battle by the Viet Minh. The Algerian War of Independence was starting: France's military were already overstretched. The Paris Agreements had just given West Germany its sovereignty, climbers had reached the summit of Everest, and four British scientists had discovered the structure of the double helix of deoxyribonucleic acid – DNA. Trieste could bow out of the footlights.

By this point in 1954 Richard Stolz's wife Betty, and their young daughter Sarah, were living in a small apartment in Monfalcone. It overlooked the main railway line that ran from Trieste Centrale, all along the top of the Adriatic. This in turn ran parallel to the road that hugged the coast. This was the road that the New Zealanders, Peter Wilkinson and the British Armoured Corps had driven down in May 1945. The road to Monfalcone from Trieste had been the last miles that Ondina Peteani had trudged in July 1945, returning from Auschwitz. It was the same road, with the same glorious view of the Adriatic, that Alfred Bowman had driven down on his first arrival on the Gulf of Trieste. It is the road and the sea and the railway and the view that everybody sees for the first time on arriving in the city. So when in 1954 Richard Stolz was finally called home to Washington for consultations, he was sad and nostalgic. An era was gone, he felt. Not just his first posting, but a period of political and historical time that would not be repeated. He was now going to work in Munich. Before he did, he had to return to Washington for consultations with his CIA superiors. So he rather sadly took the train that went from Trieste to Rome, passing through Monfalcone. The line overlooks the Adriatic, but also runs very close to the backs of houses and apartment buildings as it emerges from Monfalcone station. Stolz wrote:

> I took the night train from Trieste to Rome to fly from there to Washington. Betty had a view of the main railroad line from Trieste to Venice from the Monfalcone apartment. She knew when my train was due to pass by, and when it came she flashed lights on and off to speed me on my way. I saw them. I wept.[8]

22

The Numbers, January 1999

On the afternoon of Sunday 4 May, 1980, Yugoslav football fans gathered in front of their televisions. There was a 'derby' match scheduled that day between two of the biggest national teams. HNK Hajduk, from Split in Croatia, were playing Red Star from Belgrade. In the forty-first minute of the game, three men came into the stadium and told the referee to stop play. The president of one of the two clubs took the microphone and announced that Marshal Tito had died that afternoon in hospital. The announcement was broadcast live. Fans started to cry. Players burst into tears. Both teams and the referees stood in a moment of silence. The stadium announcer said solemnly 'may he rest in peace'. Suddenly, 50,000 fans started to sing a partisan anthem. 'Comrade Tito, we swear to you, from your path we will never depart.'

Tito had died that afternoon in a Slovenian hospital from gangrene: an operation to amputate his left leg, necessitated by arterial blockage, had failed. His funeral was held four days later on 8 May. Four kings, thirty-one presidents, six princes and forty-seven foreign ministers attended, from 128 countries. As head of the Non-Aligned Movement, his death drew leaders from both sides of the Iron Curtain.[1] The Soviet Union had just invaded Afghanistan, and Cold War tensions had rocketed. But Leonid Brezhnev, Margaret Thatcher, Chinese Premier Hua Guofeng and West German Chancellor Helmut Schmidt attended. American President Jimmy Carter was absent. But the Belgian King Baudoin, Saddam Hussein, Muammar al-Gaddafi, Nicolae Ceaușescu, Indira Gandhi, Prince Philip and Robert Mugabe were among the leaders who travelled to Belgrade. The Secretary-General of the United Nations, Kurt Waldheim, was there, as were delegations from the world's self-declared liberation movements, the Palestine Liberation Organization, the Irish Republican Army and the African National Congress. Representatives from forty-five different communist and socialist parties stood in the ranks of mourners. Up until the funeral of Pope John Paul II in 2005, and the memorial service for Nelson Mandela in 2013, it was to be the largest state funeral in history. Tito was buried in a mausoleum in Belgrade. 'Tito sought to improve life,' said the *New York Times* on 5 May 1980:

> Unlike others who rose to power on the communist wave after WWII, Tito did not long demand that his people suffer for a distant vision of a better life. After an initial Soviet-influenced bleak period, Tito moved toward radical improvement of life in the country. Yugoslavia gradually became a bright spot amid the general grayness of Eastern Europe.

And then, in the absence of his dynamic and autocratic central leadership, Yugoslavia started to tear itself apart. By 1991, the single-minded nationalism of Serbian President Slobodan Milošević led to Serb forces invading Croatia. The country declared independence. The war moved into neighbouring Bosnia. The following four and a half years saw 96,000 people die, a million witness their homes destroyed, and more than a million flee as refugees or displaced people. Forty thousand people went missing. The only incidence of genocide on European soil since the Holocaust took place in July 1995 at Srebrenica in eastern Bosnia. Exhausted by Milošević's intractable aggression and broken promises, America forced NATO's hand. The Serbs were bombed to the negotiating table. On a US airbase in Dayton, Ohio in

November 1995 a peace treaty was finally agreed, Bosnia was split into two, and once again a destroyed and shattered region tried to re-build itself. Peace in the Balkans lasted until 1998. Independence-minded ethnic Albanian rebel fighters, from the Kosovo Liberation Army, then emerged from the forests and villages of the southern Serbian province. They took the fight to Milošević's atrocity-prone soldiers and policemen. By 1999 NATO and the United Nations had once again grown exhausted of his broken promises. For two years his men had been tearing up the human-rights rulebook as they cracked down on Kosovar rebels and civilians. A total of 11,000 people, mostly Albanians, had died. To force Milošević to the negotiating table – and thence to a court room, and a prison cell – NATO unleashed the full might of its air power on targets in Serbia and its southernmost province, Kosovo. For seventy-eight days in the spring of 1999, the skies over the Adriatic and the Balkans were criss-crossed by the vapour trails of American, British, French, Dutch and German fighter bombers, pounding the military and civil infrastructure of Serbia. Milošević gave in. Kosovo was occupied by 40,000 NATO troops. Those warlords, generals and politicians from Croatia, Bosnia, Serbia and Kosovo who had been indicted for war crimes, subsequently stood in the dock at the International Criminal Tribunal for the former Yugoslavia in The Hague. If not peace, then an absence of war, shuddered slowly across the Balkans. The region drew exhausted breath into its lungs, hoping that this time, there would be no more war to look forward to.

And in January 1999, a seventy-eight-year-old Croatian man from the town of Rijeka went on trial in Rome. He stood accused of war crimes from another era, another war, but one whose roots and results seemed to differ little from the 1991–95 Yugoslav conflicts. Oskar Piskulic was a former Yugoslav partisan, accused of participating in the killings of Italian Fascists and anti-communist Slovenians in the mountains above Trieste in 1945. Fifty-four years after the event, it seemed that justice had finally caught up with one of the perpetrators. Piskulic was eventually acquitted under an obscure amnesty ruling, but the case received huge publicity in both Italy and Slovenia. It was about territorial difference, land claims, compensation, reparations and stolen property. Books, films and newspapers in both countries found the story ran and ran. Yugoslavia had, in 1983, agreed to pay Italy $110 million in compensation to relatives of Italians forced off their property in 1943–45, in what was then Yugoslavia. By 1992, the Bosnian and Croatian wars had intervened, and the old Yugoslavia fell to pieces. In the aftermath of the conflicts, Slovenia and Croatia both emerged as independent republics, agreeing to share the debt of compensation to Italy.

THE *FOIBE*, SEVENTY YEARS ON

The left-wing, Italian-speaking Slovenian population of Trieste has always insisted that the numbers of people murdered and dumped in the *foibe* are wildly exaggerated by Italians. The Italian right wing says the numbers are downplayed. Italy's politicians, however, have declared 10 February each year the National Memorial Day of Exiles and Foibe, which was first celebrated in Trieste in 2005. It has attracted eccentric supporters. One is Alessandra Mussolini, the grand-daughter of the dictator, niece of Sophia Loren, and right-wing member of the European parliament for Italy. Former actress and tireless devotee of women's rights, supporter of Israel, and previously a topless Playboy model, she says the number of Slovenian dead are exaggerated, those of Italian Fascists underestimated.

Meanwhile the lonely, ossified physical evidence of what happened between 1943 to 1946 on the windswept Karst plateau, and in wider Slovenia and Croatia, keeps coming to the light of day. While digging up victims of the 1992–95 Bosnian and Croatian wars for DNA identification, again and again forensic teams find themselves coming across the skeletal remains of soldiers and civilians from an earlier war, whose co-mingled bones never stop turning up in their hundreds.

The precise number of people who were killed and dumped in *foibe* during and after the war, in the area around Trieste and Istria, has never been formally and decisively established. The different sides to the conflict tend to disagree vehemently. Estimates range from hundreds to 20,000. It is important for the sake of clarity to distinguish between the two distinct 'caseloads' of killings and victims. The first involves those persons from Trieste, Istria and the Venezia Giulia who went missing and or were killed between 1943 and 1946. The second includes those Croat, Serb, Slovenian partisans, soldiers and civilians who died following their capture or surrender on or near the Austrian border in May 1945.

Raoul Pupo, a Professor of Contemporary History at the University of Trieste, is something of a world expert on the issue of the Trieste caseload. He is the author of some twenty books and pamphlets on the *foibe,* the history of Venezia Giulia, Trieste, and the period before, during and after World War II in the region. He estimates the total number of victims at about 5,000.[2] But this is again contested by many. Italian historian Guido Rumici estimates the number of Italians executed, or who died in Yugoslav concentration camps after the war, as between 6,000 and 11,000. Another, Mario Pacor, estimated that after the September 1943 armistice about 400–500 people were killed and dumped in *foibe* and about 4,000 were deported, many of whom were later executed. Some sources have also attempted to compile lists of locations and possible victim numbers. The numbers are highly contradictory, always incomplete, and frequently dependent on the nationality, ethnicity or political orientation of the author or researcher.

Between October and December 1943, the fire brigade in Pola recovered 159 victims of the first wave of mass killings by Germans and Italian Fascists.

Between November 1945 and April 1948, firefighters, speleologists and policemen recovered 464 corpses from *foibe,* mine shafts and mass graves in Zone A of the Free Territory of Trieste. No inspections were ever carried out in Zone B, controlled by the Yugoslavs.

Neither Italy nor Yugoslavia had initiated proper investigations until after Slovenia declared independence in 1991. In 1993 a study written by the writer and historian Gaetano La Perna provided a detailed list of the victims of Yugoslav occupation. From September 1943 to the end of the Italian presence in its former provinces, this listed 6,335 names (2,493 military, 3,842 civilians). The author considered this list 'not complete'.[3]

A 2002 joint report from Rome and Zagreb concluded that 'no less than five hundred persons of Italian nationality lost their lives between the 3rd May 1945 and 31st December 1947'. To these, it said, should be added an unknown number of 'missing'.'[4]

In March 2006, the border municipality of Nova Gorica in Slovenia released a list of names of 1,048 citizens of the Italian city of Gorizia who disappeared in May 1945 after being arrested by Yugoslav partisans.

So, what should be done? The answer is, obviously, to find and identify the dead bodies of missing persons and then reunite their remains, and their identities, with their surviving relatives. Italy initiated judicial investigations into the question of the Trieste *foibe* caseload, which resulted in the 1999 trial of Oskar Piskulic. But a national-level, coordinated judicial and forensic exhumation operation, to try and accurately assess the number of dead, has yet to take place. It is a huge undertaking. Italy has the scientific and technical ability. Decisive political will is lacking. Meanwhile, few international organisations have the knowledge or experience of how to help carry out such a task. However, the world's acknowledged expert body on handling large numbers of missing persons cases, approached by governments and organisations such as Interpol, is the International Commission on Missing Persons (ICMP).[5] Based in Sarajevo and The Hague, the organisation has, since 1996, more or less revolutionised a science and human rights-based approach to finding and identifying missing persons.

For instance, they have used highly advanced DNA identification and matching technology to put names to almost 90 per cent of the 8,000-odd Bosnian Muslim men and boys who went missing, and were killed, following the fall of Srebrenica in eastern Bosnia in 1995. They have also exhumed from mass graves and identified some 28,000 of the 40,000 persons who went missing from the 1991–99 Balkans wars. They have helped the governments of countries such as Iraq, Libya, Colombia, the Philippines and the United States deal with thousands of missing persons. And while exhuming mass graves across the Balkans, they are constantly coming across hundreds of sets of human remains from the World War II era.

National organisations in Slovenia and Croatia have started to undertake some large-scale investigations and forensic operations on mass graves containing the dead of World War Two. But no coordinated operation is yet underway around Trieste, Istria and on the Adriatic coast. So what is the best estimate of the numbers there? How many people were forcibly disappeared or went missing, were taken prisoner or were killed, in and around Trieste from the period of the Italian Armistice in September 1943, to the establishment of the Free Territory of Trieste in 1947? The answer is simple. Nobody knows. And nobody will know, until mass graves and *foibe* are exhumed to modern forensic industry standards, and until DNA extracted from the blood samples of living relatives can be cross-matched with DNA taken from the human remains of the victims. The important decision for the governments of the countries concerned – Italy, primarily – is to address the problem, and not politicise it. Until then the story of the Trieste and Istrian *foibe* will continue to swim in a small, poisoned pond of revisionist history and political exploitation, where the relatives of the victims are still left without answers three generations on.

The coalition government of Silvio Berlusconi brought the issue back into the open, and the Italian parliament has thus made each 10 February National Memorial Day of the Exiles and *Foibe.* Former Italian President Carlo Ciampi said that 'time has come for thoughtful remembrance to take the place of bitter resentment'. Left-wing leaders visited the Basovizza *foiba* and admitted the culpability of the Left in covering up the subject for decades. But the subject, like its victims, will not rest. In a provocative speech in Rome in 2007, Italian President Giorgio Napolitano said:

> Already in the unleashing of the first wave of blind and extreme violence in those lands, in the autumn of 1943, summary and tumultuous justice,

> nationalist paroxysm, social retaliation and a plan to eradicate the Italian presence intertwined in what was, and ceased to be, the Julian March. There was therefore a movement of hate and bloodthirsty fury, and a Slavic annexationist design, which prevailed above all in the peace treaty of 1947, and assumed the sinister shape of 'ethnic cleansing'. What we can say for sure is that what was achieved – in the most evident way through the inhuman ferocity of the foibe – was one of the barbarities of the past century.[6]

It took only a few days for Croatia to react. Croatian President Stjepan Mesić responded:

> It was impossible not to see overt elements of racism, historical revisionism and a desire for political revenge in Napolitano's words. Modern Europe was built on foundations ... of which anti-fascism was one of the most important.[7]

Mesić's father had been a partisan, and as President he had initiated a round of public apologies with Serbia and Montenegro for war crimes committed between 1991 and 1995. Mesić also testified at The Hague Tribunal against the army of his own country for its behaviour during the wars in Croatia and Bosnia. His government apologised to the Italians a few days after his original statement. But the story still would not lie down. And, say all sides, nor will it until a thorough investigation involving forensic science and DNA technology, justice and human rights is carried out. To truthfully establish the numbers, of who did what to whom, when, where, how and why. Until then controversy will trickle on like chemically poisoned water flowing into the large reservoir of national consciousness of Italy, Slovenia and Croatia.[8]

TRIESTE, SUMMER 2016

Summer lasts a long time on the Adriatic. In Trieste, long shadows and hot evening sun stretch endlessly across the Piazza d'Unità. The Adriatic shimmers in and out of the harbour like a tectonic plate of cobalt velvet. The air is a warm cloak. From an outside table on the corner of the Piazza della Borsa, conversations all around at *aperitivi* time, the cocktail hour, are about work, and holidays just starting or finishing. In June, the leaves on the lime and plane trees across the city still have their vivid green. Along the *Lungomare,* by the sea, the palm trees stand guard in spiky grandeur, looking over the sea. The air is warm, thick and still. The *Bora* wind does not blow. Over prosecco and chilled Peroni lager, work talk at the bar tables is about ships, coffee trading, banking links with Slovenia. Somebody's had a good day fixing a piping problem down at the huge oil terminal. Another round of beers is ordered. They come with small saucers of salami, olives, cubes of cheese, tiny curlicues of bread baked just *so.* Another table sees the staff of a travel agency celebrating: it's another busy summer. Thank God for the Germans and the Austrians, they say. And the Russians too! Chat moves on to beach plans for the weekend. Anybody going up to the Castello di Miramare on Saturday? There'll be *fuochi d'artificio,* fireworks. To celebrate the proper beginning of the summer season. *Oh come on, guys,* says the male boss. *We'll all push the boat out this weekend. Summer's here.*

By September, in the Piazza della Borsa, the two men are still staging their demonstration outside the Tezenis underwear and lingerie shop. They have a new press release this time. It turns out that it's seventy years on from the date of the signing of the 1947 Treaty of Peace with Italy. Establishing the Free Territory of Trieste. The two men are from the Free Trieste Movement, that, we're told 'defends the Free Territory of Trieste and its international Free Port from the abuses of the provisional Italian administration.' It is making a special call on the seventieth anniversary. That the Americans and the British, and their respective militaries, must return to protect Trieste. There is a large sign in the windows of their office that sits above the bikini-clad mannequins in the shopfront of Tezenis. In the first-floor windows, banners of huge black letters spell out the words: *ALLIES COME BACK!*

Epilogue

What Became of the Characters in the Book

Lieutenant-Colonel Arapeta Awatere DSO MC, 28th Maori Battalion
Araware returned home from Trieste in July 1945. He participated in two separate Maori rituals of purification to 'release himself' from the effects of war. He studied anthropology, philosophy and Maori at university, and served as a very highly respected Maori district welfare officer. He was elected to Auckland City Council for five years from 1962 to 1969. He suffered a stroke and developed diabetes. In a tragic, and unexpected, turn of events, in 1969 he stabbed to death his girlfriend's new lover. He was sentenced to life in prison for murder. He died in 1976.

Lieutenant-Colonel Peter Wilkinson KCMG OBE DSO, Number 6 Special Force SOE
Wilkinson resigned his commission in 1947, joined the Foreign Office, and was immediately posted to Vienna. Postings in Washington, Geneva, Bonn and Vietnam followed. His final diplomatic position was as ambassador to Austria from 1970 to 1971. He then became Coordinator of Intelligence in the Cabinet Office. His wife, Theresa, died in 1984 after a car accident in Kent, in 1970, had left her with brain damage. Wilkinson left the Diplomatic Service in order to nurse her and be with her.

Major Geoffrey Cox, Intelligence Corps
Cox became a television correspondent and editor in chief of Independent Television News (ITN); he was made Commander of the British Empire in 1959 and knighted in 1966.

Edward Stettinius

Stettinius became the first American Ambassador to the United Nations. He resigned in June 1946. He wanted President Truman to use the UN as a method of solving tensions with the Soviet Union. He then served as Rector of the University of Virginia and died in 1949 of a coronary thrombosis, aged 49.

Marshal Josip Broz Tito

Tito governed Yugoslavia until his death in 1980. Of the many decorations awarded to him by foreign governments, these included the Orders of the White Lion (Czechoslovakia), Elephant (Denmark), Redeemer (Greece), Chrysanthemum (Japan), Aztec Eagle (Mexico), Lenin (Soviet Union), Victory (Soviet Union), Condor (Peru), Nile (Egypt), and Bath (Great Britain.)

Ondina Peteani

Peteani lived in Trieste for the rest of her life. She turned down the offer of a job as a municipal town councillor of Monfalcone, and ran an independent charity that helped children from poor families attend summer camps each year in the mountains above Trieste. In 1960, Peteani and her husband finally succeeded in a quest to adopt. They went to a local orphanage in Trieste. When it came to choosing a child to adopt, Ondina Peteani was determined to save one who appeared to have suffered the most. So she deliberately didn't pick the brightest, healthiest one with blonde hair or blue eyes. Rather a sickly, pale and sad-looking boy with red hair. She picked him up. Both Ondina and the child smiled. 'Ah,' said the nurse, smiling too. 'He's safe.' The adopted son was called Gianni. Peteani died in 2003 in Trieste, in the hospital where she was born.

William Deakin DSO

After the war Deakin resigned from the Foreign Office, and resumed his Fellowship at Wadham College, Oxford. He took up a position as Churchill's director of historical researches. When Churchill began work on his history of the Second World War, Deakin drafted much of the text. He became the founding Warden of St Antony's College, Oxford, established as a postgraduate foundation in 1949. In 1954 Evelyn Waugh, who had also served in Yugoslavia, said 'Bill Deakin is a very lovable and complicated man. He can't decide whether to be proud or ashamed of his collaboration with Tito.' He continued to visit Tito on his island home at Brioni, and in 1980 he was part of the official British delegation at his funeral. He was knighted in 1975 and he also held the Russian Order of Valour, the Chevalier de la Legion d'Honneur and the Yugoslav Partisan Star, 1st Class.

Alfred Connor Bowman

Bowman helped develop plans for the military occupation of North Korea in 1950, while serving as chief of the army's Military Government Division and Claims Division. He was then the first Army Staff Judge Advocate. In 1953 he served as the Head of the Negotiations Committee of the United Nations Component of the Military Armistice Commission in Panmunjom, Korea. He died in August 1982.

Friedrich Rainer

The former Gauleiter of the Adriatisches Kustenland testified in twenty-four separate trials at the International War Crimes Tribunal at Nuremberg. The Allies realised that he was of far more value to them as a witness than as a defendant. And besides, another country had submitted an extradition request for the Austrian SS man. Yugoslavia was determined to track down and bring to justice those who had committed atrocities on their territory, or against their people. So Rainer was extradited to Ljubljana, the capital of the Slovenian province of Yugoslavia, on 13 March 1947. He was brought before a military court on 10 July, and charged with 'crimes against the Yugoslav people'. The trial lasted exactly a week. On 19 July he was sentenced to death. There his life supposedly ended, and the mystery began. His widow in Austria received a death certificate. But no details of any burial, or any grave she could visit. Certainly no photographs. In archives in Ljubljana and Belgrade are supposedly the documents that can provide the answer to what happened next. Did Friedrich Rainer die on 19 July 1945, or did he go on to work for the Yugoslav Department of State Security, OZNA? Nobody in the Slovenian Government Archives can find a record of his name.

SS-Obergruppenführer Karl Wolff

Wolff was arrested on 13 May 1945. He provided evidence against fellow Nazis at the Nuremberg trials, and thus escaped prosecution. He was re-arrested, having been indicted by the post-war German government as part of its denazification process. In November 1948 he was sentenced to five years' imprisonment because of his membership of the SS. Seven months later his sentence was reduced to four years. After his release, Wolff worked as an executive for an advertising agency and lived with his family.

In 1962, during the trial in Israel of Adolf Eichmann, evidence showed that Wolff had organised the deportation of Italian Jews in 1944. Tried again in West Germany in 1964, he was convicted of deporting 300,000 Jews to Treblinka, and of the deportation of Italian Jews to Auschwitz. He was sentenced to fifteen years' imprisonment but only served part of his sentence and was released in 1969 due to ill health. His full civil rights were restored in 1971. He claimed to have known nothing about the Nazi concentration camps, although he was a part of Himmler's entourage during several of his visits to them. After his release, Wolff retired in Austria. In the late 1970s and early 1980s, he returned to public life, frequently lecturing on the internal workings of the SS and his relationship with Himmler. This resulted in him appearing on television, saying that he had witnessed an execution of twenty or thirty prisoners in Minsk in 1941 with Himmler. He died in 1984.

Iosif Grigulevich

After the cancellation of the operation to assassinate Marshal Tito, he went to live in Moscow and worked as a university academic, a position arranged for him by the MGB. He was awarded a doctorate in history – without having to defend a thesis – and worked as an expert on Latin America and the Catholic Church. He wrote fifty-eight books, including a biography of Che Guevara. In 1979 he became a corresponding member of the Academy of Sciences of the USSR. Colleagues were reportedly 'puzzled by the lack of any biographical information about him prior to his forties and by his refusal to be photographed.' The details of Grigulievich's role as a Soviet agent were clarified only after the fall of the communist regime, particularly with the release of the Mitrokhin archive in the mid-1990s.

Vittorio Vidali
Vidali became a member of the Italian parliament.

Lieutenant-General Bernard Freyberg
Freyberg became Governor-General of New Zealand in 1946. He then served as Lieutenant-Governor of Windsor Castle. He died of complications from his war wounds in 1963.

Maks Milić
Milić was made a People's Hero of Yugoslavia. He became a government minister in Tito's administration and Yugoslav Ambassador to Japan and Sweden, and then resigned from the Communist Party in 1971. He retired to his home town of Split on the Dalmatian coast, a city he had helped liberate in 1945. He died aged ninety-one.

General Petar Drapšin
Drapšin was a candidate for national elections after the war. But in November 1945 he died as a result of a gunshot wound. The official explanation was that it was an accident. He was posthumously made a People's Hero of Yugoslavia.

Richard Stolz
Stolz became chief of the CIA station in Moscow in 1965, but was deported from the Soviet Union. He retired in 1991, having been brought back to the agency in the wake of the Iran-Contra scandal. He died in 2012, aged eighty-six.

Appendix

Science Finds the Evidence

Slovenia and Croatia and Trieste – autumn 2016

Barbara Rov, or the Barbara Pit, is an old deserted mine working near the village of Huda Jama. It lies in the midst of a huge forest of beech, pine and oak trees in northern Slovenia. It is about thirty miles south-east of the Austrian border town of Bleiburg. Local people had long suspected that it was the site of a secret mass grave from the World War II era. But nobody had ever done excavations, so the lost, ghostly and disused mine shaft was left deserted. Proper investigations of the Barbara Pit site only began in August 2008. And it turned out that whoever had buried and hidden the bodies that were found there had taken a huge amount of trouble and effort to conceal them. Forensic exhumations often require very large amounts of digging before any evidence of hidden human remains can be found. So it was at Huda Jama. It took the excavators eight months to remove 4,300 square feet of rock. They then found themselves up against another obstacle put in place to prevent the bodies being found. Eleven reinforced concrete partition walls, each three feet thick. They laboriously demolished them. Beyond these they found the first bodies, white, covered in decades-old lime. There were 427 of them. Who had put them there? How old were they? What condition were the corpses in?

One important thing the forensic investigators were looking at in the mineshaft was the extent to which the bodies had decomposed.

Decomposition is slowed, or sometimes halted altogether, if very little oxygen is available. And this had happened at the mine shaft in Slovenia. The bodies at Huda Jama were well-preserved, almost mummified, and the forensic investigators also discovered that the bodies were naked. Some of them were female. So they dug a further sixteen feet into the shaft, and found another 346 corpses. At this point the Slovenian government, reportedly intensely nervous and sensitive about what was being discovered, temporarily halted work. They also reportedly put a temporary halt to any further documentation of mass graves in all of Slovenia, which was being carried out by the country's own national Commission on Concealed Mass Graves in Slovenia.

Of the bodies found, 726 of them had been exhumed by the end of the first week in September 2009. Estimates were that the Huda Jama site was one of just dozens, if not hundreds of mass graves spread around Slovenia. So whose were the bodies? And who had put them there? And more than seventy years on from World War II, why was the government so nervous? Partly because the truth that was beginning to emerge with the bodies was the truth about who had killed whom, in and just after World War II. Whose grandparents or great-uncles or parents had fought with Tito? Whose relatives had actually secretly fought with the Ustashe or Chetniks? Forensic exhumations and DNA identifications tend to bring out secrets that not everybody wants to see exposed to the truthful light of day. Croatia and Slovenia are both countries still coming to terms with missing persons and the reality of war from 1991–95. Suddenly World War II has turned up as well, bigger, larger, badder, older, wanting to be listened to. Not everybody is ready for it.

The Commission on Concealed Mass Graves in Slovenia estimated that there could be upwards of 2,500 bodies in the Huda Jama mine. They said that most of the victims were believed to be Croat and Slovene soldiers, partisans and civilians who had collaborated – or were thought to have collaborated – with the Nazis and were executed, often without trial. The wartime mass graves commission had registered some 700 possible grave sites in which some 15,000 people were also believed to be buried. Before exhumations were temporarily halted, the first bodies that had been found and exhumed from Huda Jama were transferred to a memorial centre at Dobrova, west of Ljubljana. Then experts would try to use DNA to identify them. Once and if identified, the human remains would be returned to any living relatives for burial.

The Slovenian Research Centre for National Reconciliation then stated that according to eyewitness accounts from World War II, the victims were mostly German soldiers, Croatian and Slovenian militias, and that they had probably been killed by the Yugoslav Army and partisans between May and September 1945. Other Slovenian investigators believed the bodies could be those of prisoners brought to the Huda Jama site from the Slovenian partisan concentration camp at Teharje. The camp, and the sites of several mass graves near Huda Jama, are in close proximity to the Austrian border, and the town of Bleiburg. When the huge column of fleeing Croats, Serbs, Germans and Slovenian and Croatian Home Guard militias surrendered at Bleiburg in May 1945, some of them were detained in the Teharje camp. The Germans had operated a prison camp during the war in that town south of the Austrian frontier. The Yugoslav communist partisans and soldiers reactivated it at the end of May 1945. Four thousand of their prisoners were brought there between 31 May and 7 June alone. Five thousand internees who passed through the camp between May and July were estimated to have been killed.

The Slovenian Ministry of Justice provided further details at the European Public Hearing on Crimes Committed by Totalitarian Regimes:[1]

> A certain number of internees from the Teharje concentration camp were killed in its immediate vicinity, but the majority was killed in the neighbourhood of Stari Hrastnik, Trbovlje, and Laško. Many were killed there and thrown into mine pits, while some were thrown into deserted

> mine shafts. Of several thousands of internees in the concentration camps Teharje, Št. Vid and Ljubljano and Škofja Loka, only a small number of civilians and young Home Guards survived. These were released after the amnesty that was declared on 3 August 1945.[2]

On 9 March 2009, the Croatian Deputy Prime Minister, Jadranka Kosor, and her interior minister visited the site at Huda Jama. On the 10th, Croatia's then-Prime Minister Ivo Sanader called for a joint Croatian–Slovenian investigation into the grave there. Montenegro joined in: they wanted to sign an international agreement with Slovenia to help facilitate the exhumation of Montenegrin victims of the war. This was sensitive territory. It was not surprising. These exhumations, and DNA identifications, were the past coming back to haunt Slovenia and Croatia. Hardly had both countries ironed out their respective histories, their respective dead, their respective missing persons from the wars of the 'nineties, than inconvenient and shameful history from the more distant past was banging on the country's doors again, demanding to be heard, demanding to be let in.

In October 2016, the Slovenian President Borut Pahor attended a memorial and burial ceremony for some of the dead from Huda Jama. He said at the ceremony:

> During the Second World War, in the middle of the previous century, when Slovenians were being killed by foreigners, Slovenians also killed each other. The national liberation war against the occupier was a time of communist against anti-communist civil strife as well. The fighting did not end with the war. In the aftermath of the war, the defeated continued to be the victims of killings. We still find it difficult to unravel all the mysteries surrounding human beings, who since time immemorial have been capable of performing the noblest of deeds and the most horrific atrocities. We recognise the historical, political and moral mistakes that must not ever be made again, irrespective of our different political, religious, or other beliefs.[3]

DNA BRINGS THE TRUTH

Since the 1970s, thousands of people have gone missing from conflicts and human rights abuses in countries such as Bosnia, Iraq, Chile, Kosovo and El Salvador. Before the advent of mass DNA testing in 2000, human remains were mostly identified through artefacts found with the dead. Dentures, blood-stained clothing, documents and fingerprints – the stark, mundane memorabilia of violent human demise. The problem was that this method was flawed. DNA was the only reliable way forward.

How does it work? How were, and will decomposing human remains from mass graves in Slovenia, or *foibe* around Trieste be identified? The identification process for DNA profiling, or 'typing', starts with blood and bone samples. Human remains, once they are exhumed from sites such as Huda Jama, are washed, autopsied and catalogued. Bone samples, each about four to six inches long, are cut with electric saws from the long bones, such as the femurs, of the victims. These are scoured of dirt, ground down into very fine powder, washed, and broken down in a chemical solution. The resultant liquid sample is then purified and treated in devices equipped with silica membranes to which, simply put, the microscopic DNA particles adhere. The DNA strands are then analysed. The main building blocks of the DNA molecule are four nitrogen-containing compounds called nucleobases – adenine, guanine, thymine and cytosine. These four nucleobases repeat in pairs all along the human DNA strand, adenine pairing off with thymine, cytosine with guanine. The patterns in which these pairs repeat and occur on the DNA strand are different in each human being. If the DNA strand can be amplified millions of times, the patterns of these individual repeats can be identified, and a profile of them obtained. This is the human DNA profile or 'fingerprint'.

Meanwhile the bodies exhumed from Huda Jama and other graves in Slovenia started to give up their DNA. Following analysis on eleven bone samples from one hidden mass grave, in 2009 Slovenian scientists were able to obtain six useable DNA profiles. This was a 'hit' rate of over 50 per cent, which for highly degraded human samples that are more than seventy years old, was highly successful.[4] There is no precise official data about the number of missing persons from World War II buried in Slovenia, but rough estimates suggest that the approximate number could amount to tens of thousands.[5] Almost 600 hidden mass graves have been verified in the country.

SCIENCE AND HISTORY TOUCH HUMAN LIFE

The investigations into the mass graves in Slovenia have thrown up the real, human links to the past that science and history can bring. Every DNA sample and DNA match tells the story of a missing person. And a story of triumph, discovery, love and loss. And, as is so often the case, it brings huge sadness once the truth about the past is revealed by modern science. Such is the story of two Slovenian brothers who were looking for their mother. She had been missing since the autumn of 1942. According to witness statements, she was kidnapped in front of her children on 2 August 1942 from a train, by territorial workers of the Communist Security Intelligence Organisation. She was in an advanced stage of pregnancy. According to the testimony, she was murdered soon after being kidnapped.[6] Her children had searched determinedly for information about her burial place. More than seventy years after the end of the war, two grave sites were eventually identified that could possibly contain her remains. After exhumation of these, samples for DNA analysis were taken from the remains of her femur, and from swabs taken from her two sons. Scientists obtained a complete female DNA profile that was matched to both brothers with a Likelihood Ratio of 2.21×10^9.This means that the chance of the human remains being those of the mother of the two sons was 2.21 billion to one in favour. Seventy years after World War II, across Slovenia, Croatia, Istria, in Trieste and the Venezia Giulia, thousands of families are wishing that they could pick up the pieces, and put the past to bed, with such definitive certitude.

Glossary

Abwehr	German military intelligence service from 1920 to 1944
Adriatic Coastal Area	German operational area made up of provinces from around Trieste, Ljubljana and Fiume–Rijeka
AIS	Allied Information Service, a service set up in 1945 and run by British and American intelligence to to 'inform, educate and supply propaganda to the local Italian and Slovenian population'
AMG	Allied Military Government
carabinieri	Italian paramilitary police, part of the Ministry of Defence
CIA	Central Intelligence Agency, the US foreign intelligence service since 1947
CIC	Counter Intelligence Corps, the US Army's intelligence agency during World War II and the early Cold War
CLNAI	Comitato di Liberazione Nazionale Alta Italia (Council for the Liberation of Northern Italy), the umbrella body of Italian partisan groups that the Allies supported during and after World War II
Cominform	Communist Information Bureau, the Soviet agency that coordinated the communist

governments of eastern Europe and the communist parties of western Europe

Comintern Communist International, the organisation established in Russia in 1919 to stimulate world revolution

EU European Union

Gestapo Geheime Staatspolizei (Secret State Police), the secret police force in Nazi Germany

FBI Federal Bureau of Investigation, the US domestic intelligence unit

FSS Field Security Sections, units within the British Army's Intelligence Corps

GIs US Army soldiers, from the phrase 'General Issue'

GRU Glavnoe Razvedyvatel'noe Upravlenie (Main Intelligence Directorate of the General Staff), the Russian intelligence service

Heer German Army

IFC illegal frontier crosser

IRSML Istituto Regionale per la Storia del Movimento di Liberazione nel Friuli Venezia Giulia, the Regional Institute for the History of the Resistance in Friuli Venezia Giulia

JAG Judge Advocate General's Department, the department of the US Army that provides legal advice to the military

Kampfgruppe a German composite infantry battlegroup

KGB Komitet Gosudarstvennoy Bezopasnosti (State Security Committee), the Soviet Union's main security agency between 1954 and 1991

Kriegsmarine German Navy

Luftwaffe German Air Force

MGB Ministerstvo Gosudarstvennoy Bezopasnosti (Ministry of State Security), the Soviet Union's

	main security agency until Stalin's death in 1953
MI6	Military Intelligence Section 6, the British foreign intelligence service
NATO	North Atlantic Treaty Organisation
NCO	non-commissioned officer
NDH	Nazavisna Drzava Hrvatska, the Independent State of Croatia
NKVD	Narodnyi Komissariat Vnutrennikh Del (People's Commissariat for Internal Affairs) the Russian Communist Party's law enforcement arm from 1934 to 1946
OKW	Oberkommando der Wehrmacht, the armed forces high command
OSS	Office for Strategic Services, the active-operations US foreign intelligence service during World War II, superseded by the CIA
OZNA	Odjeljenje za Zaštitu Naroda (Department for National Security), Yugoslavia's security service from 1944 to 1946
PCI	Partito Comunista Italiano, the Italian Communist Party
POW	prisoner-of-war
Questura	Italian Fascist Interior Ministry
RSHA	Reichs-Sicherheitshauptamt (German Central State Security Office), the German secret police, security and home intelligence agency during World War II
SIM	Servizio Informazione Militare (Military Information Service), the wartime Italian military intelligence branch
SIS	Secret Intelligence Service, also known as MI6, the British foreign intelligence service
SOE	Special Operations Executive, the secret

	British organisation created during World War II to carry out sabotage and encourage resistance in enemy territories overseas
UDBA	Yugoslav State Security Service, which replaced OZNA in March 1946
UN	United Nations, the inter-governmental organisation established in 1945 to promote international cooperation
Ustashe	a fascist, ultra-nationalist Croat political group with armed units, which existed from 1929 to 1945
Wehrmacht	German armed forces, comprising the Heer (regular Army), Kriegsmarine (Navy), and Luftwaffe (Air Force).
YCP	Yugoslav Communist Party

Notes

Preface – This Land is my Land, June 2015

1 Alfred Connor Bowman, *Zones of Strain, A Memoir of the Early Cold War* (Stanford, CA: Hoover Press, 1982), pp. 44 and 47.

1. The Race for Trieste, April 1945

1 Papers of Edward Reilly Stettinius 1918–49, the University of Virginia Library, Charlottesville, VA. Accession Number 2723/Z.
2 Harry S. Truman, *Memoirs by Harry S. Truman: 1945 – Year of Decisions* (Old Saybrook, CT: Konecky and Konecky, 1999), p. 243.
3 Sergey Khrushchev (ed.), *The Memoirs of Nikita Khrushchev, Volume 2: Reformer (1945–1964)* (University Park, PA: Pennsylvania State University Press, 2006), p. 401.
4 Fitzroy MacLean, *Eastern Approaches* (London: Jonathan Cape, 1949), p. 324.
5 Winston S. Churchill, *The Second World War Volume VI – Triumph and Tragedy* (London: Cassell, 1956), p. 442.
6 The quotations on this and the following page are drawn from Churchill, Triumph and Tragedy, pp. 442–45; this instance is also quoted in Truman, *Memoirs* pp. 243–53.
7 Ibid.
8 Ibid.
9 Siegfried Westphal is reported to have said this to Maori Battalion's former Padre, Reverend W. D. Huata, at an Afrika Korps reunion dinner in Mainz, Germany in 1972. As quoted on the Battalion's website, www.28maoribattalion.org.nz, under the section 'The Maori Chaplains'.
10 Quoted on www.28maoribattalion.org.nz, under the section 'The Maori Chaplains'.
11 Corporal Nepia of the 28th Battalion, outside the town of Rubizzano in April 1945, quoted in J. F. Cody, *28th Maori Battalion* (Wellington, New Zealand: Historical Publications Branch, 1956), pp. 474–75.
12 28th Battalion War Diary/Cody, *28th Maori Battalion,* p. 477.

2. Holding Trieste, 29 April – 1 May

1 Museum and archives of the Risiera di San Sabba concentration camp in Trieste, recorded in the book and CD *Scritti, Lettere e Voci,* (Trieste: Civic Museum of the Risiera di San Sabba/IRSML, 2014), an official photographic and text record of the history of the camp.
2 IRSML, Trieste; also detailed in various camp inmate interviews in *Scritti, Lettere e Voci,* for instance on pp. 93–94.
3 Art Looting Intelligence Reports from 1945 to 1946 can be found at www.lootedart.com.
4 Interview testimony of Major-General Linkenbach by the British Field Security Sections, and transcripts of recorded conversations between him and SS-ObergruppenführerKarl Wolff in 1945. The testimony and transcripts from the Nuremburg International Military Tribunal and elsewhere are available from the Collection of William J. Donovan at Cornell University Library, New York, Documents number CSDIC/CMF/X167.
5 Post-war interviews with Linkenbach carried out by the British, and Nuremberg Trial testimony.
6 *Scritti, Lettere e Voci,* witness and survivors' testimony recorded in the museum of the Risiera di San Sabba camp, and in archives and on websites of Italian Holocaust survivors.

3. The Capture of Trieste, 1–2 May

1 As quoted to David Hunt, a British intelligence officer in North Africa who became a diplomat, and was on the British Committee of Historians of the Second World War. David Hunt, *A Don at War* (Abingdon: Frank Cass, 1966), pp. xv and xvi.
2 Churchill, *Triumph and Tragedy*, p. 443.
3 Peter Wilkinson, *Foreign Fields: the Story of an SOE Operative* (London: I.B. Tauris, 2002), p. 225.
4 His diary entries were later adapted into a book: Geoffrey Cox, *The Road to Trieste* (London: Heinemann, 1947), updated as *The Race for Trieste* (London: William Kimber, 1977). The quotation is from the latter volume, page 60.
5 Kay Robin, *The Official History of New Zealand in the Second World War. Italy Volume Two: From Cassino to Trieste* (Wellington, New Zealand: Historical Publications Branch, 1967), p. 521.
6 Ibid, p. 543.
7 Ibid, p. 547.

4. Kidnapped by the Partisans

1 From an Allied Information Service press background document, Allied Military Government, Trieste 1945, held in the IRSML and quoted in Bowman, *Zones of Strain*, p. 35.
2 The comments about Jasenovac made by General Edmund Glaise von Horstenau can be found in his memoir, *Ein General im Zwielicht* (Graz & Koln: Hermann Bohlaus, 1980), p. 168.
3 Ondina Peteani's story is taken from six main sources. Her biography, *E Bello Vivere Libero* (It is Good to Live in Freedom) written by Anna di Gianantonio, was published in 2010 by IRSML in Trieste. It was updated in 2016 with further editing and contributions from her son. Further information came from interviews with Gianni Peteani in 2016 and from documents on the Garibaldi partisan group held in the IRSML. Her life story is recorded on the website of Italian concentration camp inmates, www.lager.it; on that of the Fondazione Memoria della Deportazione, again devoted to Italians deported to concentration camps, www.deportati.it; and on the website of the National Association of Italian Partisans, ANPI, at www.anpi.it.

5. Revenge and Reprisals on the Dalmatian Coast

1 The nationalities of the guards at the San Sabba camp are extensively documented throughout the inmate interviews recorded in *Scritti, Lettere e Voci.*
2 Testimonies held in the Civico Museo della Risiera di San Sabba, reported in *Scritti, Lettere e Voci* on pp. 20–25.

6. Death on the Plateau, 2–3 May

1 Russian Foreign Ministry memos in Khrushchev, *Memoirs of Nikita Khrushchev,* pp. 399–433.
2 SS-Obergruppenführer Gottlob Berger, quoted in Anna Wittmann, 'Mutiny in the Balkans: Croat Volksdeutsche, the Waffen-SS and Motherhood', *East European Quarterly* XXXVI No. 3 (2002), pp. 258–60.
3 Dr Dušan Nedeljković, President of the Yugoslav State Commission for the Investigation of War Crimes, Report of the Commission, Belgrade 1946, Document D-940.
4 Raoul Pupo and Roberto Spazzali, *Foibe* (Milan: Mondadori, 2003); Robin, *History of New Zealand*; Institute for Contemporary History, Ljubljana, Slovenia.
5 A report titled *L'elenco dei mille deportati in Slovenia nel 1945* (The list of the thousand people deported in Slovenia in 1945) issued in March 2006 by the municipality of Nova Gorica.
6 Testimony of General Linkenbach and others from the Donovan Collection, Cornell, as above.

7 Pupo and Spazzali, *Foibe*; IRSML.
8 IRSML; Zadnik, *Istrian Detachment.*
9 Reports, photographs and diaries from the Trieste Fire Brigade, partisans, municipal hospital and civilians, and reports given to British and American Military Police and War Crimes Security Sections; from IRSML, photographs seen by the author.

7. Who was Marshal Tito?

1 Vladimir Dedijer, *Tito Speaks: His Self Portrait and Struggle with Stalin* (London: Weidenfeld and Nicolson, 1953).
2 The background of Josip Broz Tito comes from documents in the archives of the National Museum of Belgrade and the Musej Istorije Yugoslavije, or Museum of Yugoslav History, in Belgrade, in whose grounds Tito and his wife Jovanka Broz are buried; also from the IRSML in Trieste, and from the three best biographies of the Yugoslav leader: Jasper Ridley's *Tito: A Biography* (London: Constable, 1996); Dedijer, *Tito Speaks*; and Nicholas West, *Tito and the Rise and Fall of Yugoslavia* (London: Faber, 2012).
3 Timothy J. Colton, *Moscow: Governing the Socialist Metropolis* (Cambridge, MA: Harvard University Press, 1998) p. 100.
4 Katharine Bliss Eaton, *Daily Life in the Soviet Union* (Westport, CT: Greenwood Publishing Group, 2004) p. 70.

8. The Allies' Support for Yugoslavia

1 Citation for Lieutenant-Colonel Donovan's Medal of Honor. The Medal of Honor Citation can be found at The United States Army Center of Military History, www.army.mil.
2 Quoted in the *Daily Telegraph*'s obituary of Sir William Deakin DSO, 25 January 2005.
3 Ibid; Parachutists, Heather Williams, *Patriots and Partisans: SOE and Yugoslavia 1941–1945* (London: Hurst, 2003), p.146.
4 Maclean, *Eastern Approaches,* p. 287.
5 Ibid, p. 287.
6 Ibid.
7 Richard Smith, *OSS – A Secret History of America's First Central Intelligence Agency* (Guilford, CT: The Lyons Press, 1972, republished 2005), p. 124.
8 Major Louis Huot, quoted in Smith, *OSS – A Secret History,* p. 126.

9. Marshal Tito Plays a Double Hand

1 Peter Ruggenthaler, *The Concept of Neutrality in Stalin's Foreign Policy, 1945–1953* (Lanham, MD: Lexington Books, 2015), p. 94.
2 Churchill, *Triumph and Tragedy*, pp. 86–90.

3 OSS Memo to the President, 24 September 1944, released under the CIA's Historical Review Programme, 22 September 1993.
4 Cyril E. Black, Robert D. English, Jonathan E. Helmreich and James A. McAdams, *Rebirth: A Political History of Europe Since World War II* (Boulder, CO: Westview Press, 2000), p. 61.
5 David McCullough, *Truman* (New York: Simon and Schuster, 1992), p. 507.
6 Ruggenthaler, *Concept of Neutrality*, p. 97.
7 Quoted in Mark Laar's 2009 paper for the Centre for European Studies: 'The Power of Freedom, Central and Eastern Europe after 1945'. The original line is from Stalin to his foreign minister, Molotov in 1945, when Tito announced that he would formally take Yugoslavia out of Stalin's sphere of influence into an era of national unity defined by socialism – it appears in Molotov's personal diaries.
8 Wilson D. Miscamble, *From Roosevelt to Truman: Potsdam, Hiroshima and the Cold War* (Cambridge: Cambridge University Press, 2007), p. 52. This is also quoted in an article written by the former American Ambassador to the USSR from 1933 to 1936, William C. Bullitt, 'How We Won the War and Lost the Peace,' *Life*, 30 August 1948, p. 94.
9 Churchill, *Triumph and Tragedy*, p. 361.
10 Diary of Harry S. Truman, 17 July 1945, included in Papers of Harry S. Truman, Boxes 322/333, Harry S. Truman Library.
11 Dedijer, *Tito Speaks*.
12 Federal Reserve Bulletin September 1940, Board of Governors of the Federal Reserve System, Washington DC. Information from this, and from the Foreign and Commonwealth Office files quoted, is also found in George M. Taber, *Chasing Gold: the Incredible Story of how the Nazis Stole Europe's Bullion* (Berkeley, California: Pegasus, 2014).
13 Ruggenthaler, *Concept of Neutrality*, p. 95.
14 Published in the *New York Times* on 19 May 1945.
15 Ibid.
16 Smith, *OSS – A Secret History*, p. 46.
17 Robert Gellatelly, *Stalin's Curse: Battling for Communism in War and Cold War*, (Oxford: Oxford University Press, 2013), p. 271.

10. Dividing Trieste: June 1945

1 Lieutenant-Colonel G. R. Stephens, *The Tiger Triumphs: The Story of Three Great Divisions in Italy*, Chapter 21 Postscript: Macedonia and the Julian Marches, (HMSO India, 1946).
2 The description of the Battle of Poljana comes from Franci Strle: *Veliki Finale na Koroskem* (Ljubljana University Press, Ljubljana, 1977). (The title translates from the Slovenian as 'Final Showdown in Carinthia'. Strle was a Slovenian soldier, who also published an investigation into the events at Bleiburg in Zagreb in 1990: *Otvoreni Dossier: Bleiburg* (Open Dossier: Bleiburg).

3 Sabrina P. Ramet and Davorka Matic, ed., *Democratic Transition in Croatia: Value Transformation, Education and Media* (College Station, TX: Texas A&M University Press, 2007), p. 274.

4 Jozo Tomasevich, *Contemporary Yugoslavia: Twenty Years of Socialist Experiment* (Oakland, CA: University of California Press, 1969), pp. 113–14.

11. Spies on the Adriatic, May–August 1945

1 IWG / OSS Records – Entries 211, 213, 214 and 216.

2 Stanley P. Lovell, *Of Spies & Stratagems* (Englewood Cliffs, NJ: Prentice-Hall, 1963), p. 79.

3 The intelligence reports and notes on OSS operations before and after World War II come from one particular 'record group' and four different 'entries', namely 211, 213, 214 and 216. These are now listed under the IWG, or Inter-Agency Working Group, on Intelligence. Records are held at the United States National Archives and Records Administration at College Park, Maryland. The operations described here come from the Records of the Office of Strategic Services (Record Group 226) 1940–1947, Entry 216, Boxes 1–10. Location 250/64/33/4. CIA Accession: 92-003373R / Entry 214 Boxes 1–7. Location: 250/64/33/2. CIA Accession: 91-01046R.

4 Memo from OSS Director William Donovan to Edward R. Stettinius, 23 December 1944 reporting on meeting in Belgrade between OSS representative Bernard Yarrow and Prime Minister Ivan Subasic. State Department Memo 860H.00/12/2344, quoted in *Journal of Croatian Studies* XXIV, 1983.

5 OSS report to the President, 24 May 1945.

6 OSS Research & Analysis Department report, 1 June 1945, no. R&A33122, approved for release January 2002.

7 British Public Records Office, Class HS, SOE Operations in Western Europe, HS 6/800.

8 Imperial War Museum London, Oral Records, Catalogue no.12522.

12. Very British Intelligence

1 Douglas Lyle, 21 Port Security Section, 412 FSS Intelligence Corps, quoted on the BETFOR (British Forces Trieste) Association website: www.betforassociation.org/BETFORTSO.html. Additional information on the British Intelligence Corps' operations in Trieste also comes from: the Imperial War Museum's Oral History of John Bryan Akehurst, Catalogue no. 27184, IWM, London: Nick Van Der Bijl, *Sharing the Secret: the History of the Intelligence Corps 1940–2010* (Barnsley: Pen & Sword, 2013), Chapter 11, pp. 161–62; Records of Allied Military Government (AMG) Organizations in Venezia Giulia and Udine, Italy [AFHQ] 1943–47; Record group 331–31, UK National Archives, London.

2 Ibid.

3 Ibid.

4 BETFOR (British Forces Trieste) Association website: www.betforassociation.org/BETFORTSO.html.

13. The Capture of Friedrich Rainer and Odilo Globocnik, May 1945

1 Quoted from a paper published in 2010 by the University of Northampton's Holocaust Education Archive and Research Team (HEART), titled 'Friedrich Rainer and Odilo Globocnik – Typical Nazis, an Unusual Friendship.'
2 Wilkinson, *Foreign Fields,* pp. 210–11
3 Ibid.
4 Richard J. Aldrich, 'Unquiet in Death: The Post-war Survival of the Special Operations Executive 1945–51', in Anthony Gorst, Lewis Johnman, and W. Scott Lucas (eds.) *Contemporary British History, 1931-1961: Politics and the Limits of Policy*, (London: Pinter Pub Ltd, 1991).
5 Wilkinson, letter to Robert Knight, quoted in Robert Knight, 'Life after SOE: Peter Wilkinson's Journey from the Clowder Mission to Waldheim', *Journal for Intelligence, Propaganda and Security Studies*, 3 (1).
6 Rainer's broadcasts from Austria are quoted in the essay mentioned in Note 1 of this chapter, while slightly different versions and translations come from F. Rainer, *My Internment and Testimony at the Nuremburg Trial* (New York & Lampeter: Edwin Mellen Press, 2006), translation and editorial commentary by Maurice Williams, which details Rainer's descriptions of the Nuremburg Trials in 1945 and 1946.
7 US Counter Intelligence Corps; US Looted Art Intelligence Unit; Joseph Poprzeczny, *Odilo Globocnik, Hitler's Man in the East* (Jefferson, NC: McFarland Inc., 2004).
8 Poprzeczny, *Hitler's Man in the East,* pp. 352–53.
9 Statement given by Lieutenant William Hedley to the British Foreign and Commonwealth Office for the Austrian government, 1964; Poprzeczny, *Hitler's Man in the East*; British Public Records Office, Kew, London.

14. A New Enemy for the Allies, June 1945

1 Nella Last's diary entry from 7 May 1945 is quoted on the BBC's website, under www.bbc.co.uk/history/british/britain_wwtwo/nella_last_part2
2 Churchill, *Triumph and Tragedy*, p. 593.
3 Russia – Threat to Western Civilisation – War Cabinet File, Public Records Office, London. Number CAB 120/691 / 109040, dated, from British War Cabinet Joint Planning Staff, 22 May, 8 June, 11 July 1945.
4 Quoted in by B. C. Novak, *Trieste 1941–1954, The Ethnic, Political and Ideological Struggle* (Chicago, IL: University of Chicago Press, 1970), p. 209

5 As quoted by the British historian Sir Max Hastings in *The Daily Mail*, 26 August 2009.
6 The Allied Purge Commission was designed to circumvent this aberration in Italian law adopted by the Allies.
7 This was quoted in an address titled 'What Happened in Trieste', delivered to the students and faculty of the United States Army Ground General School, Fort Riley, Kansas, on 5 October 1949 by then-Colonel Alfred C. Bowman.

15. A New American Sheriff in Trieste, June 1945

1 Bowman, *Zones of Strain*, pp. 8–9
2 Ibid.
3 Documents referring to the workings of the Allied administration of the Emilia Romagna region are held by the ISREBO, the *Istituto per la storia della Resistenza e della societa contemporanea nella provincia di Bologna.* The Alfred Connor Bowman Papers – reports, diaries, records and assorted documents – can be found in the library of the Hoover Institution at Stanford University. Bowman also wrote an autobiography, *Zones of Strain: A Memoir of the Early Cold War.*
4 Bowman, *Zones of Strain*, p. 17.

16. Hidden Conflict, July 1945

1 The IRSML in Trieste contains almost large parts of the daily documentation of the AMG in Trieste, including that of the AIS, or Allied Information Service, effectively the AMG's press office; also in Bowman, *Zones of Strain*, pp. 85–87.
2 Ibid.
3 Bowman, *Zones of Strain*, p. 78. Bowman's instructions and memos to the AIS are also held in the archive of AIS records at IRSML in Trieste that documents its daily activities from 1945 to 1947.
4 Bowman, *Zones of Strain*, pp. 51–52.
5 IRSML – AMG Intelligence Summaries June–July 1945.
6 Bowman, *Zones of Strain*, p. 55.
7 Quoted in the Allied Military Government Executive Intelligence Summary for August 1945, held at the IRSML in Trieste, and in Bowman, *Zones of Strain*, p. 81.
8 The complete daily documentation and records of the AIS from 1945 onwards were de-classified by the American National Security Agency in 1961 and returned to Trieste. They now reside in the IRSML.
9 AIS records, July–December 1945, IRSML, Trieste. This box relates to December 1945
10 This is from Section 148 of the personal memoirs of Professor James C. Davis, from the University of Pennsylvania, recalling his time serving with the US Army in Trieste in 1952–53. His memoirs are published at www.istria.net, titled Zone A in the 1950s, as we Americans knew it. He acknowledges the

inspiration of a co-soldier, Tom Boyd, who wrote a memoir entitled *A Bowl of Cherries: the memoirs of Tom Boyd from 1932 to 1992* (Cirencester: Englang Publishing, 1992).

11 Ibid, Section 146.

12 Ibid, Section 147.

17. *OZNA Sve Dozna* (OZNA Can Find Out Anything), August–September 1945

1 Dedijer, *Tito Speaks*, p. 219.

2 Inter-Agency Working Group (IWG), Records of the Office of Strategic Services (OSS) Records Group 226 (1940–1947) Entry 214 Boxes 1–7. Location: 250/64/33/2. CIA Accession: 91-01046R.

18. A Gurkha Beheading, October–December 1945

1 Sergeant Tom Norton, British Army Intelligence Corps, 12 Field Security Section, Gorizia, November 1945. A number of accounts exist of this incident, both in Allied and Yugoslav documentation, but the clearest and most accurate version is this one, reproduced and sourced to the account of Sergeant Norton on the website of the BETFOR Assocation, www.betforassociation.org/BETFORTSO.html.

19. Bloody Compromise, February–April 1946

1 Bowman, *Zones of Strain*, p. 76.

2 President Josip Broz Tito, Address to the Yugoslav Parliament, 18 March 1946.

3 Ibid.

4 Statement by the Yugoslav Foreign Ministry, June 1946. The Yugoslavs conveniently forgot to consider their ports in Zadar, Rijeka and Split.

5 The details of the State Department of the United States' analysis of the incident is laid out in Lorraine M. Lees, *Keeping Tito Afloat: the United States, Yugoslavia and the Cold War* (University Park, PA: Pennsylvania State University Press, 1946), pp. 17–20.

6 John C. Sparrow, *History of Personnel Demobilization in the United States Army* (Center of Military History, United States Army, 1994), p. 383.

20. The Free Territory of Trieste, March–August 1947

1 Milovan Djilas and Rupert Hart-Davis, *Conversations with Stalin* (Orlando, FL: Harcourt, Brace, 1962), pp. 187–88

2 Both are quoted in Bowman, *Zones of Strain,* p. 140.

3 Richard West, *Tito and the Rise and Fall of Yugoslavia* (London: Faber & Faber, 1994).
4 www.betforassociation.org/BETFORTSO.html.
5 This is extracted from an essay entitled 'The Cominform Fights Revisionism' prepared for the Stalin Society in London by Bill Bland, 1998, published on www.marxists.org.
6 Edvard Kardelj, *Reminiscences – the Struggle for Recognition and Independence: The New Yugoslavia, 1944–1957* (London: Blond and Briggs, 1982), p. 217.

21. Killing Tito and Dividing Trieste

1 Dmitry Volkogonov, 'Stalin's Plan to Assassinate Tito', *Izvestia*, 11 June 1993. Volkogonov based his article on the original MGB report, which is also detailed in Christopher M. Andrew and Vasili Mitrokhin's *The Mitrokhin Archive: The KGB in Europe and the West* (London: Penguin Books, 1999). Further details are contained in *Spetsoperatsii – Lubyanka i Kreml 1930-1950 gody,* by Pavel Sudoplatov (Moscow: Olma Press, 2003), pp. 526 and 528–30. The title translates as 'Special Operations: Lubyanka and the Kremlin 1930–1950'.
2 Ibid.
3 The letter is quoted in Zhores Medvedev, Roy Medvedev, Matej Jeličić and Ivan Škunca, *The Unknown Stalin,* (London: I.B. Tauris, 2003), pp. 61–62. The letter itself is on display in the archives of the former NKVD in Moscow.
4 As quoted in *The Daily Beast,* 'Did Tito Kill Stalin?' by Noah Charney, 7 May 2012. Charney details the findings of a biography of Tito published in Slovenia: Jose Pirjevec, *Tito in Tovarisi* (Ljubljana: Cankarjeva Publishers, 2011).
5 Stolz's account of his first CIA duty tour in Trieste is in the Library of the Central Intelligence Agency, Studies Archive Indexes Volume 37, no.1. *A Case Officer's First Tour.*
6 William Shortland, British Field Security Section Trieste, BETFOR Association website. www.betforassociation.org/BETFORTSO.html.
7 Richard Stolz, '*A Case Officer's First Tour*', Studies Archive Indexes Volume 37, no.1, Library of the Central Intelligence Agency.
8 Ibid.

22. The Numbers

1 The Non-Aligned Movement was founded in 1961, by the prime ministers and presidents of Yugoslavia, India, Egypt, Ghana and Indonesia. It aimed to give developing states the option of a political middle ground, that did not align them either with the western or eastern power blocs in the Cold War.
2 Pupo is a member of the 'Technical Committee' of the IRSML in Trieste.
3 Gaetano La Perna, *Pola Istria Fiume 1943–1945,* (Milan: Mursia, 1993).
4 The report, *Le vittime di nazionalità italiana a Fiume e dintorni (1939-1947)* (The victims of Italian nationality in Fiume and the surrounding area (1939-1947)) was produced by the Society of Fiuman Studies, from Rome, and the Croatian Institute of History, and was published in 2002 by both parties.

5 From 2008 to 2010 the author spent two years working for the International Commission on Missing Persons, the ICMP, in Bosnia, whose staff include senior forensic anthropologists and archaeologists who have worked on hundreds of mass graves in the Western Balkans, Africa, Asia and South America.
6 President Giorgio Napolitano, official speech on the Day of Remembrance on 10 February 2007; text from Italian Presidential Bureau.
7 Zagreb, Croatia, 11 February 2007, quoted on a BBC report on 14 February 2007 entitled 'Italy-Croatia WWII massacre spat'.
8 In February 2012 a photo of Italian troops killing Slovene civilians in World War II was shown on Italian state television. But the photo made it look as though the Italians, not the Slovenes, were the victims. When the historian Alessandra Kersevan, who was a guest on the show, pointed this out to the television host, he did not apologise. A diplomatic incident then followed.

Appendix

1 The European Public Hearing on Crimes Committed by Totalitarian Regimes was an initiative of the Slovenian Presidency of the European Union, and the European Commission, from January to June 2008, the period of Slovenia's presidency. Subsequent reports and proceedings research and investigate large-scale human rights abuses carried out by 'Totalitarian Regimes' from the 1940s to the 1990s. The countries involved were Slovenia, Poland, Estonia, Romania, Lithuania and Spain.
2 Information contained on the website of the Slovenian government's Ministry of Justice. During autumn 2016 the link and web URL to it was deactivated, saying the material from the European Public Hearing could no longer be accessed. No explanation was given.
3 The speech is quoted on the website of the President of Slovenia, dated 27 October 2016.
4 Quoted in Marjanovic et al, 'Identification of Skeletal Remains of Communist Armed Forces Victims During and After World War II: Combined Y-chromosome Short Tandem Repeat (STR) and MiniSTR Approach', *Croatian Medical Journal*, June 2009, Zagreb, Croatia.
5 The Commission on Concealed Mass Graves in Slovenia, or *Komisija za Reševanje Vprašanj Prikritih Grobišč*, finds and documents mass grave sites from World War Two in Slovenia. It was set up by the Slovenian government in November 2005, and presented a report with its initial findings to the government in October 2009. It estimated that there are around 100,000 victims in 581 mass graves. Some graves contain fewer than ten bodies, others hundreds. The Croatian newspaper *Jutarnji Vijesti* reported the commission's findings on 1 October 2009.
6 The information on the case comes from the Slovenian Research Centre for National Reconciliation, while the forensic and scientific details were included in an article in the Croatian Medical Journal in June 2009.

Index

References to footnotes are indicated by fn.